Matt Dickinson

BOBBY MOORE
The Man in Full

YELLOW JERSEY PRESS

LONDON

2 4 6 8 10 9 7 5 3 1

Yellow Jersey Press, an imprint of Vintage
20 Vauxhall Bridge Road,
London SW1V 2SA

Vintage is part of the Penguin Random House group of companies whose
addresses can be found at global.penguinrandomhouse.com

Penguin
Random House
UK

Copyright © Matt Dickinson 2014

Matt Dickinson has asserted his right under the Copyright, Designs
and Patents Act 1988 to be identified as the author of this work

First published in Great Britain in hardback in 2014 by
Yellow Jersey Press

www.vintage-books.co.uk

A CIP catalogue record for this book is
available from the British Library

ISBN 9780224091732

Printed and bound by CPI Group (UK) Ltd, Croydon, CR0 4YY

For Helen, Joseph and Finlay

Matt Dickinson is Chief Sports Correspondent for *The Times*, where he has worked for 17 years and covered five World Cups. He has won numerous awards including Sports Journalist of the Year. He has previously written books with David Beckham and Gary Neville but this is his first biography.

Contents

Prologue: On A Pedestal

Many footballers become heroes. Quite a few are called legends. What fascinated me, gazing up at Bobby Moore on his plinth outside Wembley, was how he came to be English football's only saint.

Moore stands on a pedestal all of his own, though that was not always the plan. In the months following Sir Alf Ramsey's death, as they considered ideas for the new Wembley, the FA discussed erecting a statue of Moore and Ramsey as they were on the pitch in 1966, captain passing the Jules Rimet Trophy to his reluctant manager. By the time it came to the unveiling, Moore was the sole focus and it was not a scene from the World Cup final that he represented.

The statue is not an action pose, or a triumphalist one. It does not capture a moment in history. Moore stands, arms crossed, left foot on the ball, in a timeless image of leadership and heroism. At twelve feet high, twice lifesize, he is awesomely imposing, with the sort of hulking thighs and calves you normally see drawn on superheroes. Standing sentinel outside the national stadium, the statue shows an Adonis, a man-god exuding an aura of absolute self-certainty and control.

On match day the crowds gather at Moore's feet and read the inscription: 'Immaculate footballer. Imperial defender. Immortal hero of 1966. First Englishman to raise the World Cup aloft. Favourite son of London's East End. Finest legend of West Ham United. National Treasure. Master of Wembley. Lord of the game. Captain extraordinary. Gentleman of all time.' It is enough to make you wonder if, in sculpting Moore so beautifully out of two tonnes of bronze, Philip Jackson forgot to add a halo.

It was walking past that statue, reading the extravagant tribute, that I began to wonder how Moore came to be so revered. The adoration went way beyond his unique accomplishment as the only Englishman to lift the World Cup, the high point of English sport. In the *New Statesman*, Jason Cowley wrote of the 'cult of Moore' which has arisen since his death in 1993.

'National Treasure . . . Gentleman of all time.' Moore has become an idyll. In a world where we incessantly question our footballers' characters, asking if they want it enough, if they are suitable role models, picking over their love lives and salaries, passing judgement not just on their skills but their morals, Moore is held up as a figure beyond reproach, a man of almost superhuman virtue. After every indiscretion by an England player, we hear how Moore would be turning in his grave. It is almost enough to make you pity the modern star; not only doomed to World Cup failure but forced to stand comparison to a paragon.

The adoration shows no sign of diminishing – indeed, it grows with every failure of the England team – and that began to nag at me. I started to store up questions; the type it can feel uncomfortable to ask given how Moore is remembered. He is held up as a man without blemish but could he really be that perfect? Could anyone? To me, the idyll seemed implausible. It wasn't that I thought the eulogies were untrue; rather I could not believe they represented the whole truth. There is chaos and complexity in every life. Shit happens, even to saints.

I felt that doubt again, more acutely, on a radio show when there were several of us, all football writers, discussing the England captaincy. Inevitably, Moore's name popped up but, as we paid the familiar tributes, I was struck by how little we knew about him. We were passing down the approved, orthodox view – Moore the Impeccable – but it felt as though we were describing a mythical figure, not a man of flesh and blood.

We knew about the glories, but what of the adversities? I began to wonder what Moore had been through, what battles he had fought and hardships he had overcome. What was he like to play with, to confront, to share a beer with before he became a towering figure in bronze?

It seemed I was not the only one who felt there was something missing in our knowledge and understanding of Bobby Moore, a need for fresh perspective. In an article for *The Times*, Matthew Syed wrote about our tendency to beatify those in the public eye who die tragically young. He talked about this process of Dianafication, alighting on the example of England's captain and the way his memory is so zealously policed.

'The real Moore, a man of light and shade and moral complexity, has been replaced by a messianic and increasingly implausible caricature,' he observed. 'There is a real sense in which Moore has now been lost to us. Authenticity has been obscured by sentimentality.' I was not alone in wondering whether the 'real' Moore had been buried in mawkish nostalgia and a desire to see only perfection.

This was not about pulling Moore down from his pedestal but humanising him, and early inquiries made me even more curious. I had thought of Moore as a straightforward hero but he turned out to be much more enigmatic. Brian Glanville, the doyen of football writers, was one of the first people I spoke to. 'Bobby Moore? I knew him for almost forty years but I'm not sure I really knew him at all,' Brian said. Almost certainly he was offering a warning but it felt like a challenge.

So many who talked of Moore as an inspirational leader, a true friend, also revealed in the same breath that he could be almost unknowable, determinedly elusive. Jack Charlton, Moore's defensive partner on that momentous day at Wembley, described the captain as 'one of us, but not like us' – a man apart even among his fellow heroes of 1966. Among dozens of interviews, I met Tina Moore, his first wife, to discuss her late husband. 'A very strange man in some ways,' she said. It was not a description I had expected, yet it was recurring.

Moore's life turned out to be far more turbulent than I had guessed – or even many of his close friends ever knew – because he kept his agonies private. That inscrutable face on the statue at Wembley hid many secrets. Sir Michael Parkinson told me that he could have had Moore on his chat show numerous times but never invited his friend because he sensed it would be torture for both of them, particularly

Moore. 'He was a curious chap,' Parkinson said. 'You loved him because he was so friendly but, when you stopped to think, you realised you knew bugger all about him.'

1. The End

On the day he found out that his bowel cancer was terminal, that all hope of recovery had been extinguished, Bobby Moore thanked his consultant, climbed into his car and drove back to work in central London. Stephanie, his second wife, was with him and, as they approached Trafalgar Square, she could stand the silence and the stillness no more. Her body heaving, she burst into uncontrollable sobs. The grieving process had already started. Moore pulled up the car, looked at her with alarm and got out. He could bear the cancer but not the histrionics.

Stephanie wanted to tell Moore that she was distraught because she loved him so much and was going to miss him dreadfully, but it was the type of conversation he would have found very difficult. The last thing he wanted was unnecessary drama so she kept her emotions to herself. In the months ahead, as Moore fought his cancer, Stephanie never cried in front of her husband again.

Throughout the two years when he knew he was dying, Moore never did properly discuss the illness with his wife. He never talked about his fears, if he had any. He did not discuss the impact it would have on her life and how she might cope when he was gone. He never asked 'why me?', or not so that anyone heard.

He never disclosed the illness to his friends, even when they could see that something was terribly wrong. Soon after he had endured major surgery, which came too late to stop the spread of cancer, Moore went to visit Harry Redknapp down at Bournemouth. Redknapp went to pick Moore up from the station and burst into tears when he saw his old friend cross the road, looking so gaunt, a shadow of the big man he used to call 'God' in the West Ham dressing room.

Redknapp quickly composed himself before Moore could see his anguish – Bobby would not want a scene – and they headed off for a lovely weekend, visiting some horseracing stables, sharing a nice lunch chatting about good times. When Moore departed, Redknapp was none the wiser about the illness or the operation. You didn't ask Bobby those sorts of things.

If you did, he wouldn't tell you. Moore was a closed man who had a curious way with conversations, a funny habit of answering a question with a question. One friend likens it to one of those fighter planes with a defensive shield, a way of deflecting inquiries. 'You all right? How's the wife? Going anywhere nice on your holidays?' He may have been interested in the answers but, mostly, it was his way of avoiding talking about himself.

It was that familiar routine when Moore began to ring around friends early in 1993. The same old Bobby, asking about the kids and the weather. How were his mates to know that he was dying? He never said.

Alan Ball, Moore's best pal from the World Cup winning

XI, was among those who took a call at home. 'Hello, little man, how are you? Lesley OK? How are the kids?' Moore asked. After a bit of chitchat, Ball hung up and went about his business. It would only be later that he understood the significance. 'I never realised he was ringing to say goodbye. I was so mad with myself afterwards that I didn't twig,' Ball said.

The phone rang for Geoff Hurst, the hat-trick hero of 1966. Hurst was surprised because, although he and Moore had known each other since schooldays, they were not particularly close. 'Bobby called me out of the blue which was a bit unusual. "How are you? How's Judith?" It wasn't for anything particular, just to talk.' It was only some time afterwards that he, too, realised why Moore had called. It was his unspoken farewell.

The first that Ball and Hurst, or any of those friends he rang, knew about Moore having cancer was when they read it in the newspapers a few weeks later. Moore would have maintained his secret to the end, telling no one, but his condition had deteriorated to the point where people were starting to notice that he looked very sick.

His sturdy thighs had withered away. The clothes which had always fitted him so perfectly were hanging off him. He wore a black cap over thinning hair and plimsolls to soothe swollen feet. When the jaundice started showing in his yellowing eyes, there was no way he could continue to pretend that, honestly, all was well.

A public statement was released. Moore disclosed that he had undergone an operation on his colon a couple of years earlier and that he had cancer in his liver. 'I have a battle to win and would ask only that I am given the chance to do so without intrusion in my private life. I appreciate everyone's concern and above all the loving care and support of my family. Bulletins about my progress will be issued in due course but neither my wife nor myself will be making any further statements of any kind with regard to my medical condition.'

When Roberta, his daughter, came to visit him the next day, Moore asked if there was anything in the papers. She told him it was front page news.

'Has anyone said anything detrimental?' he asked.

'I went "detrimental?" He was so unassuming. He had no idea how much people thought of him. No idea.'

Moore had given the impression that he was fighting his illness but, in truth, there was not much left of this particular war. The cancer had spread from his bowels to his lungs and into his brain. His voice was starting to falter, though he was not yet on painkillers. The doctors had not given him any because he had not complained.

They never told him how long he had left to live because he never asked, but he must have known the end was close. He began to make a few last phone calls, those unspoken goodbyes. Among the final conversations, he talked to Noel Cantwell, his captain at West Ham and his best man. Cantwell promised to come to London to pay a visit. 'I'll be down next week to see you,' he said. Moore agreed, though he must have known that he would not be around long enough to keep the date.

Moore talked to Kenny Lynch, the entertainer who had been his accomplice through a few scrapes, and many late-night beers.

'I'd had a bypass about four or five weeks earlier and we spoke every day on the phone about twice a day. I remember our last conversation like it was yesterday,' Lynch recalls.

'I said "I'm worried about you".

'Bobby says, "well that's why I phoned because I was worried about you".

'His voice was weak. He said "I tell you what we'll do from now on" – and these were the last words he ever said to me – "you worry about me and I'll worry about you". I'll call you tomorrow about eleven.' But they never did speak again.

Moore spent those last days at home, cared for by Stephanie. Peaceful days, as he drifted in and out of consciousness. She wanted to ask him about funeral plans, and what she should do with his body. She hoped to talk about what his death would mean to her. She wanted to say how much she loved him, a proper goodbye. But like so much in Bobby Moore's life, it went unsaid.

2. Barking

Bobby Moore arrived in Barking at the same time as the Luftwaffe. He was four days old, a crying newborn, when Nazi bombs shook the walls, shattered the windows and ripped plaster off the ceilings in his family home.

The German bombers were aiming for Barking Power Station where his father, 'Big' Bob, worked lagging the pipes. Every day he would unchain his bike and cycle the mile to work down by the River Thames, returning home with a covering of coal dust. Living so close to the power station had always been a convenience but not in the Blitz, with enemy planes scattering their bombs across the borough as they tried to detect their target through the clouds of chimney smoke.

The air attacks on London had begun eight months earlier on Black Monday but, in the East End, they had seen nothing like Wednesday 16 April 1941. *The Times* recorded it as 'one of the most wanton and savagely indiscriminate raids of the war'. By morning, more than one thousand Londoners would be dead, unable to find safety in the underground stations or air raid shelters. There were so many fires that the night sky above the capital lit up in an orange glow.

Barking was not spared. At Blake's Corner, a busy shopping area, a direct strike demolished Killiwicks furniture shop, closing the main road. The anti-aircraft guns stationed in Barking Park fired constantly but they could not deter incessant German raids.

For Doris – Doss to friends and family – it was a terrifying homecoming just a few days after giving birth to Robert at Upney Hospital. She had spent one night on the ward before being discharged with her only child. She craved rest but a nearby blast shook the house with a tremor that ran through the floors and ceilings. The bombs never did hit the power station but they came perilously close to striking the Moores at 43 Waverley Gardens.

Bob tried to summon an ambulance to take the three of them to Doss's parents two miles away on the other side of Barking. But resources were already stretched ferrying the countless wounded. The Mayor of Barking's car had been commandeered for the night to help with emergencies and, around midnight, it came to their rescue. Driven by chauffeur – not that Bob and Doss were in any state to appreciate the luxury – they fled through the streets of blacked-out houses.

Arriving at 110 Faircross Avenue, Bob urgently rapped at the door and handed over a bundle of blankets to Aunt Ina, one of Doss's three sisters. Inside was baby Robert. Doss was carried into the house by her father, Fred Buckle, a 17-stone giant of a man.

Fred and Beatrice Buckle had taken to sleeping downstairs in the dining room because of the bombing which at least meant that there was a spare bedroom for the new arrivals. The question was what to do with the baby. Ina solved the problem by pulling out a long drawer from a chest, filling it with blankets. Robert had his bed for the night.

The next day, once the bombing had ceased, the sirens had gone quiet and Londoners had emerged blinking from their shelters, Bob returned to Waverley Gardens to inspect the damage and to start the job of clearing up the debris. It was another six weeks of the Blitz before the Moore family could go back to Robert's childhood home.

Six miles east of Canary Wharf down the A13, you join the queue of lorries turning off into River Road, with its warehouses and factories. Waverley Gardens – a flattering name for a nondescript street on the edge of an industrial estate – is first on the right. At number 43 there is no plaque to mark that this three-bedroom, end-of-terrace property once housed an icon of English sport, but it contains all the clues to understanding Bobby Moore.

A mile to the east, across the Thames View Estate, is Chelmer Crescent, where John Terry spent his childhood, but England captaincy is all they have in common. Moore was very much a product of his time; a child of the forties and fifties, austerity Britain, surviving the war and then emerging stoically from the trauma. George Best was born five years later and became the thrilling symbol of iconoclastic, rebellious, hairy Beatlemania. Moore always did look like he was more of the Spitfire generation with his creased slacks and neat parting.

In post-war Barking and the upright ways of Doss and Bob we can see the making of Moore. Neatness, tidiness, politeness. No swearing. No drink. There was a strong Salvationist streak in Doss's family. She kept her faith private but number 43 was a non-smoking, teetotal house, no small irony given how their son turned out.

Doss and Bob had married in September 1939, just a few weeks after war broke out. Petrol rationing ended honeymoon plans and there was no taxi to take the newlyweds home. They travelled back to Waverley Gardens by bus, but they were not the complaining type.

Moore spoke very little about his parents – and they preferred it that way – but we can catch the essence of them, and him, on *This Is Your Life*, the painfully stiff television programme that, in 1971, celebrated his glories as a footballer.

With a fond grin, genial 'Big' Bob starts to tell how Doss would painstakingly wash and iron young Robert's laces on the night before every schoolboy football match. Clutching her handbag, Doss tries to scold her husband for betraying her secret. 'Don't you dare,' she mutters. But inside she will have been glowing with pride at the memories of her precious Robert being so smart with his clean, pressed laces, his pristine kit and his hair neatly combed. Never did a young boy emerge more freshly scrubbed and polished from the East End of London.

Like mother, like son. Into this tidy home came an obsessively neat child. Even as a youngster, Robert laid down strict rules about his clothes. Shirts must never be folded; they must be placed on hangers and hung from the picture rail around the sitting room. He would take them upstairs to his wardrobe and place them in order, dark to light, like a filing system. A peculiar habit for a boy.

It was a trait revealed by Aunt Ina when she was interviewed for the documentary *Hero*. 'That's how particular he was,' she recalled. 'Quite fastidious really but it was very important to him.'

Perfectionism became a defining Moore characteristic and,

with it, a hatred of being shown up. Moore always recalled that his worst day at school was the time he was ordered to go up in front of his classmates and sing 'God Save The Queen'. He was mortified, and the words came out in a half-hearted drone. Talking about it years later, he could still feel the hot flush of embarrassment.

Moore looks similarly pained on *This Is Your Life* when asked to recall his childhood nicknames. 'Tubby' they called him. Or 'Fatso'. 'Nicknames which can hurt a boy,' he admitted. In a café after class, Moore sat with some friends. A gang from a nearby school were across the way. 'Is that Bobby Moore, the fat one?' one asked. Moore went crimson, stung by the casual insult. This was just puppy fat but the nicknames wormed into his mind. 'Tubby' Moore was conscious of his weight right through adult life; careful what he ate down to counting out a dozen peanuts – no more, no less – and sticking to his ration.

It is not hard to see how Moore's restraint was forged; a neat, well-behaved boy from a straightlaced home and a strict but loving mother who hated attention and fuss. Hardly any images survive of the family. According to Aunt Ina: 'Doris would never have her photograph taken. She would turn her back on the camera. I've only got one photograph of her, just tucked in at the end. She didn't know it was being taken. She didn't like to be in the limelight anywhere. She was that personality, "no, no, leave me out of it".' Moore's father was soft, with a self-deprecating sense of humour which he would pass on to his son, but he was no socialiser, declining the invitations of his workmates to join them down the pub.

Moore was an only child, fiercely protected by his mother. 'I suspect Doss decided one kid was enough,' Peter Buckle, one of Moore's cousins, says. 'And there would have been no arguing after that.'

'She idolised him,' says Brian Dear, who would become one of Moore's great pals as team-mates at West Ham United. 'Doris would be one of those mums, whatever the kid does she'd be saying "that's impossible, my Robert wouldn't have done that. Not my Robert".'

When Moore was caught short one day and ended up peeing into a milk bottle, his mother was aghast, unable to believe that her son would be so uncouth. Already Moore carried an expectation that he would live up to high standards.

This was not a household likely to foster an extrovert, and Robert Frederick Chelsea Moore was never one of those. 'Robert could be a good conversationalist – when it was necessary,' Aunt Ina noted, but he would never be known for his way with words.

It was a regimented upbringing, but far from a joyless one. The Moores had a passion, and it was for sport. Doss was a determined tom-boy who loved going to watch any contest: the dogs, speedway, boxing, professional wrestling.

'Big' Bob had a role with the supporters' association of Barking FC, the local non-league club in the Isthmian League. Right from an early age, they would take Robert to matches, home and away. Bob took his son to Wembley to watch England's international against Argentina in 1951, when Billy Wright was the blond captain of the national team and the attack was led by Tom Finney, Jackie Milburn and Stan Mortensen. The team also included a right-back called Alf Ramsey.

Robert spent his Saturday afternoons jumping on his bike

and taking the Woolwich Ferry to watch Charlton Athletic, the First Division team nearest to Barking. Standing in the crowd at The Valley, Moore thrilled to the sight of Ray Barlow for West Bromwich Albion, full of poise and intelligent passing. He adored, too, the magnificent Duncan Edwards, Manchester United's muscular midfield star, and once claimed to have bunked off school to catch a glimpse of Edwards playing against Spurs at White Hart Lane.

On Sunday mornings, he would cycle across Barking to see one of his cousins, waiting patiently outside, chucking a tennis ball against the wall, until there was a game on the local rec. Peter Buckle talks of a quiet boy who, as the youngest of the gang, would often have to wait patiently on the sidelines until there was a place in one of the teams.

'We had quite a number of lads who did quite well at football,' he says. 'A lad who went to Colchester, another boy called Webb who went to Spurs. About twenty of us would get over the park, put our coats down. Robert was a bit younger so he used to make up the numbers.

'What I do remember is that he was a pain in the butt! You'd get the ball and he was on your back, always there. You'd say, "go mark someone else!" He'd always be on you but he wasn't quick, wasn't special. You'd never look at him and imagine what he'd go on to do. You can't believe it, looking back, seeing him stand on the side of the pitch waiting to get a game.'

Moore's first success on the football field came at Westbury Primary School. He was inside-right and captain of the school team which won the Crisp Shield, a trophy almost as big as young Moore himself. The local paper carried the first published photo of Moore with his big dimples and silverware in his hand.

He was just another East End kid who loved football, playing on the streets with his mates. It took Malcolm Allison to see what he might become.

3. Big Mal

When Bobby Moore died his diary was full of preparations for a testimonial night for Malcolm Allison. Even as he was fighting cancer, Moore was still trying to repay the debt he owed to his dear friend and mentor.

Moore once went so far as to say that he loved Allison, which was highly out of character given that he was not one for gushing emotion. But as many women of Allison's acquaintance could attest, there was much about Malcolm to love.

Allison was over six feet tall with the rugged good looks of a Hollywood idol. He was ebulliently charismatic. 'Possibly the least tranquillised Englishman alive,' Michael Parkinson once said. Brian Clough called him 'the Errol Flynn of football, too handsome for his own good', a compliment which also carried hints of Allison's downfall.

Allison was a force of nature, a blast of energy, whose influence on West Ham was profound from the day he strode into Upton Park in February 1951, looked around at this becalmed Second Division club with its middling ambitions and journeymen players, and scolded them all for trundling along. In Allison's mind, what was the point of life if not reaching for the stars?

He was signed as West Ham's centre-half. He became its captain, alpha male, chief tactician, spokesman and unofficial coach, and an innovative one at that.

Much later, Big Mal's passions would become champagne, cigars, fedora hats and the prettiest woman in the room but, through his early years, Allison's boundless enthusiasm was focused on improving an English game being left behind by clever foreigners.

Allison was on the terraces at Wembley in 1953 to witness first-hand the 6-3 thrashing of the national team by Hungary, the dark day that showed up decades of English complacency and stagnation. Allison took the humiliation personally. He wanted to be part of the solution and he took himself off to coaching courses at the FA centre at Lilleshall in Shropshire. He would return laden with fresh, sometimes half-baked, ideas.

Some players were straight off to the dog track as soon as morning work was over but Allison led extra training with the approval of Ted Fenton, West Ham's pipe-smoking manager who was respected by his players but more likely to be spotted in tweeds than a tracksuit.

West Ham was not yet known as The Academy but Allison was helping to forge that reputation along with the men he regarded as fellow 'revolutionaries' like Noel Cantwell, Frank O'Farrell and John Bond. Tactics and training methods were discussed, foreign trends analysed in Cassettari's Cafe across the road from Upton Park, which was an unofficial mess for senior players.

On match day, fans would walk in there a couple of hours

before kick-off and find their heroes finishing off a mixed grill. Folklore has it that salt and pepper pots and ketchup sauce would be moved around the table in different formations, highlighting how English teams were stuck like concrete to the outmoded WM system.

Fenton's contribution to the revolution was a determination to overhaul West Ham's youth system by stopping the flow of all the best East End youngsters to Chelsea, talents like Jimmy Greaves and Terry Venables who were being lured away. Chelsea were rumoured to be offering illicit temptations to the families of the top teenage stars, with a new fridge said to be the going rate.

As Fenton fought to keep the local talent at West Ham, he paid Allison, Cantwell and other senior players to coach his young recruits. With typical modesty, Allison declared that he had 'a gift' for spotting the kids who would make it. His eye had been caught by a sturdy blond boy no one else seemed to consider outstanding.

We love to hear about the first sighting of a great player; the moment when the legend is born, his destiny mapped out. We revel in the story, even if it is apocryphal, of a Northern Irish scout sending a telegram to Matt Busby proclaiming: 'I think I found you a genius'. George Best lived up to the billing. We delight in Sir Alex Ferguson remembering the first thrilling sight of a swaying Ryan Giggs. 'He was thirteen and just floated over the ground like a cocker spaniel chasing a piece of silver paper in the wind,' the Manchester United manager lyrically recalled.

Such moments, such prodigies, come along but rarely. There was certainly no 'Eureka' moment from a scout or manager in the career of Bobby Moore. Even with the benefit of hindsight, there was no one who could wind back the clock and say they spotted a world-beater on the pitches of east London.

No one ever mistook the young Moore for a wunderkind – least of all Moore himself. 'As I recall, the faults boiled down to the fact that I wasn't very fast, I wasn't very good at heading and I wasn't very good at tackling. I can't actually remember what I was supposed to be good at.' Even if we factor in Moore's tendency for extreme self-deprecation, his modesty was based on certain indisputable facts.

From the start, Moore was one-paced, and that pace was average. The teenage Moore was a battleship rather than a speedboat; a left-half, a defensive midfield player, who would doggedly close down more creative opponents just as he did on Barking rec.

He had his schoolboy dreams. Moore would sit in classes at Tom Hood Technical College in Leyton, working towards his four GCE passes (in technical drawing, geography, woodwork and art), and imagine a career in professional sport – until reality bit and he returned to plans to become an apprentice draughtsman.

If he excelled at sport, it was as a cricketer. A stylish opening batsman, Moore progressed to London and Essex Schoolboys and then on to captaining the South of England. He led them against the North, coming up against Colin Milburn who was on his way to an England Test career.

Essex started to show an interest in the unhurried batsman who was twelfth man for England Schools, a far higher grade than he had reached in football. Doug Insole, the Essex captain, was sufficiently impressed to make an approach to Moore: 'I think you've got quite a lot of promise as a cricketer. How would you like to join the Essex groundstaff?'

Professional football might have missed him but for Tom Russell, a teacher from Hackney. Watching Leyton Boys under 15s, Russell liked the earnestness of the left-half who was not the most mobile but played with zealous application. The teacher had contacts at West Ham and added Moore's name to the list of kids they should monitor.

With Fenton's determination not to miss out on emerging talent, Jack Turner, a man of many titles at Upton Park, including Welfare Officer and Property Manager, was sent down on a winter's day in 1955. On a pitch off Flanders Road, wrapped up against the biting cold, Turner watched Moore playing against East Ham and duly sent in a scouting report which would be recalled with wry amusement decades later: 'Whilst he would not set the world alight, this boy certainly impressed me with his tenacity and industry.'

It was hardly a declaration that he had discovered a genius, but it was enough for Moore to be invited to join training on Tuesday and Thursday nights at West Ham. He had his chance, though Moore was still very unsure that he had the calibre to make it. The persuasive, charismatic Allison would soon convince him otherwise.

Moore was desperate to know how to make the professional grade, and what he needed to do to overcome his weaknesses. He had an endless list of questions; Allison appeared to have all the answers.

The teenager's natural reserve began to evaporate in the company of an extrovert who had an opinion on everything and everyone. Allison forced the young man out of his shell from the day he discovered that Moore lived on his route to Barkingside.

'Do you want a lift home?' Allison asked one day after training.

'If you could take me as far as Barking,' Moore replied.

'Do you want a lift home?'

'Barking would be great.'

'Tell the truth,' Allison snapped. 'You want a lift home but you're too frightened to ask for it.'

Moore jumped into the car.

They became regular travel partners, Moore gathering the confidence to pester Allison for advice. Others at Upton Park raved about Georgie Fenn, a brilliant young goalscorer. He had a special talent but Allison found Fenn cocky. Too flash, thought he knew it all. Moore was the opposite. Moore was desperate to learn. Moore was keen and hungry.

When it came to choosing those kids who should be invited to join as apprentices, Allison was insistent that Moore should be included and so, at sixteen, he left school to take his first job on £7 a week as a member of the West Ham groundstaff.

The job title was not misleading. Up a ladder cleaning windows at Upton Park, or on the terraces sweeping away the rubbish, the apprentices had to earn their money. Coke had to be shovelled into the boiler, floodlight girders painted, the pitch dug up in summer to lay fresh topsoil.

After every match, the cigarette butts and litter would have to be swept out from the old Chicken Run, the rickety wooden stand at Upton Park which only ever seemed one careless flick of ash away from disaster.

In the summer holidays, Moore took up a job labouring, digging the roads, mixing cement, working for a West Ham supporter who was a building contractor. The hard graft was more than compensated for by the prospect of training.

Bill Robinson was the official coach of the youth team but it was the sessions with Cantwell and Allison that Moore savoured.

Whatever Moore lacked, Allison poured into him. There was a lecture in on-pitch demeanour. Moore was told that even if he was not skipper, he must act as captain. 'Look BIG, think BIG,' Allison told him. That stature was increasingly coming naturally to Moore, who was losing the puppy fat and starting to blossom into the 6ft, 12st 10lb man he would become.

As they weaved out through the industrial East End and Moore confessed a doubt that he would ever make it, Allison barked back: 'You'll be better than all of them. Don't you worry.'

'But Malcolm . . .'

'Don't be silly. Do as I say and see who comes out on top. You're not the one to judge. I am.'

The lessons became more specific, with Allison determined to pass on his ball-playing philosophy. Sometimes he did so with brutal force. Moore would never forget the dressing down after a youth team match against Chelsea. He was deployed in defence, marking Barry Bridges. The brilliant young striker had already played for Chelsea's first team. It was a daunting test but Moore applied himself with his familiar diligence and Bridges did not get a sniff in a goalless draw. Moore was delighted with his contribution until Allison stormed angrily through the dressing-room door.

'If I ever see you play like that again, I won't waste my time with you!'

Allison berated Moore for limiting himself to a destructive role, handcuffed to Bridges, when he should have taken responsibility for building play from the back.

'Every time the goalie got the ball, what are you doing? You're running up the field looking for Bridges, chasing him like a shadow. Did you ever drop back to take the ball off the goalkeeper or help a team-mate out? What have I taught you? Don't ever let me see you play like that!'

That rant had such an impact that, years later, Moore was still explaining to his friend Harry Redknapp how Allison's anger had shaped his approach to the game.

'Bobby said that without Malcolm he wouldn't have made it,' Redknapp recalls. 'He said Malcolm took him back to the training ground, made him work every day on playing out from the back and that made him the player he became. Bobby loved Malcolm. He thought he was fantastic.'

The lessons shaped Moore for the rest of his career, none more so than the day Allison took him aside and explained that the secret of every great player was to plan how to use the ball before you received it. 'The single most valuable thing I was ever taught,' Moore would say. 'If I get the ball now, who will I give it to?' It was the question he asked himself daily, drawing pictures in his mind.

West Ham developed a training exercise in which a practice game would be stopped, the players told to shut their eyes and then instructed to pinpoint where their team-mates were standing. In that drill, Moore was always top of the class.

Moore was driven by an insecurity that he did not have outstanding natural skills. The result was that no one trained with more determination or listened more intently. When all the young players were forced to do the dreaded stomach tests – lying on their backs with both feet raised off the ground – Moore quickly established a reputation as the fittest. When Georgie Fenn was messing about, Moore was finding a ball and a wall and practising for an extra hour.

The one significant doubt that preyed on Moore's mind remained his lack of speed, trailing at the back in sprints. Eventually he confided his worries to Cantwell who tended to provide a more sympathetic ear than Allison. Moore's question was this: 'Can I be a great player if I can't run fast?'

Cantwell pondered it for a while: 'You had to be very careful with your answers to Bobby because he thought seriously about all aspects of the game. If I'd said he couldn't succeed without speed, it would have affected him terribly. I didn't want to hurt his feelings and I suggested to him that he watch some of the greats, like [Johnny] Haynes [of Fulham] and Ray Barlow, of West Bromwich.'

'Milk turns quicker than Haynes but that doesn't matter,' Cantwell told him, explaining how game intelligence could compensate for lack of speed. Moore seemed reassured. There was not much he could do about his pace but he had done everything else to learn and improve. West Ham were happy with his progress and had no hesitation in offering Moore professional terms soon after his seventeenth birthday. In May 1958 he signed his first professional contract for £12 a week, the maximum for that age. For a lad who could not run fast, head the ball or use his left foot, Moore's career was progressing quickly. Too quickly for Allison.

Mentor or protégé? The old pro desperate for one last chance or the kid with a future? Malcolm Allison or Bobby Moore? The poignancy of the choice was lost on no one when West Ham, depleted by injuries, needed to draft in an emergency left-half to face Manchester United on 8 September 1958.

It was a weighty decision on so many levels. This was West Ham's biggest match in decades. They had been promoted in May, back into the top flight for the first time in twenty-six years. Fenton and his players were eager to make an impression and there was no bigger game than hosting United. Everyone wanted to catch a glimpse of the team reborn from the Munich air disaster. United had been a source of endless sympathy and fascination since the crash in February in which twenty-three people had died, including eight players. Bobby Charlton, the twenty-year-old golden boy, was one of five survivors due to line up for Matt Busby's team at Upton Park.

West Ham's injury crisis had come at a bad time, leaving Fenton with a straight choice between Moore and Allison. After all those hours together, the lifts home and the bonding, the two men were now rivals.

Moore was still raw but he had impressed everyone with his maturity. His performances for West Ham's youth team were starting to win him international recognition. Moore left Britain for the first time in October 1957 to represent England Youth against Holland in Amsterdam.

For Fenton, Moore was the best choice among his young apprentices but Allison was desperate to play, to hear the roar of the crowd once more. It had been a shattering year for the man who had done so much to put West Ham back in the top division. Promotion should have been Allison's glory as much as anyone's but he had missed almost the entire season, stricken with tuberculosis. He had spent most of the year in hospital and then a sanatorium. He had lost a lung.

Moore was at Upton Park to collect his wages on the day that Allison's illness was confirmed and he was shocked to see his mentor – big, confident Malcolm – in tears being consoled by Cantwell. Moore had visited Allison at the sanatorium in Midhurst, Sussex on the day of the Munich air crash which had killed his hero Duncan Edwards. Had he lived, Edwards would have been twenty-nine in the summer of 1966 and, according to just about anyone who saw him play, the obvious choice as England captain.

Cantwell and Moore fidgeted uneasily while Allison moped in bed, distant, distracted and depressed by his infirmity. Six months later, Allison's mood had turned to angry defiance. He vowed to make a comeback and to play in the First Division, even on one lung. Suddenly that rash of injuries to three left-halves had given Allison a glimmer of hope. As Fenton's options decreased, so Allison's expectations grew. Young Moore was a possibility but the teenager could wait. This was his shot at the big time.

What happened next would end one career and launch another. It was like watching two men crossing on the escalators of life; one heading up, the other down.

At the stadium for some light training on the morning of the game, Fenton summoned Cantwell to his office. The Irishman had replaced the convalescent Allison as team captain.

'I've got a bit of a problem. Who would you play tonight at left-half?' Fenton asked. Cantwell squirmed, knowing that he was not just picking a team but potentially having a tremendous impact on the lives of two friends.

'If it were my decision, I would play Bobby Moore,' Cantwell replied. In purely footballing terms, he felt that it was an easy choice between the improving seventeen-year-old and an old friend who, for all the sympathy he merited, had played only two reserve matches in twelve months.

It was the right call by Cantwell and admirably unsentimental given his long friendship with Allison. But it was brutal, too. Allison never played professional football again. For him it was a shattering moment; for Moore, it presented the biggest day of his young life.

Moore's first challenge was to make it to the front of the bus queue. All of Barking seemed to be heading to the game, jostling to squeeze on board for the journey three miles east to Upton Park. Moore thought about pushing in but was too polite to queue-barge, and no one thought to usher the blond teenager through. How were they to know that the anxious young man would soon be making his debut as West Ham's new left-half?

Moore fretted in line, observing protocol. 'I thought at one stage, let alone play the game I wouldn't even see it,' he recalled. Eventually he squeezed on to a packed upper deck, glancing at his watch and praying that he would not be embarrassed by reporting late. He arrived to find a thronging mass of supporters on the streets around the ground.

The crowd was so huge that they had to shut the gates early, with more than 36,000 fans inside and many more locked out that Monday night. Moore was nearly one of those excluded. A line of police officers were stopping supporters going through the main gates and when Moore tried to squeeze through, a constable put his arm across his chest: 'Sorry, son, all these entrances are closed. Try round the corner.' Moore attempted, unsuccessfully, to persuade the officer that he was playing. He was forced to call over a club official who ushered him inside.

Moore made it through the main entrance, down the corridor and walked into the dressing room. The first person he bumped into was Allison. There was deep symbolism in the brief, awkward exchange as the young debutant and the old-timer passed each other.

Moore did not have much time to dwell on the conflicting emotions; the thrill at his promotion and what he called the 'sadness and embarrassment' that his jubilation should inflict such anguish on his old friend. There was a momentary, uncomfortable silence before the older man, masking his own rage and pain, wished the teenager all the best – then turned and departed.

Allison would save his anger for Cantwell. Somehow he had heard of his friend's role in team selection and exploded with anger. 'I could play with my ankles tied together and be better than the kid,' he shouted. It would take weeks before he calmed down.

Moore would come to say that he wished Allison had played; that he could have waited his turn; that one appearance would have meant more to his stricken mentor than it did to him. But on the night, he did what he would always do. He blocked out the emotion. He compartmentalised.

He had enough to worry about, marking Ernie Taylor, 5ft 4ins of scheming forward in size four boots best known for his years cleverly feeding the ball to Stanley Matthews at Blackpool. Fenton kept it simple to Moore: 'Keep on top of Taylor. He's the general. He needs watching all the time.'

Moore readied himself in the dressing room. There was no warm-up on the pitch. The first the crowd would see of the players was when they came out a few minutes before kick-off. He set about the preparations which would become the ritual throughout his career.

On came the shirt, he pulled up his socks, laced his boots and sat in his jockstrap. He always left his shorts to the very last minute because he did not want any unsightly streaks of linament or creases. When the buzzer sounded to summon the teams, Moore would hold his shorts by the band with two fingers. Shorts on, shirt tucked in, he was smartly turned out and ready for action.

Shortly before 7.30 p.m., as the Leyton Silver Band near the players' tunnel finished their pre-match repertoire with 'I'm Forever Blowing Bubbles', Moore walked out for his debut on a warm and humid September night. He could hardly have picked a better occasion, roared on by a packed crowd.

Moore's first notable intervention in professional football was to catch Taylor with a strong early tackle, earning a ticking-off from the referee. He settled down into his role as destructive wing-half, a man-marking job, leaving Andy Malcolm to drive West Ham forward from right-half. It was a good night to make a debut. West Ham were 2-0 up by half-time.

Upton Park was delirious when Malcolm Musgrove added the third after the break. Manchester United looked bedraggled, effectively playing with ten men after Wilf McGuinness pulled a thigh muscle and had to play on with his leg heavily strapped. No substitutes in those days; not for another seven years in the Football League.

It seemed over as a contest but, exhausted by their early intensity, West Ham gradually began to lose control of midfield, tiring after an hour of hard pressure. First Colin Webster struck, then, miraculously, McGuinness.

It was a fraught finale but West Ham clung on to win 3-2 and walk off top of the First Division with four wins from six games. Matt Busby put his head around the dressing-room door: 'You were great, lads. You won well.'

At seventeen, the self-proclaimed schoolboy plodder had

made it into the First Division, though his joy was short-lived. From the high of his debut against United, the return to earth came with a bump when Moore kept his place against Nottingham Forest the following Saturday.

He took a terrible chasing from Johnny Quigley in a 4-0 defeat but it was not the score that lodged in his memory, rather one lone shout from the crowd as the teams came out for the second half: 'Play on the left-half, he's the weak link.' One heckle made Moore feel sick to his stomach.

Moore still had much to learn and, following those two appearances, he was back in the youth team and the reserves. He played only three more league games that season. It took the arrival of Ron Greenwood at West Ham to unlock Moore's full potential.

4. Ron

About all that Ron Greenwood shared with Malcolm Allison was a love of coaching and a certainty that, in the young Bobby Moore, there was a talent to nurture. As characters, they were from opposite ends of the spectrum (and Moore would soon discover that he preferred the end which came with champagne).

'Big Mal' was a playboy who married a Bunny Girl, an extrovert and a hellraiser who entranced Moore, opening his eyes to his youthful promise and, eventually, to new social horizons. Greenwood would prove no less influential but he came about it in the rather more studied way you might expect from a man known to his players as Reverend Ron.

Greenwood brought idealism to his work, a belief that he was on a mission to show that the game was not about victory by any means but the pursuit of excellence. It was about artistry. 'Football is a battle of wits or nothing at all,' Greenwood said. He abhorred the win-at-all-costs culture he felt was taking a pernicious hold in professional football. Preaching those principles would inspire that 'Reverend' tag.

While Allison came to spend his managerial life at war

with football's authorities for his many, intemperate attacks, Greenwood was exactly the sort of upstanding chap welcomed into FA circles. While coaching the Oxford University team, Greenwood impressed Harold Thompson, a chemistry don who was on his way to becoming the notoriously autocratic chairman of the FA. Thompson brought Greenwood into the England fold and put him in charge of England Youth.

It was while scouting for new talent that Greenwood would first come across Moore as a sturdy sixteen-year-old, an early sighting that may say more about his discerning eye than Moore's outstanding abilities. Greenwood was at Stamford Bridge looking for recruits for his junior international team and he liked the blond teenager playing centre-half for London Grammar Schools against their Glasgow counterparts. Greenwood called up Moore and handed him a record seventeen appearances for England Youth in 1957–8. He championed Moore around the FA.

At West Ham, they were still not sure about Moore's quality, or even his best position, moving him around defence and midfield. Greenwood saw a ball-playing centre-half and a boy with the temperament to go a long way.

To Greenwood, at least in those early days, Moore seemed a manager's dream; enthusiastic to the point of being a teacher's pet. 'I rarely had a conversation with young Moore,' Greenwood said. 'He simply asked questions. He wanted to know everything.' How to defend against this player? Where to pass? When to bring the ball out? Just the type for a thoughtful coach like Greenwood who, even as he was winning a championship medal with Chelsea and one cap for England at centre-half, sensed that his greatest achievements might come as a coach.

After the England Youth team, Greenwood was promoted

to take charge of the national under 23s and he was soon bringing Moore along with him. Greenwood had kept track of Moore as he tried to establish himself at West Ham, captaining the apprentices to the FA Youth Cup final in 1959. Nine of that teenage team would go on to play for the first XI, justifying all Fenton's busy recruitment as well as the input of Allison and Cantwell on the training ground.

Moore had started a longer spell in the West Ham first team when John Smith, the left-half, was sold to Spurs in the spring of 1960. Greenwood lobbied for him to be elevated to the England under 23s. Moore discovered his international promotion in September 1960 when he was flicking through the evening paper on the underground after a night in central London.

Some days later a letter arrived from the FA – 'Dear Moore' – which included travel arrangements. Third-class rail would be provided. There was a list of Do's and Don'ts including the necessity of polished shoes and 'laces washed bearing no unseemly marks of mud'. Not a problem for Doss's son.

Moore represented the England under 23s for the first time alongside Gordon Banks and Bobby Charlton. His and Greenwood's careers were about to become entwined even more closely when West Ham looked for a new manager in April 1961. The team's progress had slowed and, the directors decided to oust only the third manager they had employed in sixty years. Fenton departed.

When the news emerged that Greenwood was his replacement, lured from his full-time job as assistant at Arsenal, the West Ham players rushed to ask Moore what the new boss was like. A proper coach, he said. 'If you want to learn, there's no better teacher,' he told them.

Moore had particular reason to be thrilled. After Fenton's sacking he had been dropped by West Ham. Phil Woosnam, the captain, had taken over as caretaker and replaced Moore with Geoff Hurst as the new left-half.

The first knock on the door when Greenwood installed himself in his new office in the main stand at Upton Park was a fretful Moore. The young man was desperate to know what lay ahead of him. He wanted to know if he had prospects. He wanted reassurance that he had a future given that he could not find a place in the side.

Greenwood looked at Moore and made a bold promise which would stick in both men's minds: 'I know you, I like you and I am going to build this club around you.'

From a manager who had barely started in his first significant job to a twenty-year-old midfield player who was not in West Ham's XI, it was a leap of faith. But, of course, Greenwood already knew the quality of the young man in front of him. The chance to build a team around Moore was one of the reasons he had been attracted to the job at Upton Park. 'I was not flattering him,' Greenwood remarked. 'I meant it. There was always something about Moore.'

There *was* something about Moore, but what was it? Greenwood talked of 'the determined jaw, the cool knowing eyes' and he quickly noticed that behind them lay a peculiar mind. Greenwood was struck by a lad who seemed a little apart from his team-mates; so diligent about his game that, whenever his team scored, he would not rush over to celebrate but turn on his heels and walk back to his position ready for the restart. 'Only once in all my years with him did he congratulate a player for scoring a goal,' Greenwood remarked.

It would have been a fascinating experiment to put a heart-rate monitor on Moore to find out if his pulse registered any leaps in moments of stress or ecstasy. It seemed as though he was immune to emotion, never more obviously than in his goal celebrations – the total absence of them.

It didn't matter who scored, or how spectacularly. When Moore once advanced thirty yards and smacked a cannonball shot into the top corner against Queens Park Rangers, team-mates ran over to mob him. Moore shrugged his shoulders. You can still find the clip on YouTube. Watch it enough times and you start to make out a barely perceptible smile, though only just.

Greenwood reckoned that Moore regarded celebrations as 'a waste of energy'. Moore himself would dismiss it as simply keeping his concentration at a vulnerable time for a team, but this went beyond practicality. One writer called Moore 'as emotional as a computer' and it was an unnatural reaction, cool and composed yet almost robotic.

'The most calculated footballer you could ever meet,' says Brian James, who covered Moore's career extensively for the *Daily Mail*. 'He calculated everything. How he behaved on the pitch, everything he said off it.'

It was a similar story with Moore and discipline. At Manchester City one night in November 1961, Moore suffered a rush of blood. He was facing the winger David Wagstaffe; two young bucks jostling for the upper hand. Moore won the first duel, Wagstaffe got stroppy. There was an edge, a fractiousness, for the rest of the night. Right at the final whistle, Wagstaffe sneaked in one last kick as he chased Moore down the touchline. The young defender lashed back with a boot. Wagstaffe crumpled to the floor. The evidence was damning, even if Moore thought that Wagstaffe was guilty of exaggerating the impact.

It was a momentary aberration but Moore was sent off for the first time in his career, and shortly before he was about to meet up with England under 23s. Questions were asked in the newspapers, and within the FA, about the temperament of a young man who could be dismissed so idiotically right at the end of a game in which West Ham had trailed 3-1 at half-time but had fought back magnificently to win 5-3.

Moore was suspended by the FA for a week. He would say that the lesson lasted a lifetime. In *My Soccer Story*, his first autobiography, Moore talked about never again falling for provocation, never again allowing himself to react. 'I have my own way of annoying this kind of opposition. I pretend they don't exist,' he wrote.

He went on: ' "I'm not coming down to your level mate" is the attitude I try to convey and this infuriates the niggler – who immediately thinks you are some kind of stuck-up snob – so much he loses his temper.'

There are numerous examples of Moore subsequently refusing to fall for the wind-ups, the stray elbow, spit in the face. The tale is told of how he wiped an opponent's saliva from his cheek, held out his sleeve to his assailant and said, 'I believe that's yours'. It could be dismissed as apocryphal if it involved any footballer other than Bobby Moore.

Opponents would snap and snarl. Moore would smile back, killing them with politeness. 'I am not being goody-goody about this,' he explained. 'In fact, it's a cold-blooded decision. By staying aloof from "all that" you plant the idea in their heads (or hope to) that you are superior all round. It's like psychological warfare.'

Moore was no soft touch. Denis Law once pulled aside Hugh McIlvanney, the journalist, and made it plain that Moore should never be confused with Mother Teresa: 'You're always praising that Moore,' Law said. 'But you're not there when he's standing on my fucking feet.' Moore could stand up for himself but, after the Wagstaffe incident, retaliation would always be inflicted with a cool head, not in the heat of confrontation.

McIlvanney saw him once inflict revenge with that calculated ruthlessness. 'A guy fouled him a couple of times badly. Bobby looked to check the guy's number which was a bit pointless because he could see the guy's face, but there was something very deliberate about it. Next time the guy came up, nothing. The second time, nothing. But the third time, over the boundary wall the guy went. That was the thing about Bobby. Don't act immediately so the referee doesn't connect the two. He was smart like that.'

Moore's cold detachment would eventually give him a reputation for haughtiness. Greenwood would come to curse Moore's restraint, but in those early days he saw it as a sign of a young man's maturity and fanatical dedication. He was sure that Moore could be the rock of his new West Ham, but he had to work out how.

Bob Dylan sang that the times were a'changing. English football was a'changing, too. Among all the great revolutions of the sixties, the decade of rock and roll and rockets to the moon, the arrival of the back four was not sexy or swinging but it has endured long after mop tops and psychedelic prints have gone out of fashion.

At the 1958 World Cup finals, Brazil had caused a stir and not just because of a teenage sensation called Pelé. With attacking

full-backs and two centre-backs, the South Americans popu-
larised a new 4-2-4 strategy. In England, Greenwood was
one of the trendsetters, recognising the benefits of the back
four – and, most importantly, how it could work perfectly for
Bobby Moore.

Moore had moved around several positions. Greenwood
had seen him in the junior England teams as a traditional
centre-half. In the WM formation which English clubs had
slavishly followed for decades, the position was essentially
destructive. In *The Soccer Syndrome*, John Moynihan wrote
that the stopper's only task was to track the centre-forward
'like a casino manager watching a con man'.

According to Brian Glanville, it had 'become the
Frankenstein's monster of modern football', the least demanding position on the field with no creative responsibility. There
were skilful exceptions, but mostly it had been a role for tall
bruisers, and Moore could be exposed there.

In West Ham's youth team, some of his team-mates fretted
when he faced quick centre-forwards or specialists in the air.
They worried about Moore being isolated in that key position
because of his lack of pace and reluctance to join aerial battle.
'Bobby didn't particularly like heading the ball because it was
untidy,' says Ken Jones, who covered Moore's career for the
Daily Mirror. 'Bobby wasn't interested in untidy.'

In the first team, Moore had mostly been used as a destructive
half-back, a midfield scuffler sent out to close down a particular
opponent but one day in February 1962, Greenwood pulled
Moore aside on the training ground ahead of a match against
Leicester City. He explained that he was withdrawing him
into defence: 'I want you to drop back, to play deeper and play
loose.' He was playing him as a 'spare' centre-half alongside

Ken Brown, effectively making a back four.

They hardly sound like the words to change a career, and certainly not the course of English football. No one hailed the new role at the time, but Geoff Hurst is in no doubt about the deep and lasting significance of that tactical switch. 'Perhaps Ron's masterstroke,' he says, which is quite an accolade considering that Hurst himself was transformed, in a brilliant piece of coaching alchemy, from a middling midfielder to a powerhouse centre-forward who would make an historic impact.

A masterstroke it was. Moore immediately thrived in his role off Brown, seeing problems and smothering them. As Brown battled with the centre-forward, Moore tidied up, bringing order to the defence the way he brought it to his sock drawer and his rack of shirts.

He was always more perceptive than most thanks to the lessons of Allison. Dropping back from the hustle and bustle of midfield allowed his awareness to flourish. It was the skill which, many years later, would prompt the great Scottish manager Jock Stein to say 'there should be a law against Moore – he can see things twenty minutes before everyone else'.

With the game now laid out in front of him, Moore could use good judgement to help compensate for the lack of pace. His distaste for heading was no longer such an obvious drawback as he learned to drop off and, far more elegantly, take the ball on his chest.

As Moynihan put it, Moore was 'a smooth, streamlined young Londoner with the appearance of a male model, whose methods have been built for the new emancipated soccer of 4-2-4 and 4-3-3'. The game was changing and Moore had all the qualities to adapt with it. 'Moore had found his niche,' Greenwood said, with pride and delight.

Ken Jones, for decades one of Fleet Street's most perceptive readers of the game, believes that it is hard to overstate how the new tactics shaped Moore's career: 'I'm convinced that the change in the way the game was played helped to make Bobby Moore a truly great player.' Without Greenwood Moore might not have been a world-class defender; he might not have been a defender at all.

This was not just about tactics boards. Great players redefine positions by their own unique, and unmistakeable, qualities. Plenty of English teams embraced the new era but it was Moore who showed just how influential the new role could become.

He described himself as a 'sweeper' which, Greenwood noted proudly, 'was not a position anyone had heard of before'. Yet the label does not quite fit. Typically, Moore was being too self-deprecating. He was not stationed behind a back line in the *libero* position that was becoming so common in Italy into the sixties, but just to the left of a stopping centre-back with the freedom to stride forward. 'Sweeper' does not begin to do justice to Moore's range and influence; watching him build play from the back was like watching a team with rear-wheel drive.

One of Greenwood's constant demands of his players was 'can you hurt them?', demanding that his players always look for an attacking opportunity. That included Moore in central defence. He was encouraged by his manager always to look for the quick pass that could turn defence to attack.

He had the accuracy to do it. The sight of Moore striding into midfield and chipping the ball forward would become so commonplace that the players used to joke that Geoff Hurst must have a bull's-eye on his chest, so frequently could

Moore find the target. He played like a gridiron quarter-back, initiating moves with flighted, angled passes.

Allison had always encouraged him to play from deep, and Greenwood preached from the same gospel. When Moore's ambition proved costly in one game, possession lost and a goal conceded as he tried to carry the ball out of defence, Greenwood told the press that he would much prefer to see a well-intentioned mistake of over-elaboration than a clearance hoofed into the stands.

To a twenty-first-century eye, Moore's range of influence is startling. What central defender of the modern era would you see breaking forward so boldly, imposing a pattern on the game from centre-half? Modern football has its ball-playing defenders and those with adventurous spirit, but in a game with such aversion to risk, the surging centre-back is almost as extinct as the old five-man attacks. To wish for another Moore may be as romantic, and as pointless, as yearning for another Sinatra.

Gerard Piqué, encouraged to take the ball from the back at Barcelona, certainly has the poise. Others, such as David Luiz, have the intention. But in English football, the defender who strides into midfield has been bred out of existence. Hurst bemoans the loss: 'We haven't produced anybody who plays that way as a sweeper, who is composed, a leader and good on the ball, taking responsibility. Nowhere near. We produce a lot of the markers, Terry Butcher, Dave Watson or the John Terry of today but no one who can play a totally different way alongside. A defender who can play into midfield, it's a huge advantage in top-class football if you have that.'

There were high hopes that Rio Ferdinand might be the successor to Moore, a man schooled at West Ham and an assured central defender capable of joining midfield, but he was rarely encouraged to carry the ball forward by club or country.

The last great exponent was Matthias Sammer for Germany at Euro 96. Perhaps the game's evolution will bring us back one day to a centre-half as one of his team's most creative influences, but this is not just about quality of player but force of personality, too. To watch Moore play is to see a majestic presence, prowling the pitch with his head held high, pushing the ball ahead and running after it, though never hurriedly, looking for the forward pass.

Moore seized his moment in time and the role first carved out for him by Greenwood against Leicester. Eddie Bovington played just in front of Moore, as a scurrying midfield terrier in the evolving 4-4-2 system.

'Sometimes it felt like Bobby was getting all the praise and you were doing all the hard work,' he says. 'You'd be marking tight and he had the nice job of mopping up behind. But you could hardly complain because he was unique. He had the special quality of making time on the ball. The great players do, don't they? He was in control. The rest of us were chasing around.'

Moore had his fixed place in the West Ham team, a new position carved out by his manager – and his debt to Greenwood would not end there. In May 1962, on the night before the FA Cup final, Moore performed superbly for a junior England side against the senior international team at Highbury. It was a good time to impress Walter Winterbottom, the England manager, who was running into trouble with his half-back positions as he finalised his squad for the World Cup finals in Chile.

Winterbottom was looking for a fringe player as back-up. He chatted to Greenwood about his predicament. 'Why not take Bobby Moore?' the West Ham United manager counselled. 'He won't let you down.'

Winterbottom hesitated about taking an uncapped player but Moore came with the advantage that he could be useful cover in several positions. He was coming off the back of a strong campaign. West Ham had finished a highly respectable eighth in their first season under new management.

Greenwood had vouched for Moore's temperament, saying that he would not be overawed if needed in an emergency. It was a huge step up but Winterbottom decided to take the young man in whom Greenwood had such faith. At twenty-two, Moore found himself propelled into a World Cup having never appeared in a senior England squad.

Greenwood had the privilege of being the messenger, though his method was a little unorthodox. When Moore was summoned to see his manager, he was expecting an update on the end-of-season tour to Africa with West Ham. 'You won't be coming with us,' Greenwood said with mock gravitas. Moore's face dropped.

The manager made him squirm before, finally, breaking the tension. 'You're going to Chile with England,' Greenwood said. 'You're going to the World Cup.'

It was a thrill for Moore just to be travelling in the senior squad, with Flowers, Charlton, Greaves and one of his foot-balling heroes, Johnny Haynes, the pass master. Moore thought he was just going along for the ride so he was thrilled to be promoted for his England debut for a pre-World Cup friendly in Lima, Peru. He replaced Bobby Robson, coming in at his old position as a defensive wing-half. Moore applied himself well enough though the headlines all belonged to Jimmy Greaves, the hat-trick hero.

Moore expected to revert to the bench but everything changed when Winterbottom accepted an invitation to face a local team in Chile. Robson was kicked, painfully, on the ankle. The swelling in his leg ruled him out for the World Cup group stages. 'The beneficiary was Bobby Moore. Not a bad guy to lose your place to,' Robson recalled, wryly.

It would be quite an international baptism in Chile. England headed by single-track train to their base in Coya, a remote community run by the Braden Copper Company as a rest camp for miners and their families. 'For those of us who had been in the army, and most of us had for our national service, it wasn't too bad,' Jimmy Armfield remembers.

The distractions were a bowling alley and a cinema showing Italian films with Spanish sub-titles. To ease the boredom, the players delighted in putting a plastic spider in Ron Springett's bed in the hope of convincing him it was a tarantula. The young players messed about with itching powder, but most of the senior pros hated being cut off from the world.

Those interminable hours would cement the friendship between Greaves and Moore, who was drawn to the cheeky irreverence of his fellow East Ender. When Winterbottom con-cluded a long-winded instruction about an elaborate passing sequence with Greaves as the focal point, the Spurs striker rolled his eyes. 'Do you want me to score that with my left foot, Walter, or my right?'

The reserve in Moore was drawn to the rebel in Greaves, his willingness to challenge authority. He liked Greaves' sardonic wit and the fact that he came from Manor Park, not too far from Barking. Greaves could afford to be lippy because, even at twenty-two, England were hugely reliant on his goalscoring prowess and they also had Bobby Charlton, at twenty-four, coming into his prime. Moore's promotion was a sign of midfield weakness in an England team which would prove far too reliant on the creativity of Haynes.

Moore's first competitive game for his country was a 2-1 defeat to Hungary in front of a few thousand spectators in Rancagua. He was used to bigger crowds to watch the West Ham reserves. The games were not being broadcast live back in England but grainy black and white footage shows Moore, in the number sixteen shirt, constantly seeking to be involved, dashing over to take corners and throw-ins, keen and busy from his position on the right side of midfield.

Looking a little stiff with his coat-hanger shoulders and a noticeably upright bearing, chasing after the game rather than conducting it as he would in his prime, it is easy to see why Moore was seen by Greenwood as better suited for defence not midfield. Moore was far more comfortable with the game coming on to him, but he was not found wanting.

'It wasn't an easy baptism for him,' Armfield says. 'But one thing you did notice was that he was unflappable.' Brian Glanville described Moore in that tournament as 'precociously and impeccably calm'.

With Moore performing the role of water-carrier alongside his hero Haynes, England beat Argentina 3-1 in their second group game. A desultory draw against Bulgaria secured a place in the quarter-finals and a confrontation with Brazil, the world champions. Even without the injured Pelé, the South Americans had more flair than England could handle.

Garrincha dazzled, scoring twice and had a hand in the other. It was a chastening experience for Moore who admitted 'if I hadn't been so busy defending I would have applauded some of their football'. He realised how far England had to travel to be on top of the world but he departed Chile with his first five England caps and the sense that, while international football represented a step-up, he was not out of his depth.

From the sidelines, Robson noted that Moore was 'a studious player, not a vigorous one. He never hunted opponents to bury them with a tackle. He waited for people to come on to him and then dealt with the threat. Bobby worked out that the hole in front of you is less dangerous than the hole behind you.' Like Greenwood, he saw a future for the young man not in midfield but defence.

Robson said that he would never have guessed then that his replacement would become the golden boy of English football. But he also recognised the diligence of 'the nice, earnest young man . . . very respectful, very polite and trained well. He was the guy you wanted your daughter or sister to marry.'

But by the time Moore returned from Chile he already had a bride waiting for him.

5. The First WAG

History suggests that the metrosexual footballer is an entirely modern phenomenon. As Tina Moore sits in an upmarket restaurant in Chelsea, picking at a sea bass while also trying to prise open the closed character of her former husband, it appears that history might have got it wrong.

Tina talks about a side of Bobby Moore that few saw, and, even as his wife of twenty-six years, she acknowledges that there were chambers which remained locked. 'He wasn't a typical male,' Tina says. 'He had a lot of feminine side, Bobby.'

She talks of his passion for fashion (his and hers), and how he loved to buy her gifts; a tortoiseshell powder compact not long after they had started going out, a designer handbag if he had been on a foreign trip, a new outfit. 'Bobby would love to go shopping with me. If he heard me say to a girlfriend "oh, I like your dress", he'd appear with it a few weeks later. He was amazing like that.'

Tina describes how she went away for a weekend when they were dating as teenagers and came back to find her bedroom newly decorated; and how, using his GCE in woodwork, he made her a jewellery box, lining the interior with pretty fabric.

She talks of a husband who took just as much care with his own appearance as she did with hers, laughing at the memory of Moore's painstaking effort to sunbathe with the backs of his hands facing the sun so that the tan would show up well against his dazzling white shirt cuffs.

He was a working-class boy from the East End who had a drive to better himself, and not just as a footballer. Tina describes an obsessive groomer who wanted to learn how to look the part, to move up in the world, to hang around the smart joints, to be classy and admired. He would even seek advice on dining etiquette and table manners.

The more she talks, the more he sounds like another famous England captain in his aspirations. 'The manners, teaching himself to be better, always immaculate – I was watching Beckham on the television the other night and I could see the similarities' Tina says. 'Very, very similar, I've always thought that.'

To mention the two men in the same sentence is heresy among many of Moore's most loyal supporters. 'Beckham's not fit to lace his boots,' they hurrumph. They say that Moore was all about the substance of the game; Beckham the froth.

But in stoutly defending Moore's honour, they miss the point. Comparisons between the two men as footballers will always be fatuous – different eras, different positions – but similarities in personality, demeanour and particularly in ambition and aspiration are very worthwhile. They are so obvious as to become almost uncanny when Tina also mentions that her husband was, like Beckham, a slave to a form of obsessive compulsive disorder.

Psychiatrists call it an anankastic personality – neatness, perfectionism, a need for order often accompanied by a highly developed sense of conscientiousness. It can be a strength, as it certainly was for Moore and Beckham, in driving them to perfect their skills. Practice, practice, practice. The inner drive, the long hours honing their abilities, laid the foundation for all their success. Neither stinted when it came to the self-improvement necessary to be a top player.

As Moore himself once expressed, possibly with a little help from a ghost writer: 'The standards I set myself are limitless. I can only draw a parallel perhaps with a ballet dancer who seeks the ultimate of performance by timeless practice; or even the concert pianist who strives to play the perfect Beethoven concerto. It is the endless search for perfection and expression.'

But the trait also comes with compulsive habits. Beckham has talked of how he becomes uneasy and restless around clutter. In his home(s), he must put objects in straight lines or pairs; throw out a can from the fridge if there is an odd number; tidy away the leaflets in a hotel room because he cannot stand the disorder, needing everything 'to be perfect'.

Moore had very similar rituals; not just a desire for order, but a need. Shoes had to be lined up like soldiers on parade. He would turn all the pans in the kitchen so that they were neatly stacked a particular way in the cupboards. The labels on cans must all face out. He would fiddle with the towels so that they were all folded in a certain manner.

'Bobby didn't like the edge of the towel to show,' Tina recalls. 'He preferred them folded in three so you didn't see each end. If I didn't do it right, he would come behind and get it right. I still do it now.

'When I met Bobby, it was very difficult because I wasn't used to doing anything. I was so spoilt and there you had this man who was totally and utterly pernickety about all these things, fussing around the house.' OCD? 'Oh yes, I'd say so. He compartmentalised everything. He couldn't cope with disorder and disarray.'

This was no longer just about his clothes being colour coordinated, hung from light to dark, as they had been since he was a child. Tina has described how 'it was almost an aesthetic pleasure to open the wardrobe'. The whole house had to be neat. Cushions would have to be plumped so that when he came down in the morning it was as though no one had been there the previous day. When guests came round and lit up a cigarette, Moore would all but follow them around checking no ash was being carelessly flicked on to the carpet.

On trips, he took his own travel iron. There are tales of him pressing his money. The stories are almost hackneyed about Moore stacking loose change by the side of his bed every night, different denominations in separate and perfect pillars; how he always folded his dirty kit after training and placed it in a neat pile while team-mates hurled theirs into a filthy heap; how he wiped the mud of his boots with his socks while others just chucked them straight into a kit skip.

'He's the only person I've ever met who gets out of the bath dry,' Mike Summerbee said. Moore had developed a technique for preventing a drop of water falling on to the floor when climbing out of the bath. He would flick the water off one leg, dry it with a towel and then step out on that dry leg, continuing the process with the rest of his body. Moore was appalled one day when his room-mate Brian Dear told him not to let the water out because he would jump in the bath afterwards. 'You dirty bugger,' he said.

His friends always spoke about these habits as though they were amusing little quirks but the desire for neatness and order, perfection and control, went to the heart of his character. With or without a ball, Moore was the perfectionist's perfectionist.

He liked his fun, too, and that is what he saw in Tina. It was the pretty blonde looks he fell for first and then he quickly grew to love the vivacious personality. She was bubbly and outgoing, leading the conversation. Just his type.

It was a union of teenage sweethearts. Moore fell for his bride across the dance floor of the Ilford Palais. Loitering with his fellow young players from West Ham up on the balcony, scanning for pretty girls, he eyed her up for weeks, trying to summon the courage to ask her for a dance. His fearfulness of rejection and public embarrassment held him back.

Finally one night, as 'Blue Moon' played, he found the boldness to wander over and introduce himself to fifteen-year-old Christina Elizabeth Dean. There was no reason why the name Bobby Moore would mean anything to her. In 1957 he was just a sixteen-year-old youth player. Tina stood up Bobby on their first date. If it had not been for the intervention of her mother, the romance might have died after one chaste dance.

Some weeks later, travelling down the Ilford High Road in a taxi, Tina pointed out the boy who was chasing her. Her mother liked the look of the handsome, smartly dressed young footballer. She suggested he come over for tea and an inspection. 'My mother always had great aspirations for me,' Tina noted. 'She must have had this in-built antenna and recognised that he had prospects.'

Tina's mother was a pushy sort, a single mum desperate for her daughter to do well. She sent Tina to elocution lessons, thrusting her in front of modelling agencies. Now, in this polite young footballer, Tina's mother believed they had landed a great catch. She took Moore under her wing. 'Bobby latched on to my mother because she had very good manners and he wanted to learn. He craved to learn about everything. He wanted to be the best at everything, Mr Perfect,' she says. 'He was quite mannered and manicured.'

First they had to get past Doss's protective shield. Tina had to prove that she would dote on Robert as his mother did, right down to cutting the little Vs into the side of his football shorts as Doss had always done.

Eventually Tina received the seal of approval though only after a strict lecture on the first night she stayed over in the spare room in Waverley Gardens. Doss took her aside: 'My Bobby's a good boy. You'd better not be getting him into trouble.'

With that blessing, on 30 June 1962, just a fortnight after England's rising star returned from the World Cup in Chile, the new Mr and Mrs Bobby Moore walked out of St Clement's in Ilford. The bride wore an Alexandrine tiara, the groom a dark blue mohair suit.

Press photographers gathered outside the church, a sign of Moore's rising status now that he was an England international. The happy couple obliged the waiting snappers by skipping under an archway of boots held up by a guard of honour, formed by West Ham's first team. Then they headed to Gants Hill, to the reception in the Valentine. The pub is still there hosting big-screen football and karaoke every Wednesday night.

The honeymoon took the Moores to Mallorca and featured the first, but by no means last, drunken row of their marriage. Noel Cantwell, Moore's best man, and Malcolm Allison had both arranged to take their wives to the Mediterranean island at the same time. Allison had been broadening Moore's social horizons in London, introducing him to the good life. Moore was developing a taste for socialising in the West End and for halves of lager.

In Mallorca, the couples met up, the champagne and gin and tonics flowed. Tina liked a drink but, by the time she was begging her husband to come back to their apartment, he was slurring his refusals. Words became heated. The evening concluded with Bobby throwing up in one room while Tina was sobbing next door on to the shoulder of Cantwell's wife.

They returned to a three-bedroom house in Gants Hill, the first marital home bought at a cost of £3,650. At twenty-three, Moore owned a better property than his parents, and he added a Siamese cat called Pelé and a fire-engine-red Ford Zephyr, which was his pride and joy.

Bobby and Tina were both keen on the best things in life, with Moore's ambitions fuelled by a wife who also enjoyed socialising and fashion, eager to be seen at the trendy places wearing the latest outfits. Jimmy Armfield, Moore's England team-mate, puts it succinctly: 'Tina wasn't quite a WAG but she may have been the prototype.'

It was the need to afford this lifestyle that was uppermost in Moore's mind when he sat down to negotiate his new contract at West Ham in that busy summer of 1962. Since signing his first professional contract on £12 a week, Moore had moved up to the £20 limit but that was before the end of the maximum wage in 1961. The ceiling had been smashed, the limit abolished after the campaign by Jimmy Hill and the players' union, the Professional Footballers' Association.

Money had become the topic of fevered conversation in every dressing room around the country. Who was earning what? Was Johnny Haynes of Fulham and England really on £100 a week? How much could a player hope for now that there was no limit?

For most players, the new era did not herald a gold rush, more of a trickle. Club directors were not about to be held to ransom, and fought to keep basic wages down. They preferred to pay incentives, with bonuses linked to appearances, victories or even crowd attendance. Liverpool paid their players an extra £1 for every thousand fans over 28,000 who came through the turnstiles at Anfield.

The players had to fight hard for every penny and they had to conduct their own negotiations. Agents were banned by the Football League. In this new era, there was no limit to what a player could demand but few knew where to start and how to go about it.

The abolition of the maximum wage made for strains between many clubs and their star players. Ron Greenwood hated this new requirement to be haggling in his office when he could be outside with a ball. How was a manager supposed to squabble with his players over pay and then go out to the training pitch and demand they give blood?

Greenwood did not enjoy the confrontation. Indeed, he loathed it. What he certainly did not anticipate was that the most awkward, demanding West Ham player of all would be the diligent, dedicated Bobby Moore.

As far as Moore was concerned, he was owed a good income. 'People often say footballers don't deserve to get such high wages,' he said. 'But we are, after all, basically entertainers. Thousands pay to watch a match just as they do to see a pop group . . . and they mostly earn far more than we do.'

Moore felt he had every right to bargain hard. He had become captain of West Ham in April 1962, taking over the armband from Phil Woosnam. None of his team-mates questioned the promotion. Moore had their complete admiration simply through the rapid development of his game. Eddie Bovington summed up the standing of their new skipper: 'Whatever you could do, he could do it better. You had to respect him just for that.'

Brian Dear, the striker, says he used to tell Jack Burkett, a jobbing left-back: 'Just pass it straight to Bobby and make yourself look good.' Greenwood had promised that he would build a team around Moore, and the armband confirmed his stature. 'I like being a captain,' Moore explained. 'I like the feeling of responsibility, that if something happens on the field I have to make a decision.'

He spoke about the role with characteristic seriousness: 'In boys' teams the captain is generally the outstanding player – simply because boys are impressed purely by ability and very little by knowledge. But in professional terms the captain – if he means anything at all – must be a natural leader, the kind of individual whose play and conduct sets an example to the others. If he is slack and cynical and doesn't seem to care much about training then the rest of the team will take the hint. I try to be the other kind.'

Moore was the conscientious leader of a team that was starting to go places. On that Good Friday when he first took the armband, Martin Peters made his debut and announced himself as a young star in the making.

In February 1962, Greenwood had set a new club transfer record by signing the mercurial Johnny 'Budgie' Byrne from

Crystal Palace for £65,000. The incessant chatterbox – hence the nickname – was a brilliant forward of touch, flicks and goals as well as an unceasing fount of dressing-room banter.

West Ham were showing ambition, and proving they had money to spend. As their captain, an England international with a family and a new house to pay for, Moore was certain that his soaring status should be recognised financially.

When Greenwood offered £28 a week, Moore replied that he would not settle for less than £30. 'A violent disagreement over £2 a week,' Moore would say later, though there were no screaming rows, just long, stubborn silences.

The stand-off went on like that for six weeks with Greenwood repeating that £28 was the best he could do and Moore, steely and unflinching, reiterating politely but firmly that it was not enough.

One of the curiosities of Moore was the unshakeable certainty, the hard-headedness he would bring to pay discussions when, generally, the last thing he sought was conflict. Moore knew full well, even back then, that his demands flew in the face of his image as a 'goody-goody figure, a loyal servant of the firm, always ready to touch a forelock to a superior'. But if he was an unlikely rebel, he was also an unapologetic one. He believed in his value. (By way of comparison, Jimmy Greaves was on £60 a week at Spurs, which the England striker described as 'very good money in 1961'.)

The rest of the players caved in at £28 but still Moore held out. Eventually, his stubbornness secured a comprehensive victory. Greenwood relented, and not only was the captain paid the full £30 a week, backdated, but the rest of the senior players were as well. Moore's popularity in the dressing room reached a new peak after that.

For Moore, this was an important victory – not just for the immediate future but in setting a precedent for subsequent battles. From that moment, there was not a contract signed by Moore at West Ham which did not involve pained, sometimes bitter, confrontation with Greenwood as the captain demanded more than the club were willing to offer.

Moore would always be the very last player to agree terms to stay on at West Ham, once doing so only a couple of hours before the first match of the season, as he and Greenwood pushed and pulled over terms. But Moore had his aspirations to move up in the world, and that required money.

'West Ham had always been good to me,' Moore reasoned, 'but the way I saw it was that a footballer's career lasts a comparatively short time, and I felt that I had to do the best for myself and my wife.'

He had a standard of living to maintain. Geoff Hurst remembers chatting to Moore one Christmas and saying that he was planning to buy his wife, Judith, a new Hillman Imp. 'Bloody hell,' Moore replied. 'I'll have to buy Tina a coach.'

6. The Best Footballer in the Country

Asked to pick his favourite game, Bobby Moore would sometimes surprise his interrogator by passing over the obvious moments of international greatness, famous days at Wembley and the Maracanã, for a sodden day in Sheffield. He would cite the afternoon when he first forged his reputation for saving his best for when it really mattered.

At Hillsborough, West Ham needed their captain to be at his finest. On 14 March 1964, the odds were stacked against Ron Greenwood's team as they prepared to face the might of Manchester United in the FA Cup semi-final. A place at Wembley, in the showpiece occasion of the sporting year, was at stake.

This was the United of Charlton, Law and a teenage prodigy called George Best. They were the holders of the FA Cup. The previous Saturday, even United's second string had proved too much for West Ham. Matt Busby had brought a weakened side to Upton Park for a First Division fixture, resting his Holy Trinity, yet United still won 2-0.

As the players trooped off at the end, Dave Gaskell, the United goalkeeper, could not resist a condescending dig, muttering something about West Ham wasting their time even turning up for the big cup tie the following weekend when Law, Best and Charlton would all be back.

Nothing suggested that West Ham had much of a chance. Greenwood's team were enjoying a fine season, reaching the semi-finals of the League Cup, too, but United were a cut above, chasing the title. Even the conditions seemed to be conspiring against the underdogs. It was a grim day up north, precisely the type of filthy and difficult conditions which seemed ill-suited to a West Ham team who could pass the ball beautifully under Greenwood's painstaking instruction but were sometimes dismissed as effete southern boys.

Hard March rain lashed down against the windows as the West Ham players sat down at midday for their usual pre-match meal: fillet steak for strength, rice pudding for energy. To look at the menu is to marvel that they could play at all, yet Greenwood sensed a glimmer of a chance. In the stadium, he wandered out into the tunnel where the Dagenham Girl Pipers were preparing the pre-match entertainment. Half the United team were mooching around, chatting them up. Greenwood marched back into the dressing room. 'They think it's going to be easy,' he told his players, trying to fire them up.

As Hurst flicked a ball to and fro with Ronnie Boyce, trying to shake out the nerves, Moore was going through his silent routine, taking out a pot of Vaseline and dabbing it on his forehead to stop the sweat running into his eyes. Then he led West Ham out on to the quagmire. As the players prepared to kick off, the commentator on Pathé News remarked drily: 'Manchester United in white – but for how long remains to be seen.'

The pitch at Hillsborough was so sodden that the 65,000 spectators feared the game would have to be abandoned. Paddy Crerand, the United midfield player, walked out with the referee and laughed bitterly at the idea of such a big match going ahead: 'It was horrendous. The referee had a ball in his hands. He went to bounce it and it just stuck in the ground. I said to him "what are we doing? If you had a cart horse and a race horse, the cart horse would win on that pitch". We shouldn't have played but we did, and West Ham raised their game. As for Bobby, he was magnificent.'

Greenwood's team excelled, no one more than the captain. At the heart of West Ham's defence, he radiated an assurance which began to convince every one of his team-mates that perhaps an upset was possible. In midfield, Eddie Bovington shadowed Charlton's every move, marking him out of the game. Ronnie Boyce – known as 'Ticker' for his ability as the heartbeat of the side – scored twice.

West Ham deserved their lead but United came back into the game in farcical circumstances. Diving for the ball, Jim Standen, the West Ham goalkeeper, had mud kicked into one of his eyes. He was blinded. Moore ran off the pitch for a bucket of water, returning to pour it over the goalkeeper's head to wash the eye clean. Standen's vision was still blurred when United swung in a cross. He didn't see the ball until Denis Law headed it past him.

At 2-1 up, with nerves straining and United pressing for an equaliser, Moore made the decisive intervention. When the ball ran loose just inside the West Ham half, he stormed through the gloop like a tank through a muddy battlefield. His momentum carried him past two United players out on the left touchline, running off the pitch and back on.

Moore, the centre-half, was haring down the flank.

United were exposed and, even on this morass, Moore managed to play the perfect through ball to Hurst. The striker's shot flew past Gaskell from edge of the area. It was the combination of Hurst's run and Moore's accuracy that had been worked on for so many hours on the training ground. 'Moore and Hurst; no one else was needed,' Greenwood noted, with delight.

When the final whistle blew, West Ham's players clasped each other. Tears were shed. In the dressing room, with steam rising from the bath and off the backs of sodden jerseys, Moore and his team-mates celebrated West Ham's place in the FA Cup final for the first time since the White Horse final of 1923. The next day's papers would be filled with acclaim for 'Moore's Muddy Marvels'.

Reporting on the match, Nigel Clarke recalls: 'Bobby was absolutely, totally imperious and afterwards in the dressing room absolutely full of himself but in the loveliest, nicest way, so self-contained and so quiet. He couldn't stop grinning, couldn't stop smiling because he knew what he'd done, knew how great he'd been marshalling that side in the worst conditions. But he wouldn't shout it.'

The players celebrated wildly on the train back, the lager flowing. Family, friends and fans joined them, and there were so many people crammed into the team carriage that Greenwood became visibly upset. 'It was like the January Sales, Wembley Way and the London rush-hour all rolled into one,' he complained.

When Moore and Byrne asked the manager why he looked so downcast, he said the day was being ruined by hangers-on. 'I wanted the journey home to be memorable,' he told them.

'But this is a disgrace. We don't need all these people. Is this success?'

The players were baffled, and returned to their boozing. If they could not party now, when could they? West Ham were in the big time. This was a victory which carried a young side over the threshold from a team which had promise to one capable of delivering silverware. 'Suddenly the whole picture had changed,' Moore said. 'This was going to be our year.' It was his year more than anyone's.

According to the first edition of the *Sun* which appeared in 1964, relaunched from the ashes of the old *Daily Herald*, most of Britain had never had it so good. The newspaper heralded an era of optimism and prosperity.

Its first editorial trumpeted: 'Five million Britons now holiday abroad every year. Half our population is under 35 years of age. Steaks, cars, houses, refrigerators, washing-machines are no longer the prerogative of the "upper crust", but the right of all. People believe, and the *Sun* believes with them, that the division of Britain into social classes is happily out of date.'

Britain was a nation in which opportunity knocked. The class system was breaking down and wages rising. Consumerism was rampant, with money to spend and new goods to buy. There was a craze for DIY and home improvements.

Television was creating new stars from the working classes in music, sport and films. The first *Ready, Steady, Go!* was broadcast in 1963; the Beatles were invading America. *Match of the Day* would arrive in the autumn of 1964, taking footballers into the country's living rooms every week and not just a few select occasions each year. In this fast-changing world, few rose to prominence more quickly than Bobby Moore.

He was the up-and-coming star of English football, an increasingly central figure in the new England team being shaped by Alf Ramsey who had taken over as manager from Walter Winterbottom after the 1962 World Cup. On the end-of-season tour in May 1963, Moore had captained England for the first time in the absence of Jimmy Armfield. At twenty-two years and forty-seven days, he was England's youngest ever skipper as Ramsey's side won in Czechoslovakia.

As the captain of West Ham, he was the leader of a young, dynamic team who were picking up admirers for their attractive, passing football. Greenwood was not just opening the minds of his players to new tactics – attacking space at the near post with early crosses was a favourite innovation – but fresh experiences and broader horizons.

In the summer of 1963, he had led West Ham on a summer tour to New York, facing opponents from Europe and South America. Although they eventually lost to Dukla Prague over two legs, the players revelled in the chance to see the world and to pit themselves against exotic opposition.

It was a good bonding experience for a team who had largely grown up through West Ham's blossoming Academy. As their leader, Moore was growing in confidence and authority on the back of his England appearances, though not everything came to him naturally. On the American tour, Moore was asked to drum up some publicity by appearing on the television show *What's My Line?* He was shy and nervous as the panel tried to guess his trade, asking if it was 'some kind of rugger soccer'.

Afterwards, one of the American producers went up to Greenwood and nodded at the chattering, extrovert Budgie

Byrne: 'What a pity Bobby hasn't got the personality of that little guy.'

Moore was not a vocal captain but his performances spoke for themselves. His maturity with England and that run to the FA Cup final won him national acclaim

On the Thursday night before the final, he was crowned Footballer of the Year, lauded by the country's sports writers. At the Café Royal on Regent Street in London, Moore was saluted as the country's outstanding player ahead of Charlie Hurley, the Sunderland and Republic of Ireland defender, and Law, the prolific United striker.

Twelve months earlier it had been Stanley Matthews standing in Moore's place, his name engraved on the trophy. Matthews had won the award at forty-eight – Moore at just twenty-three, the youngest winner. A new era appeared to be dawning in the English game and Moore was at the vanguard. Fleet Street toasted his brilliance in a banqueting hall.

Less than forty-eight hours later, Moore led out West Ham at Wembley for the biggest occasion in the English sporting calendar. The FA Cup final was a dramatic contest, largely because Greenwood's side played poorly against Preston North End, underdogs from the Second Division.

Losing 2-1 at half-time, Greenwood made tactical changes, pushing Bovington forward in midfield, using Moore to mark man-to-man rather than sweeping. The more adventurous approach paid off when Hurst equalised with a header and, in the last minute, Boyce nodded across goal to win the cup.

Moore led his team up the Wembley steps, the first time any West Ham side had had their hands on major silverware. As his team-mates paraded the trophy on their lap of honour, Moore trotted around clutching a giant-sized hammer.

Victory sparked the biggest East End celebrations since the end of the war. The players had wondered if crowds would turn out when they began an open-top bus ride in central London but once they were past Aldgate the fans became ten to twenty deep. 'Without exaggeration there must have been a million people out on the streets,' Moore noted. 'This was what success meant – not money or glamour, but the satisfaction of knowing you've made your own folk proud of you.'

But it meant money, too. Moore was never slow to understand that success could be measured not just in glory, but pound notes. 'What does Wembley mean to professional footballers?' he mused. 'Well, there's cash involved, of course.'

For footballers still fighting to be paid their dues, Wembley meant a windfall. The West Ham squad produced a cup final colour booklet and a commemorative tie. They found sponsors, sold interviews, made public appearances for cash. Moore estimated that each player made around £170 from the commercial pool, far more than the club's official bonus of £25 for reaching Wembley – and that was just via legitimate means.

He failed to mention that the real profits came from the illicit trade in tickets. That was the biggest perk of reaching the final. Each player received twenty and most seemed to end up in the hands of Stan Flashman, the big-time London tout. John Sissons revealed that he made about £600, a fortune at the time, and bought a Morris 1100 with the proceeds. Moore must have sold his allocation because Doss queued up with thousands of West Ham fans rather than pester her son for a seat for the big match.

The players had complimentary tickets for all the West Ham games and Moore, along with other players, would sell their spares on through Terry Creasy, an amiable East End rogue who became one of the captain's best pals. They grabbed what they could in an era when footballers did not get much for free, apart from the odd drink. Selling tickets was the most reliable means of supplementing their modest income.

Moore found more legitimate ways of cashing in on his stature as the new poster boy of English football. He was in demand, and not just on the sports' pages. He appeared in *Vogue* magazine, squatting on his haunches in West Ham kit with models posing behind him.

Noel Cantwell, Moore's best man who had moved on to Manchester United, remarked on the transformation in his old team-mate. He was struck by how the cautious teenager had grown into a fashion icon and model, describing his friend as 'a perfect example of the new type of soccer player. Successful, and more of a star image. Good clothes, big cars and all that gear.'

Moore had the looks and the style, right down to the way he would lead West Ham on to the pitch, a ball clasped to his hip before nonchalantly knocking it out of his left hand with his right fist. 'West Ham had an image and when they came on the field it was like eleven models running out,' Mike Summerbee says. 'And of course Bobby was the smartest, the best-looking, the leader at the front.' It was as though James Bond had put down his Walther PPK to play sweeper for West Ham.

Harry Redknapp was among the young apprentices who looked on in awe. 'To us, he was the governor. Everybody loved him, everybody who came into contact with him wanted Bobby as a friend. You couldn't help it.' Redknapp would soon bestow the nickname 'God'.

Moore's team-mates started copying all his little habits. 'Bobby put his shorts on last so everyone started doing the same,' Redknapp says. 'Bobby had a little key-ring on a gold chain that used to dangle off his belt so soon everyone had one of those.'

Moore had marketability and Jack Turner, who had first scouted him for West Ham as a fifteen-year-old, was the man to transform fame into gold. Turner's office in the West Stand at Upton Park bore the sign 'Property Manager'. He helped the players with mortgages, insurance and, for those with more potential, pushed commercial deals their way. At a club where the postbag was now one giant heap for Moore, a smaller one for Budgie Byrne and bits and bobs for the rest, setting up Bobby Moore Ltd became a full-time job.

On Turner's advice, Bobby Moore Sports Wear was opened across the road from Upton Park on Green Street. It became a little family business, with Tina's mother in daily control. A column in *Titbits* magazine followed. There was a brief dabble with a Brylcreem advert, though Moore's curls were not made to be slicked back.

Average weekly earnings in Britain rose by 130 per cent between 1955 and 1969, and Moore did his best to keep up. After more haggling with Greenwood, his seniority was recognised when he was given a pay rise to more than £60 a week, considerably more than most of his team-mates.

The salaries of most footballers were comparable to the local bank manager but Moore's stature ensured that there was plenty of scope to enhance his income with off-field deals. As the leading footballer in England, the captain of his country, a stylish role model, Moore was becoming more than just a footballer. He was a celebrity. For him in particular, the sixties were starting to swing.

7. Alf

Alf Ramsey must have believed that he was appointing the school swot when he chose Bobby Moore as England captain in May 1963, in only his twelfth international. The West Ham defender was by no means the only option. He was certainly not the most experienced. Moore's dozen caps gave him junior ranking compared to the forty-two of Bobby Charlton, the twenty-seven of Jimmy Greaves and Ray Wilson's seventeen.

But when Ramsey took the twenty-two-year-old Moore aside and asked if he wanted the honour, it seemed so natural – to Moore and to everyone else – as to render further discussion pointless. The captaincy fitted Moore as neatly as a slipper on Cinderella.

A manager likes his captain to reflect his own world view and Moore's earnestness seemed to chime with the disciplined and highly professional regime that Ramsey was determined to instil when he took over the national team in 1963.

Walter Winterbottom had been a decent chap, and a progressive coach, but the former school teacher was a pipe-smoking theoriser. He had also been required to defer in selecting the

England team to an FA committee. Ramsey ushered in a new uncompromising age in which the manager was boss.

Ramsey could speak to the players with the benefit of hardened experience. He had been a full-back of some distinction for Spurs and England, and had the scars to show for it after appearing in two of the national team's most infamous defeats: 1-0 to the unfancied United States in the 1950 World Cup in Brazil, and the calamitous 6-3 to Hungary at Wembley in 1953.

As a manager he brought a fiercely patriotic determination to put England among the world's best, as well as a formidable track record after leading Ipswich Town from the depths of the Football League, the Third Division South, to the First Division title.

Intolerant of mavericks (and foreigners which, in Ramsey's mind, included Scotsmen), he wanted serious, committed men and Moore quickly struck him as someone he could rely on. Even amid the wreckage of a 5-2 thrashing by France in the manager's first game, Ramsey had been struck by the composed young defender. Like Greenwood, he saw a player mature way beyond his years.

That impression was confirmed when Ramsey sat beside Moore on the coach after that nightmare in Paris. As they chatted at length, he began to admire the young man's insight.

In the absence of Jimmy Armfield in Bratislava, Ramsey had no hesitation in promoting Moore, though he chose to test the young man's mettle first: 'I'd like you to captain but I will understand if you would prefer not to.' Ramsey wanted to be sure that Moore was up for the challenge. Moore looked him in the eye and replied that nothing would be a greater honour.

Moore skippered England to a 4-2 victory against the Czechs, the beaten World Cup finalists from a year earlier, with two goals from Jimmy Greaves and one each from Bobby Charlton and Bobby Smith. It was the first win of Ramsey's reign.

It was on that summer tour that Ramsey would declare, or perhaps blurt out, that 'England WILL win the World Cup'. With the bar set high, ludicrously so according to many sceptics in the media, Ramsey had to drag the team forward or risk embarrassment. He was demanding of his players, expecting high levels of commitment and discipline. He cannot have anticipated that his keen young captain would be one of the first to let him down.

It must have been a heady cocktail for Moore in May 1964. After his crowning as Footballer of the Year and lifting the FA Cup, his final honour in a remarkable personal hat-trick came when he led England out against Uruguay four days later – and this time not just as stand-in skipper.

Armfield had lost his place after an April defeat against Scotland – the one opponent Ramsey could not abide losing to – and George Cohen was about to start a long run in his stead at right-back. Moore had the armband for a second time and it was unlikely to be taken off him, especially following England's 2-1 victory over Uruguay, with Byrne scoring twice. Moore was on the crest of a wave.

When the chance came to wander out of the England team base of White's Hotel, in Lancaster Gate, on the night before the squad flew out for a friendly in Portugal, Moore could not resist. Suggesting a stroll for a relaxing pint, he found willing accomplices in Byrne and Greaves. That trio were joined by

George Eastham, Ray Wilson, Gordon Banks and, probably not knowing what he was getting himself into, Bobby Charlton. Off they trooped down the Bayswater Road, with Greaves steering the Mischievous Seven towards a bar called the Beachcomber.

One beer became half a dozen and the players tottered back after midnight. When they returned to their rooms, it was to find a passport lying on each of their pillows. The message could not have been more stark if the miscreants had come back to find their bags packed.

At 11.30 p.m. Ramsey and his assistant Harold Shepherdson had gone around the bedrooms. A curfew had been broken and Ramsey recognised an important moment to flex his disciplinary muscles. To make the drinkers sweat, the manager said nothing as they flew off to Lisbon that Thursday morning and kept silent on the matter for forty-eight hours. It was not until the end of the training session on the eve of the match that he called the squad together. 'You may all go and get changed now, except that is, those players who I believe would like to stay and talk with me.'

Like naughty schoolboys, they stood and stared at their feet. Ramsey's reaction to the seven boozers was controlled fury. 'If there had been enough players in this squad, I would have sent you all home when back in London,' he told them. 'Gentlemen, may I for the first and last time remind you of our responsibilities as members of the England team. All I hope is that you have learned your lesson and will not behave in such an irrational and irresponsible manner again.'

You would have thought it was a lesson to heed but Moore would continue to push his luck. Less than two weeks later when England flew to New York to play the United States en route to a friendly tournament in Brazil, Ramsey gave orders that the players were to drink nothing stronger than orange juice. But as soon as the manager was asleep, Moore and Byrne tucked into gin and tonics and champagne.

Out in New York, staying at the Waldorf Astoria, Moore could not resist breaking curfew, telling Greaves that they were going out. 'I want to see Ella Fitzgerald,' he said. They headed down to a crammed bar, strained their necks for a glimpse of 'The First Lady of Song' and listened awhile before sneaking back to their beds. But as Greaves admitted: 'Alf got to know about it and wasn't happy. Mooro got me into a lot of scrapes.' There was no punishment but the next morning Ramsey blanked the pair at breakfast. He had made a mental note.

The paradox of Moore the upstanding skipper set against the errant drinker is a strange one, but there is no doubt that the contradiction existed. It was touched on in Ramsey's most eloquent quote about Moore. 'He was my captain and my right-hand man. Bobby was the heartbeat of the England team, the king of the castle, my representative on the field. He made things work on the pitch. I had the deepest trust in him as a man, as a captain, as a confidant . . . I could easily overlook his indiscretions, his thirst for the good life, because he was the supreme professional, the best I ever worked with.'

That was said when Ramsey could afford to reflect generously on all Moore's qualities but, through 1963 and 1964, those 'indiscretions' drove him to fury. When training started, Moore's focus could not be doubted. Ramsey, like Greenwood, saw the unquestionable logic of building a defence around Moore's anticipation and composure on the ball.

But away from practice, Moore was always drawn back to

the irreverent bunch, smirking at the back of class with Byrne and Greaves. 'Bob was not Mr Perfect. He always lived with a bit of danger,' Greaves wrote. 'I think we were good for each other, Bob and I. But I'm not sure Alf would have thought that.' Moore's dry sense of humour was beginning to take on a sharp, cynical edge.

Legend had it that Ramsey was of gypsy origin, a connection which made him extremely sensitive. The story is told of Moore making a joke when passing some gypsy caravans on a Balkans tour along the lines that the manager should drop in to see his relatives. Ramsey seethed at the slight.

Ramsey's accent provided endless mirth. Like Moore, he was a working-class East Ender – from Dagenham – but, striving to present himself as a worldly, educated man, Ramsey spoke with an accent that Brian Glanville described as 'sergeant-major posh'. The affectation in his voice became even more pronounced during his time as England manager, prompting rumours of elocution lessons. It became a running joke among Moore and Greaves.

Ken Jones says that Ramsey was tested close to breaking point by the occasional bouts of mockery: 'There was a match, when Bobby and Jimmy played, and Alf got the impression they were taking the piss as they got on the coach, taking the piss out of his accent and the way he spoke. I heard Alf say it, and Brian James heard it because we were standing there, "I'll win the World Cup without those two bastards".

'Alf would do his best for the team so I'm sure he wouldn't have carried that out really, but it was something in his mind. I think it got to the stage that Bobby realised that he was going too far and if he wasn't careful he wouldn't go up any further. He had to be careful with all that nonsense.'

That 'nonsense' would never quite be eradicated. Boys will be boys. Moore and Greaves regularly escaped from the team base in Hendon Hall in north London, off in search of a pub. Jack Charlton and Gordon Banks shared a bedroom at the back which was the most discreet exit route for the drinkers. 'They'd come back through the room and we pulled them back in again,' Charlton recalls. 'I never went. I would never dream of going, what with Alf.'

Alan Mullery tells of sharing a room with Moore on England duty and as he prepared for bed, the captain was pulling on his best suit. Moore clambered out of the window near midnight with the words 'just off out'. He slid down the drainpipe and away. Mullery heard him scuttle back in at 5 a.m. He did not dare ask where Moore had been and he never did find out.

'He said he was off "on business",' Mullery recalls. 'It was Hendon Hall, one floor up, out of the window, down a gully pipe. He went off into London and came back at five in the morning in time to get back for training, looking spick and span.'

Moore thought it was all good fun but eventually Ramsey had enough. On a trip to Northern Ireland in October 1964, they had what would be called 'showdown talks' in modern journalese. The manager could tolerate no more following the boisterous summer tour, the trip to the Beachcomber, late nights in New York and a South American leg which had featured other bouts of high living.

A 5-1 thrashing by Brazil, inspired by the peerless Pelé, a bruising 1-1 draw against Portugal and a 1-0 defeat by a formidable Argentina had offered a chastening revision of England's chances of living up to Ramsey's promise to land the World Cup on home soil. Unwavering dedication was required if the manager's prediction was not to become a noose around his neck.

Ramsey worried that splits were building up between the London lads and some of the other players. The misbehaviour among Greaves, Moore and Byrne was starting to affect morale. Cliques were forming, and the captain was not setting the right example. Some of the players loved that behind the squeaky clean image, there was a mischievous side to Moore. But Ramsey decided that he needed to crack down.

It was traditional for the captain to be formally named when the squad was selected but, this time, Ramsey waited eight days. Fleet Street began to wonder if they were on to a story. Meanwhile, Ramsey took Moore aside in Belfast for a stern chat.

The manager, with his unblinking stare, reminded Moore of his responsibilities, the size of the prize they were chasing and the need for greater trust between manager and his on-pitch leader. 'I want you as my captain. But I want to be sure of your 100 per cent backing and support in everything I do or say,' he said. In short, he asked Moore whether they were pulling the same way, or not. Otherwise they would have a problem.

The captain respected the straight talk, and it was a critical juncture on the road to '66, according to Geoffrey Green, football correspondent of *The Times*. 'Up till then Moore had tended, with one or two others, to go his own way,' Green wrote. 'A splinter group was developing within the team at the top. But the split was mended in time by Ramsey's firm action. The manager, after one year in the saddle, made it abundantly clear who was to be the boss, and duly the deviationists were brought to heel.'

*

Following their wobble in 1964, Ramsey increasingly began to take Moore into his confidence. The captain had no strong influence on decisions – Ramsey was far too much his own man for that – but Moore began to gain unique access to his thought processes. Ramsey would occasionally explain his intentions. In turn, Moore could have a quiet chat with a player, bracing him for promotion or the axe.

A quiet word was as far as it went. Moore didn't shout or bawl or play power games within the dressing room. He would never bollock a team-mate, or interject in a team talk. 'Bobby would never be so arrogant,' Cohen says. 'We were an experienced squad with plenty of club captains and leader-types.' It is why Moore found captaincy of England easier than he ever did with West Ham.

At club level, there was an expectation on Moore to provide vocal leadership, and to set the daily mood. It did not come naturally. When, in December 1963, West Ham had suffered the heaviest home defeat in the club's history, an 8-2 humiliation by Blackburn Rovers, Moore's quietness and lack of animation had featured prominently in the inquest among the players and Greenwood.

Jack Burkett, the full-back, described the crisis talks: 'Someone started by having a real go at Bobby, saying he was our captain and should have taken more responsibility in terms of talking to us. We all accepted that Bobby wasn't a great talker on the pitch and he led by example. But the point was, when we were getting turned over to that extent on our own pitch, then we needed something more from our captain.'

With England, Ramsey surrounded himself with the sort of big, strong personalities that made Moore feel at ease. Geoff

Hurst tells of players turning up for training with England, lasting a few days and disappearing never to be seen again. 'You would see someone come and go,' he says. 'Alf would have decided that he wasn't the right type of character. He wanted a hardnosed bunch of professionals who, to use his own great expression, that we heard so often "will not let me down". He weeded out the other types.'

It was a long slow process, and not without its setbacks. Public confidence in the team was shaky. In 1964–5, England won six and drew four of their ten matches but Ramsey's relationship with most of the press was one of mutual hostility, and the public's view was inevitably shaped by a sceptical media.

Expectations were low but gradually Ramsey began to find those players who gave him the unceasing toil and devotion that he felt was necessary for a winning system against nations with more flair. The defence came together for the first time in April 1965 in a 2-2 draw against Scotland, Jack Charlton alongside Moore. The Leeds United centre-half was a shrewd choice by Ramsey and not the obvious one given that Charlton, just a month short of his thirtieth birthday, was very late to be coming to the international game.

On ability, a more obvious pick seemed Brian Labone, the Everton captain who was elegant yet also powerful in the air. Ramsey put his trust in Charlton and Labone eventually asked not to be considered for the World Cup, arranging his wedding for that historic summer.

Charlton hardly represented the future but Ramsey spotted that he was the perfect complement to Moore: strong in the air, belligerent, tough, and a committed, destructive stopper whose natural inclination was to attack crosses and fill in behind the captain whenever he went roaming upfield.

Charlton was so surprised by his promotion that he challenged Ramsey once to ask exactly what the manager had seen in an ungainly centre-half, or 'that bloody giraffe' as brother Bobby was known to call him. Ramsey coolly explained that he looked for a functioning team. 'I don't,' he told Charlton, 'always pick the best players.'

It was on that same day against Scotland that Nobby Stiles made his debut as a terrier-like midfield player, another redoubtable personality. Alan Ball's first international appearance followed a month later in May 1965 against Yugoslavia. He was a flame-haired midfield runner from Blackpool who epitomised Ramsey's work ethic. The squad was coming together, with Ramsey certain of his strategy and always attentive to detail.

Ball recalled one exchange when the manager approached him at half-time.

'Do you think Bobby Moore can pass the ball?' Ramsey asked.

'Yes, he's one of the best passers in English football,' Ball replied.

'Then why do you keep going back and taking the ball off him? If he can pass it to you fifteen yards further up the pitch then you are much nearer to the opposition and the danger area.'

Ball was a small man but another big personality who quickly grew to be one of Moore's closest friends in the England team. 'I wanted to be a better player so he'd respect me for that. I wanted to be great so he'd be proud of me,' Ball remarked, sounding like the younger brother Moore never had.

Ball talked of looking up to Moore not just as a footballer but for his metropolitan style, his dress sense. Moore was cool. He had class. In many parts of the country – mainly around northern grounds – the regal manner was earning Moore a reputation for being haughty. Ball and Jack Charlton would return home from an England gathering to be asked 'What's that Bobby Moore really like?' The inference was always that Moore was a little up himself.

Top bloke, his England colleagues would reply. Brilliant skipper, modest, great lad. Likes a laugh, loves a drink. They would tell tales of his mischief – and still do – like those moments just before an international when they were filled with nerves. It was Moore's job to walk down the line to introduce the England XI to some foreign ambassador or suited administrator. The players were never sure about what was to come next, but the uncertainty was part of the fun.

As he approached with the VIPs, Moore, their straight-laced captain, might pretend to forget a player's name. 'This is, er . . .' he would stutter, feigning absent-mindedness. Alternatively if he was introducing Jimmy Greaves, he might suddenly christen him Roger Hunt. Alan Ball would become Martin Peters. The names would come out jumbled up.

If the bigwigs ever spotted the joke, they never said. Down the line Moore would go, players smirking. Even in the moments before a big game, Moore could ease the tension with his dry wit and unnatural calm.

Initally, Jack Charlton was bemused by Moore's quiet approach. The two defenders would change next to each other and Charlton found the captain's silence disconcerting, on and off the pitch. 'I believe all centre-backs should be shouters because they are the people who do less than anybody else on the football field,' Charlton says. 'But not Bob.'

In an interview with Tony Palmer for *Hero*, the documentary about Moore, Charlton became almost soulful when describing his old team-mate: 'He wasn't like us. He was one of us, but he wasn't like us.'

When I spoke to Charlton about that remark, he still knew what he meant, but he struggled to explain it. 'When we won, most of us were boisterous,' Charlton said. 'Bobby would take his shirt off and sit there and smile. He did things differently to us.'

The warrior leader has long been lauded in English culture but Moore must have been the nation's least voluble skipper. According to Hugh McIlvanney, his leadership flowed from a composure which radiated through the rest of the side 'like solar energy', a warm, reassuring glow.

He looked unflappable and the players, even those like Cohen and Bobby Charlton who never felt particularly close to him, felt instantly at ease when they looked over at their skipper. What they did not know was that behind that calm veneer lay a dreadful secret.

8. Cancer

Even now, when the facts are irrefutable, one of Bobby Moore's closest friends disputes that the England captain suffered with testicular cancer at twenty-three because, well, Bobby would have told him something so vitally important. But Moore did not tell anybody. Had Tina Moore not told the story after her husband died, the secret of his illness would have gone with him to the grave. History would record that Moore suffered a passing groin problem in 1964–5 rather than the disease which was a harrowing ordeal.

There was no mention of this serious affliction in his authorised biography. In another version of his life story he talked, with ludicrous understatement, of 'a minor groin operation'. He chose to brush over his illness as though it were a slight strain even though Tina remembers it as a tormenting experience that made Moore fear for much more than just his football career. 'It was an awful thing and it had a terrible impact,' she says.

Here he was, invincible Bobby Moore; captain of club and country, the outstanding footballer in England, and, by late 1964, a first child on the way, too. His life seemed charmed. But then a lump appeared from nowhere. Moore could not bring himself to think the worst and so he ignored the problem. He would later confide in the doctors that he had borne the growth for a year.

A year of anxiety. A whole year of silence and secrecy with all his worries bottled up inside. 'It's not like there were all those publicity campaigns you see now,' Tina says. 'It's not like you could look it up on the internet.'

By the autumn of 1964, he was feeling the odd twinge in training. When Moore ran, there would be a sharp tweak in his groin. Never one to complain, he got on with his job. Be a man, he told himself. As the pain grew worse, Moore carried on, chest out, trying to ignore his body's warning lights and clanging alarms.

'Running it off' was the cure-all for footballers but this was one injury that would not go away. Team-mates started to notice the captain grimace. Then, in the dressing room, they saw a swelling. It would be seen in the showers, as he was getting changed. Moore's fastidious habit of standing on a bench to prevent the bottom of his trousers scraping on the wet and muddy floor was not exactly designed for discretion.

'Fuck me, Mooro, that's taken a few overs, hasn't it,' Eddie Presland, the young full-back, blurted out one day. Presland thought the growth was a cricket injury or, as Moore tried to convince himself, perhaps a kick in the groin during a match.

Oncologists say that such visible swelling was probably a hydrocele, a collection of fluid in the scrotum secondary to the tumour; a condition much more likely in cases of delayed diagnosis. Still he ignored it – and Presland's remark aside, so did his team-mates. Moore's delicate complaint, whatever it was, was no one else's business. 'We could see it,' Brian Dear says, 'but Bobby wasn't the type to make a fuss and he would never want a fuss making of him.'

Crossing fingers, hoping it would go away could only work for so long. The swelling was causing Moore severe daily pain. Eventually he went to see Bill Jenkins, the club physiotherapist. Rob Jenkins succeeded his father and still runs a practice opposite the stadium: 'My dad looked at the swelling and told Bobby they had to get it seen to. It was my dad who got it taken care of.'

Tina Moore's recollection is a little different. She says that Moore and Bill Jenkins decided between them that he had been injured by a kick, and left it in the hope that it would disappear. It was only when she heard Bobby yelp in the night and found him doubled up in agony that she forced him to seek help. Six months pregnant, she had banged into him with her bump.

An appointment was made to see the GP and suddenly everything moved fast, terrifyingly so. Moore was immediately referred to a specialist who ruled him out of the Saturday game against Blackburn Rovers the following day, 7 November 1964. Moore would undergo surgery on Monday.

The surgeon's prompt insistence that he needed to conduct an exploratory operation induced panic in Bobby and Tina. 'Bobby had to sign something saying that if they found what was wrong, they could remove whatever part was necessary,' Tina says. 'He was terribly frightened but still clung to the hope that it was just a sports injury. Cancer was the last thing you thought about.'

Moore was operated on at the London Hospital in Whitechapel by Gerald Tresidder, a consultant urologist. After surgery, he explained to a shell-shocked Moore that, yes, it was cancer. A tumour had been found. He had performed an orchidectomy, the removal of one of Moore's testicles. 'Bobby was worried out of his life,' Tina says. 'In those days, cancer sounded like a death sentence.'

In fact, cure rates for testicular cancer were on the increase, climbing from 60 per cent in the fifties to around 75 per cent thanks to more effective radiotherapy from cobalt machines (these days it stands at 99 per cent). But for all the reassurance from the doctors that the operation had been successful, Moore was beset with anxieties.

Even if he survived, would he be able to have more children? Would he be the same player? What if the cancer returned? And, typically, he dreaded what people might say if they discovered he had undergone such a delicate operation. Imagine if word got out not just among his friends but the fans.

Of course he did not show a flicker of these troubles to the outside world; not even to close friends or family. The patient spent just over a fortnight in hospital, a private room with a TV and a record player. There was a constant stream of visitors yet as they arrived, Moore told Tina: 'Don't tell anyone what I'm in here for.'

Heavily pregnant, she had her own anxieties. What did testicular cancer mean? Could she be widowed? With Moore unwilling to discuss the specific illness even with his wife – he never once used the C-word throughout the crisis – she had to badger the doctors for information. She visited the local library to scour medical journals. This was not the blissful life she had imagined little more than two years into marriage.

Was it not odd that they never discussed the illness together? She says that it was Bobby's way, and this was an age long before celebrity confessionals and inspirational books. It was a private battle which, at his strict insistence, they would fight alone.

Eddie Bovington, Moore's team-mate, says: 'I don't know why he had to keep it quiet, it don't make sense to me. These days, you'd be on the television saying "get yourself screened" and it would become a big issue about how you handle it. It was swept under the carpet to be honest with you and even now I can't understand why.

'I never discussed it with him and I roomed with him for a long, long while which now seems pretty stupid when you think about it. He couldn't exactly hide it once he was back in the dressing room that he'd had a testicle removed. It was there to see, wasn't it. But because he didn't discuss it, we all skirted around it. Budgie Byrne would have said he'd dropped a bollock.

'But it was different times, you know, forty years ago. We are all feeling ourselves now to check if we've got it or not. Years ago you didn't touch it because you were frightened you might have it. You didn't have a clue what it meant. You've got to be a hard man. You can't have cancer, can you?'

'That's how Bobby got the OBE,' Brian Dear says with a rueful smile. 'One Boiled Egg.' But it wasn't a joke he ever shared with his pal.

The fans had to be told something. Moore would be missing for three months in the middle of the season. A routine groin operation was the story. The press were happy to go along with the ruse. Word crept out to a well-connected few that Bobby had a more significant problem 'down there' probably caused by a kick, but they stuck, to a man, to the little white lie.

The pretence continued for decades. The subject remained

so delicate that when Terry Venables co-wrote the novel *They Used to Play On Grass* in 1970, featuring a captain with one testicle, a dismayed Tina was straight on the phone asking how he could be so insensitive. Venables knew nothing about Moore's illness, even though he was a close friend.

'Tina said "you shouldn't have written that. What will Bobby think?" I had to explain to her that I simply didn't know,' Venables recalls. 'My father had had an accident climbing over a railing and that was the reason behind the character. Bobby never mentioned it. He would have been embarrassed to bring it up.'

Moore's need for secrecy presented ongoing challenges because he required abdominal radiotherapy as an outpatient. Two blue crosses had to be drawn on Moore's back to mark the para-aortic lymph nodes to guide the radiographers. The crosses were applied with indelible ink so, even though his treatment was limited to three weeks, the marks lasted for months.

Moore was paranoid about those blue marks being seen in the dressing room which meant all sorts of difficult manoeuvres in the showers. He would wait until the rest of the players had departed, or sidle in with his back to the wall.

He kept his secret until Tina told all to the *Mail on Sunday* in June 1993, the day before the Thanksgiving Service in his honour at Westminster Abbey, she said: 'I wanted him to tell people at the time. It could have been so very inspirational. But he felt he couldn't, wouldn't share it. Today, I think everyone should know. And no, I don't feel I am betraying him. Now he has died, I feel it can do nothing but enhance his memory.'

'When that service goes ahead tomorrow,' she added. 'I want people to know just how much of a hero he was.'

The FA initially proposed a statue of Bobby Moore and Alf Ramsey but it is the captain who stands alone outside Wembley. Twice life-size, the bronze sculpture was unveiled in 2007.

Moore was presented with his first trophy, the Crisp Shield, while at Westbury Primary School where he was inside-right and captain for the under 11s.

Flanked by fellow West Ham apprentices Andy Smillie (*left*) and Tony Scott (*right*) before the 1958–59 season, Moore could not have guessed that he was only weeks from his first-team debut.

(*Left*) With his striking looks and extrovert personality, Malcolm Allison was a force of nature as West Ham captain. The charismatic leader became Moore's mentor.

(*Below*) Moore became known as the most dedicated trainer at Upton Park with a determination to be the best at every discipline from press-ups to stomach exercises.

Greenwood arrived at West Ham in April 1961 and quickly promised Moore that he would d a team around the young defender. The new manager is pictured with Malcolm Musgrove, Brown, Moore, John Dick and John Bond.

Moore's first competitive victory in an England shirt came in the 1962 World Cup finals in Chile, a win against Argentina in front of fewer than 10,000 spectators. Maurice Norman, Ron Flowers and Johnny Haynes leave the field with him in Rancagua.

Moore with his future wife, Tina Dean. They would marry in Ilford shortly after the World Cup, following a five-year courtship. The reception took place in the Valentine pub, Gants Hill.

(*Above*) Moore's status soared in 1962 as the new captain of West Ham and a regular England international. Young fans surround him before pre-season training at Chadwell Heath.

(*Below*) Alf Ramsey took charge of England in 1963 and quickly made plain that he would not tolerate indiscipline. He also declared that England would win the World Cup.

West Ham twice had to come from behind against Preston North End in the 1964 FA Cup final. Geoff Hurst scored the second equaliser with his head.

Eddie Bovington replaced Martin Peters on the run to the Cup final, adding more steel to a midfield which beat Preston 3-2 at Wembley.

Moore was the first captain of West Ham to lift a major trophy, receiving the FA Cup from the Earl of Harewood.

Victory celebrations began with milk in the dressing room but Moore and his team-mates were developing a taste for something stronger.

(*Above*) Martin Peters and Geoff Hurst hold the captain aloft after a victory which Ron Greenwood regarded as his team's crowning glory, the triumph over 1860 Munich in the 1965 European Cup Winners' Cup Final at Wembley.

(*Below*) West Ham's influence on the England team grew in World Cup year with Geoff Hurst making his international debut in February 1966 and Martin Peters capped for the first time in May.

*

Whether Moore's first illness was related to the later, fatal bowel cancer which killed him is entirely speculative. Both consultants who dealt with Moore for the latter illness, Peter Hawley and Professor John Smyth, are doubtful. But Tim Oliver, consultant oncologist and Professor Emeritus of Medical Oncology, St Bartholomew's and The Royal London Hospital School, has conducted extensive research after becoming suspicious about a higher prevalence of cancers in those who had undergone previous radiotherapy treatment.

He explains that the cobalt machine used to treat Moore was far less precise than modern methods. With Moore's radiotherapy targeted around the abdomen in an inverted T-shape, the bowel would have been within that field. There is the possibility that the radiotherapy could have left lasting cell damage which resurfaced as bowel cancer more than twenty years later.

'You could never say definitively that one individual would not have got cancer in any case,' Professor Oliver says. 'But I found that cancer frequency increased among those who had radiation because of the damage done to tissue. The probability has increased by between two times and two and a half times by having the radiotherapy.'

It is impossible to be certain but, in at least one significant sense, we do know that Moore never fully recovered from his testicular cancer. The tumour was removed but the lasting legacy was, according to Tina, the insomnia that stayed with Moore through his adult life. 'It affected him very deeply psychologically,' she says.

Moore never discussed how the sleeplessness came on – well, he wouldn't – and in the eyes of most of his friends it was part of his nocturnal lifestyle. It made sense that Mooro liked to stay up: more time to drink. He was increasingly enjoying the social life, sinking halves of lager.

But Tina was convinced that his insomnia was brought on by the stress. Over the three long months of inactivity, he had fretted whether he would be the same player. One of his visitors in hospital was Ron Greenwood who, with good intentions but lack of managerial tact, told his stricken captain: 'You're not to worry, Bobby. The team is doing just fine without you.' From his bed, Moore grimaced at the idea that West Ham were sailing happily on without their captain.

To lose a testicle through cancer was a challenge not just to his health and career, but to his manhood and his self-esteem. Though Roberta was born in January 1965, Moore inevitably worried if he could have another child. He was even paranoid that he might look different in shorts.

'He needed to prove he was still a man,' Tina says. 'It was very important. Although the doctors had told him there would be no problems, he needed to prove that to himself.' She quickly became pregnant again after Roberta's birth but miscarried. Dean, their son, was born three years later.

Tina believes that his sleeplessness was one reason he became so attached to Roberta, in particular. 'He'd get up and take her for a ride in the car at all sorts of strange times,' she says. 'He never slept well from then on. He internalised it all.' She would frequently wake up alone in bed and find her husband downstairs or taking his baby daughter out for a walk at odd hours.

As the insomnia became a regular, aggravating part of Moore's life, at West Ham they quickly became used to the late-night habits of their captain. Rob Jenkins was a frequent companion sought out by Moore to help him through his long nights. On the evening before a game, the captain would wander down the corridor in the team hotel seeking the physio's company and a nightcap. They would sit up, sipping a lager or two. Then Jenkins would give Moore a sleeping pill, washed down with a swig of beer, and the captain would wander off back to his bed.

'I used to get him one every Friday night before a game. Mandrax or mogadon, a strong one, but they are not available now, just so he could get a good night's sleep,' Jenkins says. 'It would be that and a couple of lagers. We'd just have a drink and a chat and then he'd turn in sometime around midnight if it was the night before a match.'

Moore was developing as a drinker and the booze brought him comfort, helping him to sleep and relax. He drank because he enjoyed it. He drank because his hollow legs could take it. But mostly he drank because it loosened him up. It helped him conquer the insomnia and, on a more casual basis, it enabled him to throw off the overcoat of reserve. It took away the strains and, even after surviving testicular cancer, Moore carried more of those than he would let on.

Particularly after he had been elevated to England captain, Moore felt on parade twenty-four hours a day. To be always smart, always polite, always considerate came more easily to him than most, but it must have been wearying to feel constantly scrutinised. A friendly pub, with half a lager in his hand and trustworthy friends around him, was the sanctuary where Moore could start to relax.

Out with Brian 'Stag' Dear and Budgie Byrne at West Ham, or Jimmy Greaves and Alan Ball with England, a few drinks allowed Moore to become one of the chaps. He would shed his inhibitions. According to Tina, 'he went from being the repressed, uptight son of teetotal Doss and Bob, ever-conscious of what behove him as England captain, to a different Bobby, mischievous and irresponsible'.

Moore liked to lean against the bar and watch the action unfold around him: the jokes, the footballers' banter, the tall tales. He would watch the fun from a little distance, chuckling as, for example, others tried to slip a Bacardi to lace the Cokes of any of the few non-drinkers (the straight-man role later performed by Trevor Brooking).

He was such a private man yet Moore craved company – and the more voluble the better. Back to his earlier adoration of Malcolm Allison, he loved to hang around with those who had a lot to say for themselves, like Greaves and Ball, Byrne and Dear, or Rob Jenkins on those Friday nights before a game, because then there was no expectation on him to perform.

It is why he became great pals with entertainers, notably Kenny Lynch and Jimmy Tarbuck. They wouldn't pester him about football. They would fill the room with their stories and their warmth. No longer the centre of attention, Moore felt at ease with his chatty mates, and his regularly topped-up half-pint.

Eddie Bovington was a regular socialiser with Moore: 'Some people used to think Bobby was aloof because he'd often stand in the corner of the pub, not say much. But it was more because he was a bit shy. He could be funny, a dry sense of humour, but it would take someone else to promote the conversation. He wouldn't promote himself. It wasn't that he didn't want to talk, it was just that sometimes he had nothing to say. He wasn't going to come and start telling jokes and all that business. He wasn't like Johnny Byrne who would come in and start rabbiting straight away and drive you crackers.'

Moore's friends knew him as this bone-dry mickey-taker after a beer or two but, as Terry Venables acknowledges, 'a lot of people maybe didn't see that side of him because he felt he had to behave a certain way in public.'

The lager brought relaxation, but the insomnia was Moore's most obdurate opponent. Moore made clear in one comment to Jeff Powell that his sleeplessness went beyond simply staying up late. 'If you don't have trouble sleeping you don't know what a hell it can be,' he said.

The former Manchester City and England player Mike Summerbee tells a story of Moore coming to stay at his home in the North West. Summerbee woke to find the lights on in the spare room and Moore down the corridor, curled up next to his son in a big double bed. 'Bobby never liked to sleep on his own,' he says. 'As a footballer, you are used to sleeping in a twin room and I think he was just after a bit of company.

'He loved company but he was also very lonely in a certain way. You looked at him sometimes, he looked lonely. I don't know what it was, but I felt it. Even when he was surrounded by people, he was such a private person.'

Moore returned from his three-month absence to find that West Ham had indeed been thriving without him, especially in Europe. Greenwood loved the challenge of continental football – different tactics, exotic opponents – and, just as they had enjoyed that tournament in America in 1963, the players had learned to share their manager's relish for these exciting trips abroad as they were pitched into the European Cup Winners' Cup.

For the first-round tie against La Gantoise, of Ghent, Greenwood prepared detailed dossiers on the opposition for the first time. On the ferry to Belgium, the players gathered in the café, sipping coffee and studying the paperwork. In later rounds, Greenwood sent delegations of players abroad on scouting trips to report back on the opposition. It was commendable diligence in an age when pretty much all foreign opponents were mysterious strangers.

Moore had missed the second round because of his cancer, but the captain was back for the quarter-final victory over Lausanne of Switzerland – beaten 6-4 on aggregate – and the semi-final against the daunting Real Zaragoza. The Spaniards had one of best attacks in Europe, *Los Cincos Magnificos*, the Magnificent Five. West Ham had Brian Dear on the best run of his career and he scored one, Byrne the other, in a 2-1 victory at Upton Park in the first leg. Sadly for Byrne, a serious knee injury while representing England against Scotland in his next game cost him a place in the final. His gifts were never seen again for his country.

Ahead of the second leg in Spain, Ken Jones of the *Daily Mirror* tells of finding Moore in a bar late at night, around 1 a.m. The captain was having a quiet drink as the insomnia gripped him. 'Christ, Bobby, there's fans in here, you'd best get to bed,' Jones told him. Moore downed his beer and slipped away back to the hotel. A 1-1 draw carried West Ham through and if it was their luck that the final against TSV Munich 1860 was to be played at Wembley, it was good fortune they did not squander.

To watch the game even now is to delight in that rarity, a final played without inhibition by both sides. From the moment that Moore led his team out of the tunnel and into the warm evening sunlight, it was a match of daring and skill which could have finished with ten goals and not just the two from Alan Sealey in three minutes midway through the second half. Moore was immense as he always seemed to be on the biggest occasions, constantly demanding the ball and always – always – seeking not the easy pass but the one that could make a difference. 'Technical perfection,' Greenwood said of his captain. Watch the tape and it is striking to see that, at one point, Moore is not just the furthest West Ham player forward but caught offside. On another occasion, he overlaps the left-winger. Moore appears to be playing half a dozen positions, all of them immaculately.

J. L. Manning, in the *Daily Mail*, lauded West Ham's victory as: 'The best football match I have seen at Wembley since the stadium opened 42 years ago.' Geoffrey Green of *The Times*, wrote: 'It was more than a victory for West Ham. It was a triumph for football itself.' Greenwood could not have imagined a better testimonial.

For the manager that final was the summit he would never reclaim, though he was not to know that as he reflected with a dash of lyricism: 'We proved that football at its best is a game of beauty and intelligence. Players and the ball were in happy harmony, while skill and method flourished together. Ideas and passes flowed. For me it was fulfilment.'

For Moore, 'it felt like winning something with your school team', reflecting on the fact that West Ham had won a European trophy not just with eleven Englishmen but with a squad largely raised on the working-class streets of the East End, most of them products of The Academy. This was not quite the Lisbon Lions, all born within thirty miles of Celtic Park, but there was a rare connection between the squad and the tens of thousands of fans singing 'Bubbles' at Wembley on a warm, spring night.

When Moore climbed the thirty-nine steps of Wembley to lift the trophy, it was the apogee of his West Ham years – the high point in the club's history. As millions watched the BBC's first live transmission of a European final, they had no inkling of his traumatic journey. They saw only the blond captain of West Ham and England, a man at the peak of his form and health, and not a man who only months earlier had feared for his life.

There is a revealing modern parallel in Eric Abidal who had a cancerous tumour removed from his liver in March 2011 but returned to play in the Champions League final at Wembley only two months after surgery. In Abidal's case, there was no one in football unaware of his story. There was a global outpouring of support. When Barcelona won, it was Abidal who was sent up to the Royal Box to lift the cup. He was welcomed back like a hero, a warrior who had beaten the most dangerous opponent of them all.

Moore suffered a similar torment – and made an equally remarkable and triumphant comeback at Wembley. But he suffered his agony in private. Moore hid his pain. There were no special T-shirts or goodwill messages from around the planet. It would have been wonderful if Moore could have received the same mass public support as Abidal but, then, perhaps not. If it was a trade-off between adulation and privacy, Moore would take the latter every time.

Only one English club had won a European trophy before, when Spurs had claimed the Cup Winners' Cup two years earlier. In a newspaper column Billy Wright, the former England captain, predicted a great future for this youthful West Ham team with its slick, passing game, intellectual coach, imperious captain and core of internationals: 'West Ham have the potential to dominate the English game for years to come. They are a young team and there are no limits to the heights that they can attain.'

Except the bubbles were going flat even before the night was over. After a buffet at Wembley for players, officials and directors – but not wives, who were forced to loiter outside – the players were taken back on a coach to Upton Park. They arrived back at midnight in darkness. Some slipped off to find a late-night bar. Others had a few beers at the ground.

The dispersal of the conquering heroes was not how Moore believed the club should enjoy what remains the greatest night in its history. Spotting Greenwood heading to his car to go home, the captain told his manager: 'You know the trouble with this club, boss? We don't know how to celebrate and enjoy the good times.'

Moore and Greenwood would soon be at odds over something much more serious than a good night out.

9. Spurs

One day in early April 1966, just a couple of months before the World Cup finals, Ron Greenwood called Bobby Moore into his office, told his stalwart defender to sit down and then sacked him as captain. There was no row, just cold, silent acceptance. 'Moore did not show a flicker of emotion when I told him,' Greenwood said. 'I am not sure he ever did show any.'

Perhaps it was Moore's refusal to react which provoked Greenwood to go even further. He not only stripped Moore of the armband but went to a newspaper with a remarkable public attack on the deposed captain. The outburst was untypical of a measured man and very oddly timed coming just a week before the first leg of the Cup Winners' Cup semi-final against Borussia Dortmund, the biggest match of West Ham's season. But Greenwood felt a need to pour out his frustration.

Brian Scovell was the reporter handed the exclusive. The *Daily Sketch* writer was one of a group of journalists who would spend long hours in Greenwood's office after matches at Upton Park, listening to him expound on tactics. He caught up with Greenwood in a London hotel and could not believe his luck as the scoop fell into his lap.

The article on Monday 4 April was headlined 'WEST HAM SACK MOORE'. Scovell breathlessly informed his readers that 'England's World Cup skipper Bobby Moore has been sacked as West Ham's captain. Any club that wants him can have him.'

If the headline was eye-catching, the quotes from Greenwood were even more extraordinary. According to Greenwood, Moore had been coasting since the momentous Cup Winners' Cup victory the previous May. From the high of Wembley, West Ham had spent much of the winter in distress in the relegation zone. Was Moore one of the main reasons for the decline?

'I am absolutely sure of it,' Greenwood told Scovell. 'Moore has not been really playing for us for eight months.'

Greenwood went on, scathingly: 'We got into the big time with that Cup Final win at Wembley and some of the players think they are still playing at Wembley. They have been playing in the past. To be a big time player you've got to play like a big time player every time. Since Wembley some of them think they have it made. But they haven't.'

After the glories of the previous two seasons, West Ham had not lived up to their reputation as England's coming force. They had done well enough in the cups, reaching the League Cup final. Their defence of the European Cup Winners' Cup had reached the semi-final stage. But the league campaign had been disastrous with long months spent perilously close to the relegation zone.

Greenwood was infuriated by his team's inconsistent form and convinced himself that Moore was distracted. He explained that Moore had been stripped of the captaincy because 'we can't have a man leading the side who doesn't want to play for us'. And that was the practical nub of the matter. Moore was refusing to sign a new contract at West Ham. He had been tapped up.

The idea of Moore wanting to leave Upton Park offends the sensibilities of West Ham supporters and jars with the idyllic memories of the club's greatest servant. But Moore had a pragmatic view rather than a romantic one. He wanted to do the best for himself, financially and professionally, and that meant getting away.

The problem was how to go about it. We love to romanticise the loyal players of yesteryear but the truth is that they were shackled to their clubs. They were loyal at gunpoint. Johnny Haynes is celebrated at Fulham as a marvellous one-club man, his statue outside Craven Cottage, but he itched to escape to Spurs for more money and medals. He was thwarted by the legal restraints of the time because there was no free agency when a player ran out of contract. Moore was in a similar position, intent on leave West Ham for north London, but mindful that his employers were not obliged to sell.

He had toyed with a move to Spurs in 1963 when Dave Mackay broke his leg. Alerted to interest from White Hart Lane, Moore approached Greenwood to say that he was keen to leave if a bid came in. Nothing came of it except the knowledge that Bill Nicholson, the Spurs manager, was a keen admirer. By 1966, Nicholson was more eager than ever to lure the England captain. Moore was even more receptive to the idea of moving to White Hart Lane.

His desire to leave was understandable. Here was the chance to join one of the top clubs in the country. West Ham had won two cups but Spurs were the team of the early sixties. They had won the Double in 1961, retained the FA Cup the following year and claimed the Cup Winners' Cup in 1963.

For Moore, there was a real prospect of winning the First Division title at Spurs, plus the chance to more than double his wages. There was the added bonus, too, of sharing a dressing room with Jimmy Greaves, one of his favourite drinking buddies.

The plan was that he would be joined at White Hart Lane by another good friend, Terry Venables. The Chelsea midfielder was also on Spurs' wish-list in the spring of 1966 and plotted the move with Moore. They had known each other from the London football scene as apprentices, sharing tea and toast in Cassettari's Cafe.

Venables lived just a couple of streets away – Moore in Glenwood Gardens, Venables in Beechwood Gardens – in Gants Hill. They went for a few drinks to talk excitedly about how they could fit into the Spurs team and win the title. 'We were in the thick of it together,' Venables says.

Greenwood was sure that Nicholson, the Spurs manager, would not be so disrespectful as to approach Moore behind his back. But that may just have been Reverend Ron's idealism. Sounding out a player was easy enough to do. As Moore's great friend, Greaves could easily act as a go-between.

Someone had clearly done the groundwork to set up the transfer of the England captain across London. According to Venables, Moore was 'virtually agreed' on the deal with Spurs.

As Moore would explain later, he felt that a move was necessary to 'start afresh and recapture some real drive and enthusiasm'. A transfer to White Hart Lane must have seemed more attractive with each week that the Hammers spent in the depths of the First Division. Moore craved the opportunity to further his career – and to get away from Ron.

Sir Alex Ferguson once explained a tenet of good management: 'For a player – and for any human being – there is nothing better than hearing "well done". Those are the two best words ever invented in sport.'

If Greenwood ever said them, Moore never heard.

Even as he was England captain, one of the most admired players in the country, Moore wanted Greenwood to tell him how good he was. But it was not in a dour manager's nature. Even as Moore seemed so commanding on a football pitch, he still had some of those teenage insecurities locked away deep inside. 'Beneath my exterior has always lurked a doubt and question mark of my own potential,' he confessed. He wanted reassurance, a pat on the back, a simple 'well done'.

Moore was still muttering darkly about Greenwood's lack of vocal support and affection years later. He confided in his good friend Harry Redknapp, who was struck by Moore's strength of feeling against his manager. ·

'I remember Bobby saying to me one day when we were chatting in Seattle – and it was a big lesson I learnt in management – he said, "you know, Harry, all the time I played at West Ham, Ron never ever said 'well done' to me".

'I said "Bobby, you were England captain, one of the best defenders in the world". He replied "yeah, but we all need that some days. We all need a pat on the back. There's nothing better than someone coming up and saying 'effing well done"'.

Redknapp goes on: 'It made a big impression on me. Doesn't matter who you are, it means something if you go up to a player and just say "you were great today". Ron was a genius, a fantastic coach and the cleverest football man I've come across. But he found it hard to show his emotions. Bobby felt as though he wasn't appreciated as he'd like to have been by Ron.'

Even at the height of West Ham's success, as they had each done so much for the other's career, Moore and Greenwood were far from a perfect match. 'I suppose it was basically a case of different personalities not gelling – and this was my fault as much as his,' Greenwood wrote. He described them as 'both proud and reserved men'.

Greenwood at least took his share of responsibility for the awkwardness. Moore saw it entirely as his manager's fault. He had a list of grievances, all of which added up to him feeling undervalued. He started to amass a set of gripes against Greenwood, little aggravations that formed into a wider sense of restlessness and dissatisfaction.

When Moore had been crowned Footballer of the Year in May 1964, he saw it as typically unfeeling that Greenwood had not arranged for anyone from West Ham to attend the banquet. Coming just two nights before the FA Cup final, Greenwood was keen to minimise distractions. He did not want his players out socialising – he never could see the point of boozing – but Moore was right. It would not have taken much for the club to have sent a delegation before slipping away early on such a momentous occasion.

The irritation was still festering in Moore's mind when, at the end of the cup final, he went to embrace his manager in the warm glow of victory. Moore told Jeff Powell: 'I went to cuddle him at the end but he didn't want that from me. Ron felt deeply about people without showing it on the outside. I knew then that although he respected me, he didn't like me.' That was a sweeping conclusion from one moment of standoffishness but, in Moore's eyes, a distance had formed towards his undemonstrative manager that could never close.

There had been other differences, little slights like Greenwood forcing him to haggle for every pay rise. But it was mostly a matter of personalities that never quite clicked. Greenwood had always liked to push Moore, knowing that he was driven to respond productively. He admitted that he was deliberately unkind to Moore at times, goading him to be even more determined on the training ground. But this withholding of praise had begun to grate.

Eddie Bovington was another player who had similar issues with Greenwood. Bovington, who retired from football early to work in the rag trade, says: 'Ron knew the game but his communication, his man management was useless. He never once ever put his arm around me. He'd never done it to anybody. Some people need to be cuddled and some need to be bollocked, and Ron didn't do either. I think loads of us could have been much better players if we had encouragement. The more confident you feel the better you play in all sports.'

This lack of empathy between Moore and Greenwood had not stopped West Ham winning two trophies. They had become one of the most pleasing sides to watch in the country, and Greenwood did not dispute that his captain did as much as he could ask on the pitch.

But if Moore was frustrated by Greenwood's lack of expansiveness, the manager felt that his captain was also infuriatingly cold and distant. Greenwood was capable of warm relationships with players, including Geoff Hurst and Martin Peters. Laughter would bellow out of his office if Budgie Byrne was in there playing the fool. But he came up against Moore's reserve and could not find a way through, a cause of frustration which he expressed in his most famous remark about his captain.

'Ask me to talk about Bobby Moore the footballer and I will talk for days,' Greenwood said. 'Ask me about the man and I will dry up in a minute. That's not because he's uninteresting, cold or unfriendly, but because the inner part of his personality remains a mystery to me and, I'm sure, to the great majority of those who come in contact with him.'

It was not just the manager who could find Moore hard to get close to but many of his team-mates, too. Hurst knew Moore from their teenage days in the youth team. He spent more than a decade in the same dressing room as Moore for club and country. They socialised together. Their wives were friends.

But Hurst readily accepts that he never knew Moore; not really. They never discussed much beyond daily trivia even in all those years sharing a dressing room or hotel. They shared many fun times but Moore always seemed to be holding something back.

As for praise, for all Moore's complaints about Greenwood withholding appreciation, the captain was not much better. When Moore sought out Hurst after one match to say how brilliantly he had played, the striker remembered the moment precisely because it was so rare.

Hurst was soaking in the bath after a victory at Sunderland in September 1967. He was in the prime of his career, basking in another two goals after a 5-1 victory, when Moore came past. 'You were fucking great today,' Moore said. Hurst was so surprised he might have drowned.

'Mooro never did this, ever. "You were fucking great today" and that was it. He just walked off and that was the only time he ever said it. He probably thought it at other times, at least I hope so, but I never heard,' Hurst says.

'I don't think many of us got to know him. Certainly I always felt, although I have the utmost respect for him, I could never be totally sure it was mutual appreciation. We were never mates. For a while I thought it was me because we had this little bit of a barrier but I think he was like that with a lot of people. I certainly relaxed with Mooro when he had a drink and many people would say that. They'd say he was a god and respect him as an individual but in terms of knowing someone, that's another story.'

Martin Peters makes a very similar observation, remarking that he hoped for Moore's admiration but could never be certain it was forthcoming: 'I had huge respect for him as a player and a person but I was never quite sure whether he felt the same about me, or any of his other team-mates for that matter.'

It is inevitable in any dressing room that there will be different cliques, and Moore's mates were the heavy socialisers. Hurst and Peters were the straight men. But it is a recurring theme at West Ham that Moore remained an enigma – an amiable, modest enigma – to many in the dressing room.

Some players, particularly Moore's drinking buddies like Byrne and Bovington, did not see his disinclination to be vocal in the dressing room as the slightest problem. And none of the squad, least of all in the happy glow provided by two trophies, was ever going to question the stature of their captain.

He was Bobby Moore, the England captain. Bobby Moore, their best player, the man who set the standards. But the problem lay on both sides, with Greenwood and Moore. Trevor Brooking was just starting to work around the first team, a young apprentice coming through, and he could detect a growing rift.

'Budgie Byrne could drive you loopy but he was the absolute hub of the dressing room,' Brooking says. 'Bob didn't allow people to get close to him and I'm sure, well, I know, that Ron would have liked a closer working relationship with his captain. But then the trouble is that Ron wouldn't have confronted that either.'

This was the awkwardness which had worsened by 1966, as Moore dreamed of a new career at Tottenham and Greenwood grew increasingly exasperated at his captain's refusal to commit to West Ham.

Knowing that his career was on the rise, Moore had taken to signing twelve-month deals which gave him the chance to renegotiate better terms each summer. As he kept rebuffing invitations by Greenwood to extend his deal, the manager became convinced that Moore's eagerness to leave was undermining his game. There was some evidence to back him up. For the first time Moore was starting to earn a reputation for saving his best for the biggest matches. He was coasting against lesser opposition, exacerbating the inconsistency which seems always to have plagued West Ham.

The impasse over the contract, and his future, would have to be resolved but Moore had expected to talk at the end of the season. What he had not expected was that Greenwood should not only take away the armband but then blurt out all his frustrations to a reporter.

Moore, ever mindful of his image, was furious with Greenwood. He demanded to know why, after months of discussions in private, he had not only had the captaincy taken away but been singled out by his manager in public.

Why were West Ham fans now asking him if it was true that he was off to Spurs or Arsenal or Chelsea? Why was he being asked if the newspapers were correct in saying that he could expect to pocket a £10,000 signing-on fee from a £100,000 move? It was Greenwood's prerogative if he wanted to take away the armband, but what angered Moore were the slurs, the accusation that he was not trying.

Manager and captain had a forty-minute confrontation after the story appeared. Years later, Greenwood would say that he had no regrets; that he was simply putting the club's interests first and that Moore had not been giving everything to the job.

Greenwood wrote: 'His attitude clearly meant he was less than a hundred per cent for the club and I gave the [captain's] job to Johnny Byrne who bubbled with enthusiasm. It was not a difficult decision because it made the important point that no player is bigger than his club.'

But at the time his tone was far more contrite, and it is clear who won the row. Greenwood made an extraordinary admission the following day to Scovell, and other journalists, that he had spoken out of turn.

'He [Moore] saw me last week and we discussed the situation and I agreed to make an announcement at the proper time,' Greenwood said. 'Unfortunately I let it slip over lunch and it all came out. The boy has been honest with me and my opinion about him hasn't changed. He always has been a great player and I think he still is'.

Moore's biting reaction showed that he was far from appeased. He told the same reporters that the meeting with his manager 'was mainly about character and principles. I honoured the agreement. He chose not to.'

Less inclined than ever to agree a new deal, Moore dug in

his heels and refused to sign with West Ham as the season concluded. But as the row dragged on, it threw up a practical nightmare. Moore's contract was due to expire at the end of June and FA rules stipulated that players could only be picked for England if registered with a club. Without a contract, Moore would not be allowed to play in the World Cup.

10. 1966

Hindsight beguiles us. It fills us with a sense of destiny. Bobby Moore as England's hero? Why, of course. He seemed born for the role of victorious leader. The film star Michael Caine once said that if you had held auditions for the job of England captain, you would choose Moore without even seeing him kick a ball.

Looking back, the glorious events of 1966 seem so natural, so perfect. But Alf Ramsey did not have the benefit of knowing everything would turn out well, and he was certainly no believer in fate. He was a hard pragmatist with the pressing need of making sure his England team was in the best possible shape for the World Cup and, like Greenwood, he had worries about Bobby Moore.

For all Moore's qualities as captain and his undeniable class as a defender, that business over the West Ham contract and Moore's lapses in form had raised doubts in Ramsey's mind about his skipper's concentration. Was Moore focused on his game? Ramsey was not so sure. Could he contemplate the unthinkable and drop his captain? It seems ridiculous now, but Moore's team-mates confirm that it was a real debate in the tense weeks counting down to the start of the World Cup.

The initial England squad of twenty-seven gathered at the National Recreation Centre in Lilleshall for a fortnight's boot camp to begin their World Cup preparations. The players would call it Stalag Lilleshall; eighteen days of hard training under Les Cocker, the Leeds United and England trainer. They were on a strict regime, each day mapped out from 9 a.m. to 9 p.m., filled with fitness sessions, practice matches, films of the opposition, set-piece drills. Ramsey brought such attention to detail that Alan Bass, the doctor, explained to the squad how to cut their toenails.

Alcohol was banned and the players confined to barracks, though that was not so much an order as a challenge to the usual drinking crew. A small group, inevitably including Moore and Greaves, sneaked away to the clubhouse of a local golf course for a few relaxing beers. There they were discovered by Harold Shepherdson, Ramsey's second in command, and dragged back to base like errant schoolboys.

Behind the scenes, FA staff were growing increasingly twitchy about Moore's unresolved position with West Ham. They checked the small print of the regulations, then checked again. It was clear that Moore could not play for England unless registered with a club and he would be out of contract on 30 June. England's opening match against Uruguay was on 11 July.

Ramsey did not care about the rights and wrongs of the argument. He just wanted it sorted out, and Moore left to concentrate on the tournament. With this cloud hanging over the player, he kept his best defender on the sidelines for the first two preparation matches for the World Cup.

It was entirely sensible that Ramsey wanted to experiment

and try different combinations. In February 1966, in a friendly against West Germany, Ramsey paired Jack Charlton and Norman Hunter in central defence, just as they played for Leeds United. Moore was deployed in defensive midfield. The Wembley crowd did not like the caution, even booing when the Germans had a goal inexplicably disallowed, though England did claim a 1-0 victory through the only goal of Nobby Stiles' international career.

Moore was restored to centre-back for the 4-3 victory over Scotland in April, a chaotic win at Hampden Park which featured some hapless defending by both sides. Moore was rooted to the spot when Denis Law headed Scotland's first and tackled recklessly in the fraught closing stages of a draining, if ultimately victorious, afternoon.

But it was when Ramsey eased Moore out for consecutive games against Yugoslavia, in May 1966, and Finland in June – the first in a series of four pre-World Cup matches – that doubts over the captain as an automatic pick became more than idle speculation. Hunter was seen by some as the coming man. His attitude was the opposite of the languid captain. 'Bites Yer Legs' – a far more accomplished player than the violent nickname implied – was full-blooded even in five-a-sides. On club form, Hunter versus Moore was a fair debate, and Moore himself acknowledged it. The need to stay on top of his game was one of the reasons he had resolved to leave West Ham.

Hunter was a central pillar of a Leeds team which had become a major force in the English game. He was left-sided, like Moore, and could carry the ball forward into midfield. He could not match Moore's composure or elegance, but he was a credible alternative. Was Ramsey deliberating between the two centre-backs? Would he seriously make such a critical change to his team after two years with Moore as his captain, his lieutenant?

George Cohen gained unique insight one day as he sat in the team hotel on the Scandinavian tour ahead of the World Cup and inadvertently overheard a conversation between Ramsey and his two coaches, Shepherdson and Cocker. Cohen was reading a book when he overheard the coaching staff debate their ideal centre-back pairing. As the discussion continued, he dare not move in case they thought he was earwigging. The impression he came away with was that Moore's place was far from guaranteed.

'It was Les or Harold who began it, "Norman's playing very well, isn't he". That sort of thing. The inference went on that Norman was pushing very close to getting in the team. The more it went on, I was thinking "heck, I shouldn't be hearing this".'

Cohen confided in Geoff Hurst who subsequently wrote in his autobiography that Moore might have been axed. But Hurst added the twist in his version that Ramsey was considering dropping Moore for the World Cup final and not the opening fixture.

'I wish it had never come out really,' Cohen says. 'I wasn't going to talk about it but it's best cleared up exactly what happened. I heard that conversation and, yes, it certainly made me think about what Alf was going to do with Bobby and Norman.'

Cohen struggles to imagine how England could have embarked on their World Cup campaign without their captain at the heart of defence. He is certain that every player in the team would have wanted Moore for his quality, composure and that extraordinary capacity to excel on the big occasion.

'There was a sophistication about Bob in the way he played,' Cohen says. 'The understanding of the game was far greater than Norman Hunter's. He also had this knack of raising his game but that is something that is special to Bobby. When he played in a tournament like 1966 he simply played differently. He had something about him that is almost difficult to understand.'

At heart, Ramsey must have been sure of that too but he wanted Moore to fight for his place, to prove that he was not coasting for England as he had, at times, for West Ham. When he left Moore out against Finland, Ramsey did so without explaining why. It was a very deliberate, premeditated jolt. 'It may have been his way of saying, "I know what's going on, show me you want it". It did create a doubt, showed me I'd got to work at it,' Moore told the journalist David Miller.

Even at this late stage, Ramsey wanted Moore not to take anything for granted and his psychology worked. Moore returned from his two-game absence for a 6-1 victory in Norway (playing alongside Ron Flowers) and scored with a Charltonesque twenty-five yard cannonball. As England's preparations continued with victories over Denmark and Poland, the partnership of Jack Charlton and Moore was restored, with Hunter reverting to the bench.

At Elland Road, the management team of Don Revie and Syd Owen would often ask Les Cocker, who doubled up as fitness coach for Leeds and England, why Hunter was not being picked for his country. Wasn't he starring for a club which was competing for the championship, unlike Moore at West Ham? Wasn't he a ferociously consistent performer?

'Listen, for fifty cup and league games a season, yes, I'll have

Norman every time,' Cocker would tell them. 'But for the big games, Bobby Moore, he's a different class.'

Or, as Greenwood put it: 'Bobby is not a bread-and-butter player. He is made for the biggest occasion. The more extreme the challenge, the more commanding he will be. He should play at Wembley every week.' Even with all the differences between them, Greenwood knew that Moore was essential if England were going to succeed.

A year before the World Cup, a journalist had visited West Ham's training ground and picked Greenwood's brains about the hosts' prospects of lifting the Jules Rimet Trophy for the first time. Greenwood pointed across the training pitch to where Moore was practising with a ball and said: 'We're going to win and that man's the reason why. He can already see in his mind's eye a picture of himself holding up the World Cup and he's calculated what that will mean to him.'

But none of this lauding of Moore, or his big game temperament, would mean much if he was ineligible.

Moore's form had reassured Ramsey, but he still had no contract when the players gathered at Hendon Hall for the final few days of preparation before the opening match of the World Cup. Still hopeful of a move to Spurs, Moore did not want to commit to a long-term deal at Upton Park but he was coming under pressure from all sides. As the clock ticked down to England's opening match, Ramsey demanded that the matter was resolved so that there could be no distractions.

Greenwood was instructed that he must break the impasse for England's sake. He travelled up to England's base just off the North Circular, to reach a compromise. Ramsey and Moore waited in the lobby. Ramsey told West Ham's manager and captain to go to a room and sort out their differences. 'You've got a minute,' Ramsey supposedly told the uncommunicative pair. It was all they required.

With the scribble of a pen and barely a word to Greenwood, Moore signed a one-month contract with West Ham, extending his deal until 31 July when the tournament would be over. He would be a West Ham player on paper, though not in his heart.

For England, at least, the crisis was over though Moore, still resentful over being stripped of the captaincy and Greenwood's public criticism, felt blackmailed into signing even that short-term deal. He felt defeated. 'Gambling on my pride and ambition, Ron had won his point,' he said.

Moore felt let down, which would have long term consequences for his relationship with Greenwood, but that was for another day. His immediate priority was the World Cup and, not for the last time, he found that quality to set aside any turbulence to concentrate on the challenge in front of him. Moore was free to play in the defining games of his life.

On 11 July 1966, Moore led out the England team at Wembley Stadium for the opening game of the World Cup finals. It would be wrong to say that the nation was gripped by feverish excitement. There were more than 20,000 empty seats. Touts outside the ground clasped handfuls of tickets, unable to sell them. Far from convinced by Ramsey's claim that England would win the tournament, the public needed a reason to believe.

The press remained sceptical and their doubts seemed justified by an indifferent performance against Uruguay. Ramsey began with John Connelly, the Manchester United winger, in the starting XI. Twice he hit the woodwork in a frustrating goalless draw against defensive opponents. It highlights how fickle a sporting career can be that, had either of those chances gone in, Connelly might have stayed in the team. Instead he was dropped and never played for his country again.

For the first time in twelve games, England had failed to score. Despite some scathing write-ups, Ramsey was upbeat afterwards, reassuring the players that the most important thing had been to avoid defeat. He had expected first-game nerves. 'After the game they booed us off the pitch for a little while and the press weren't too clever towards us,' George Cohen says. 'They said we were no-hopers, we didn't have a clue. But Alf came in and said we didn't lose and we're going to win the rest of them.'

To soothe his players, the day after the Uruguay game Ramsey took the squad to Pinewood Studios to mix with film stars. It was a break from his usual routine of leading them off to the cinema to see one of his favourite westerns. At the end of the studio tour, Ramsey said a few words of thanks to the assembled film stars including Sean Connery, who was filming *You Only Live Twice* in his role as 007. Except, with his odd, clipped accent, Ramsey thanked 'SEEN' Connery, to the undisguised mirth of the usual suspects.

Moore and Greaves collapsed with laughter as Connery tried to stifle his giggles. 'It's true Alf had acquired a voice but, actually, I admired him for that,' Cohen says. 'He'd come from Dagenham from the cloth-cap era and had come a long way. But Bobby and Jimmy found it very amusing.' Eventually Moore stopped laughing and turned to a few of the lads. 'Now I've SEEN everything,' he deadpanned, to more laddish guffaws.

The good-time boys were determined to make sure that it

was not all work and no fun during the World Cup. When Nigel Clarke was at Hendon Hall one day to interview the players, he heard a couple of familiar voices whispering down from an upstairs window, 'Nige, Nige'. It was Alan Ball and Moore. 'Come up here and have a look,' they grinned.

Clarke's immediate thought was that they must have smuggled a woman into the hotel. 'I went up and it was all "shush, shush, is the coast clear?" They opened up the bathroom door and in the bath cooling off were six crates of lager.'

For the second match, against Mexico, out went Alan Ball and Connelly. In came Martin Peters and Terry Paine in Ramsey's lopsided 4-3-3, with Paine replacing Connelly as the sole winger to the right of Roger Hunt and Jimmy Greaves. In the crowd to watch England was Moore's father, 'Big' Bob, in a section reserved for the players' families.

It was an improved performance from England, ahead through Bobby Charlton in the first half and the lead doubled by Hunt in the second, but Bob Moore's enjoyment of the game kept being disturbed by a loudmouth in front. After a while even this mild-mannered man could take no more and he reached over. 'Excuse me, would you mind sitting down so we can watch?'

Big Mouth turned around. 'Do you know who I am? I'm Terry Paine's father.' Without mention of his own, far more impressive connections, Bob Moore sat down without a fuss.

Doss was so eager to stay out of the way that she did not attend a single game during the World Cup. Robert's soaring fame had made his parents more wary than ever of the limelight. Following the 1965 European Cup Winners' Cup final, Doss and Bob had been invited for a special screening but went along only after encouragement from the family. It had been the chance to watch their son at the peak of his powers among a hall full of well-wishers, but they had instantly regretted turning up.

'We're honoured tonight to be joined by Mr and Mrs Moore,' the organiser announced as they took their seats in the local community centre in Dagenham. Doss and Bob were asked to stand up but, as the crowd cheered, they tried to hide under their seats. Graham Hardwick, one of Moore's cousins, was with them: 'They were appalled by the attention. They practically had to be stopped from walking out.'

Doss preferred to stay away from Wembley where Ramsey continued to tinker with his team. The 2-0 victory over Mexico had soothed English nerves but the manager had still not found his ideal combination. Ball seethed at his omission and, always emotional, threatened to seek out the manager for an argument. He was persuaded by Moore, Greaves and some of the others to knuckle down and win back his place which, eventually, proved sound advice.

For the third game against France, the team was changed again. Ian Callaghan came in on the right wing, with Paine dropped and Ball still on the bench. Hunt scored both goals in a 2-0 win but victory came at the cost of an injury to Jimmy Greaves who badly gashed his shin and needed fourteen stitches. Whether the Spurs striker could play again in the tournament depended on how long England survived.

Greaves was the country's outstanding goalscorer, but he had not been at his sharpest. He had suffered from hepatitis six months before the World Cup and knew himself that he was half a yard off his peak. No one doubted Greaves's class as a finisher yet some of the England players said that his absence was not as devastating to them as it seemed to the outside world and, of course, to Greaves himself.

In came Geoff Hurst, who had only made his international debut five months before the tournament. He was a very different type of player from Greaves, a more muscular, mobile striker coming off a prolific season at West Ham, with forty goals in fifty-nine games. Some inside the camp were convinced that his physical approach would be more effective.

Jimmy Armfield insists that he saw the benefits of Hurst's introduction, without hindsight. 'We had looked all right but we hadn't convinced,' he says. 'We were sitting around one day at Hendon, I think Bob Moore, me, Alf, Harold, maybe one or two others and I said that "funny thing is, English teams I've played for in my football life, we always seem more comfortable with what I call a bigger centre-forward, a player you can hit with the ball".'

Cohen agrees. 'I think in every successful World Cup campaign there is a bit of luck, something that happens that makes you win it. That may have been Alf's, put it that way, though I could never ever put that to my old friend Jimmy,' he says. 'We had Roger Hunt who I thought was a terrific, marvellous player, and terribly brave in those days when defenders didn't think twice about kicking forwards from behind. When Geoff came in it worked beautifully, they worked off each other. Two strong boys, bloody effective.'

As well as Hurst's introduction for Greaves for the quarter-final against Argentina, Ball was restored for the game that England expected to be their toughest test. Ramsey had ditched all his conventional wingers for the first time in the tournament, a switch from 4-3-3 to a version of 4-4-2, using a modern midfield diamond. Ball and Peters were deployed as narrow, versatile midfield players, Nobby Stiles holding and Bobby Charlton at the apex.

Was the 'wingless wonders' a masterplan? Or, as Brian Glanville wrote, had Ramsey come across his winning formula 'only as the product of trial and frequent error'? He had played a team without wingers in a 4-3-3 formation against Spain in 1965. England's final preparation match before the tournament, a 1-0 victory in Poland, had featured ten of the team he now sent out to face Argentina, with Ball and Peters in midfield and the only change being Hurst for Greaves.

Did he always have this side in mind? Peters was convinced that Ramsey's preference was always for one outright winger. Whether by luck or design, Ramsey's plan challenged the orthodoxy. It defied the expectations of supporters raised on a strong tradition of wide men, and it would need to work if Ramsey was not going to face stinging criticism from many of the sports writers he had never attempted to charm.

As it turned out, it was not formations that anyone was talking about at the end of a hugely controversial, bruising quarter-final. After thirty-five minutes, Rudi Kreitlein, the referee, dismissed Antonio Rattín, the Argentine captain, for persistent fouling. Chaos followed as Rattín refused to leave the field, towering over the German official and demanding that an interpreter be found to explain the decision. The row continued for eight minutes, the game at a standstill as players milled around and fans jeered. Ken Aston, the head of refereeing, came down from his seat to the side of the pitch to demand that Rattín leave the field.

Eventually the Argentina captain walked off slowly down to the dressing rooms, pausing to wipe his hand contemptuously on one of the corner flags, and the game resumed, but it remained a horrible, niggly contest. It was a game when even Bobby Charlton was booked. It would be the only time in his career that he was cautioned but because referees did not carry yellow or red cards until the 1970 World Cup, he did not realise till years later.

For England, it was enough simply to win. When Peters crossed to the near post, Hurst was there to score with a header, a move that had been played out numerous times for West Ham. England were through to the semi-finals but Ramsey fumed at the end, refusing to allow the players to swap shirts and deriding the Argentinians as 'animals'. By the time the squad had returned to Hendon Hall, his anger had turned to satisfaction. He was so pleased that he even allowed the players a drink. Some needed no encouragement.

Four games into the World Cup and England had not conceded a goal. Ramsey's team had many strengths but the organisation of the back four underpinned everything. 'We moved very well as a unit,' Cohen says. 'Very organised. We swivelled around Big Jack. You always knew that he was there if myself or Ray Wilson or Bob made a move forward.'

Charlton was the fixed point, the old-fashioned centre-half, but Moore was the brain of the defence, constantly offering little words of instruction to ensure they kept their positioning. This was when he would become vocal. 'It needed somebody that was in overall charge if you like,' Cohen says. 'With Bob, it would be "come on, let's get out of the area" or he would be calling for you to give him the ball on your blind side. You never ever felt that you were isolated.'

Moore was never flustered, always taking the ball, accepting responsibility. The acclaimed sports writer Simon Barnes remembers watching the tournament at home in south London. Barnes wrote of an opposing striker advancing on England's goal and Moore appearing out of the corner of the screen: 'It was not the action that is significant here, it was the deep certainty that Moore would put everything right. That was what he was best at. Good to feel in Streatham: how much more wonderful to feel such a thing if you were a member of the England team.'

With the knowledge that Banks was in great form, Moore imperious and Hurst now on the scoresheet, Bobby Charlton says there began to be a shift in mood after the victory over Argentina. They had lost Greaves but still prevailed against one of the best teams in the world. 'I think that's when we began to think we can win the World Cup, really,' he says. 'Everything felt right; the captain, the trainer, the manager, the coach and the group of players. If you wanted to play 4-3-3 we could. If you wanted to play 4-2-4, we could change. We had it all there with a group of committed lads.'

They had friends in high places, too. The semi-final was due to be staged at Goodison Park but it was switched to Wembley. Sir Stanley Rous, the former FA secretary, was now president of Fifa and a man who could push through this late change, justifying it on the grounds of Wembley's greater capacity.

The semi-final between England and Portugal was a match which deserved the largest possible audience; it was the outstanding game of the tournament. The reigning European Footballer of the Year, Eusebio had been the individual star of the World Cup, outshining the injured Pelé. With the maestro cut down, Brazil had not even made it out of their group, losing to Portugal on the way out.

Eusebio had scored seven goals, including four in the

quarter-final victory over North Korea, and presented the obvious threat to England's advance. Stiles was ordered to shadow him, with Ramsey never squeamish about using destructive force to win a football game. When Jack Charlton had asked the best means of stifling José Torres, the giant Portugal striker, Ramsey replied: 'You'll do what's necessary.'

It was Bobby Charlton's night, the first goal a low follow-up shot from the edge of the area after Hunt's effort had been blocked, the second a typical rasping drive. Jack Charlton gave away a late penalty with a goalline handball so blatant he might have been dismissed under modern rules but, despite Eusebio scoring his eighth goal in five games, England won 2-1 at a rapturous Wembley. England were through to the World Cup final.

They would face West Germany, who had never inflicted defeat on England. Ninety minutes – or so they hoped – separated them from the ultimate triumph. The nation could look forward in thrilled anticipation; all except Greaves who was fit to play but quick to sense that Hurst would keep his place and he would spend the biggest day of his professional career on the sidelines.

Some versions suggest that Moore tried to talk Greaves back into the team with a quiet word to Ramsey but, if the manager ever discussed his selection with his captain, it was with his mind as good as made up. In any case, the majority of the players felt that it would be wrong to change a winning line-up.

According to one documentary, Greaves and Moore went to the Playboy Club for lunch two days before the final where the captain commiserated with his old friend, though it was not till the morning of the game that Greaves knew for certain that he would be a spectator on the biggest day in English sporting history. Moore stirred on the morning of the final to find his old friend and room-mate sombrely packing his bags.

'What are you doing?'

'It's all over for me, mate. I'm just getting ready for a quick getaway once the final is over,' Greaves replied.

'You can do that tomorrow morning,' Moore said. 'We'll all enjoy a few bevvies tonight together to celebrate us winning the World Cup.'

11. On Top of the World

The list of the most watched British television events is an eclectic mix; the funeral of Princess Diana, the stricken Apollo 13 splashing back down to earth, Dirty Den divorcing Angie in *EastEnders*. But nothing tops the day that England played West Germany for the World Cup.

The final was watched by an estimated 32.3 million people, which, considering that only fifteen million households owned a TV set (compared to more than twenty-five million in 2014) meant lots of huddling around a small screen in family living rooms. On 30 July 1966 the streets were hushed, the roads cleared of traffic; a nation gathered to see if England could stand on top of the sporting world.

One person who could not bear to watch was Doss. The closer England came to the final, the harder the captain's mother had found it to cope with the stress. As the game approached that Saturday afternoon, she went out into the backyard of Waverley Gardens and started fiddling nervously with the plants. She did not come back indoors for more than two hours, until the final whistle had blown and the match was done.

Doss was not the only parent absent from Wembley. Martin

Peters' mother and father were also at home, though not out of choice. In a moment of greed he would come deeply to regret, Peters sold his two complimentary tickets for the final to Stan Flashman. Peters' parents were part of that unprecedented TV audience rather than sitting among the 93,000 on tenterhooks.

For the final, there was good money to be made on the black market. As the air crackled with nervous excitement, everyone wanted a seat for the climax against West Germany. Muhammad Ali was there; the heavyweight champion knew that Wembley was the only place to be that afternoon.

In the *Observer*, Hugh McIlvanney wrote of his journey up Olympic Way, approaching the Twin Towers through the excited crowds. 'It was like walking into an ordinary, familiar room and knowing instinctively that something vital and unbearably dramatic was happening, perhaps a matter of life and death,' he noted. '"It's bloody electric," said one of the doormen. He had found the word.'

In the England dressing room, it was not just electric but chaotic, too.

The players had passed the morning of the final in relative peace and seclusion up at Hendon Hall. Some of them jumped on a bus down to Golders Green to pass the time shopping. Bobby Charlton went off with Ray Wilson to buy a new shirt. Alan Ball, flush with a £1,000 bonus in cash for wearing Adidas boots, treated himself to a new watch. Nobby Stiles went to church, as usual. None of them were pestered.

It was the bus ride to Wembley which confirmed to the players that this was the biggest game of their lives. The streets were lined with well-wishers. There was a clamour from supporters as the team coach eased through the crowds, and the frenzy continued when Ramsey and his players arrived in the dressing room. Half an hour before kick-off, the private sanctum was still jostling with television crews. For once, even the captain was agitated. Bobby Moore was trying to change but there were so many photographers that he could barely find a place to sit down.

'Aren't we supposed to be getting ready for a big match?' Moore said, with irritation, to Jack Charlton who was next to him. 'This is the most important game of my life and look at this lot. I can't even start getting changed yet.'

'That's why it is the most important game of your life, isn't it?' grinned Charlton.

The throng in the dressing room was eventually cleared and on came the kit. Red shirt, red socks, boots, tie-ups. When the buzzer went in the dressing room, the captain slipped on his white shorts.

'Let's go,' he said, leading the players into the broad tunnel which sloped up towards the sunlight, and out into a great bowl of noise.

At three o'clock, the World Cup final kicks off, the start of two hours of unrelenting drama.

When Helmut Haller puts the Germans ahead following a poor headed clearance by Ray Wilson after only twelve minutes, it is the first goal England have conceded from open play in the whole tournament, and the first time they have fallen behind. A less-assured team might be undermined by such an uncharacteristic lapse.

The equaliser comes just six minutes later. Moore is instrumental; Ron Greenwood, too. When Moore is fouled by Wolfgang Overath as he turns to shield possession midway into the German half, the captain quickly gathers the ball to take the free-kick. He is looking up, alert to the possibilities, just as he has been taught on West Ham's training ground.

Geoff Hurst knows exactly what is coming next. Timing his run to attack space in the heart of the penalty area, the striker can rely on Moore's chipped free-kick arriving precisely when and where he needs it. 'It was just like Ron always coached us,' Hurst says. 'If something is on quick, take it.' It is a move straight out of the Greenwood manual as Moore flights the ball into the German penalty area and Hurst's header draws England level at 1-1.

On a typical English summer's day of clouds, showers and sunshine, England are playing with all the purpose and resolve that Ramsey has instilled over the previous three years. Franz Beckenbauer and Bobby Charlton have been ordered to mark each other out of the game and they both do so, effectively, but England have other lines of attack through the relentless running of Peters and the indefatigable Ball, who has chosen the right day to put in the performance of his life.

In defence, Moore looks masterful, striding into midfield as England begin to exert control. 'Moving among opponents like a bank manager among junior clerks, correcting, re-directing and discreetly scolding. He never seemed to be short of time, the hallmark of any great player,' David Miller wrote.

'Moore, showing again that he is stimulated by the demands of the great occasion, played with an imaginative self-confidence that made it unnecessary for anyone to ask who was the England captain,' McIlvanney reported.

There are chances at both ends but, of the two goalkeepers, Hans Tilkowski, is busier. England feel they have done enough to earn a break and when Hurst tries a shot from the edge of the box in the seventy-eighth minute, the ball is half blocked, spinning into the air and looping across the penalty box. It could fall anywhere but it is England's good fortune that it drops perfectly for Peters whose controlled volley from six yards appears to have put the World Cup in England's hands.

Even Moore celebrates that goal, rushing over to Peters to join the hugs, a great grin of delight on his face. They think it's all over. England's reserves come down from the stand to crowd behind the bench ready for the final whistle. The final seconds are ticking away when the Germans launch one last raid. Sigi Held, the German striker, has his back to goal, trying to protect a bouncing ball. Jack Charlton leaps over him to make a clearing header. Gottfried Dienst, the Swiss referee, rules there has been a foul despite Charlton's furious protests.

The England players shout frantic instructions at each other, desperate to repel this last opportunity. The free-kick is played up into the penalty area. A melee, a block, a whiff of German handball. Moore raises his arm to appeal but there is no whistle. The ball spins off across the six-yard box. Players strain to reach it but Wolfgang Weber gets there first. In the dying seconds the Germans have made it 2-2.

When the final whistle blows as England kick to restart, Wembley is crestfallen. Ramsey's task is to make sure that his players do not suffer the same deflation. If ever the England manager must prove his ability to tap into the minds of his players, it is in those minutes as he first instructs Moore and the rest of the team to get to their feet to show the Germans that they are not fatigued.

Ramsey does not berate his players but, as they munch on segments of oranges, exhorts them to dig deep once more. 'Keep at it. You've run them ragged. Just have a look at them.

They can't live with you for another half an hour, not through extra-time,' he says.

And then comes the immortal, Churchillian line: 'You've won the World Cup once. Now go out and do it again.'

In Ball, England have a player capable of running all day. As tiredness drains the rest of energy, the redhead seems to be playing in several positions all at the same time. Inevitably, he is involved when England go ahead in extra-time. Ball charges into space down the right wing and is picked out by a pass from Stiles, stretching the German defence once more. Ball's cross finds Hurst at the near post. The German defence stand off as Hurst turns and shoots with power.

It must be the most replayed shot of all time, the ball striking the underside of the crossbar, bouncing down and out of the goal. Roger Hunt turns away to celebrate, certain that a goal has been scored. There is confusion, and German protests. Dienst runs over to consult Tofik Bahkramov, the grey-haired Azerbaijan linesman, who signifies that it is a goal. Countless replays, computer analysis and a 1996 study within the Department of Engineering at Oxford University have emphasised England's good fortune. Using ground plane homography, transforming primitives, grainy footage and an excess of free time, the boffins have calculated that Hurst's shot failed to cross the line by a minimum of six centimetres. What does Hurst care? England lead 3-2. They have one hand on the World Cup.

To concede another goal now feels unforgivable though, with five minutes left of extra-time, Moore still pops up deep in enemy territory to lead an attack. Back come the Germans and Jack Charlton begins to panic. Every time he heads the ball away from England's goalmouth, it comes flying back. Almost two hours since they kicked off the game of their lives, players of both teams are struggling to stand never mind run, but still the Germans, those relentless Germans, are pressing and pounding and pushing for an equaliser.

In comes the ball again from Willi Shulz, curling into the goalmouth. This time Charlton does not need to strain or leap. Moore is in front of him and takes the brown leather ball on his broad chest, a captain in control.

'Get rid of it! Kick it! Kill the bloody thing!' Charlton screams.

But Moore knocks it left-footed to Hunt just outside the penalty area. Then, moving towards the corner flag, Moore calls for the ball back. 'Get shot of the bloody ball! In the stands!' Charlton shouts again. But he might as well exhort Moore in an alien language.

The whistle is in the mouth of referee Dienst and players are looking at the official to blow up. Wembley resounds with thousands of piercing whistles. But Dienst waves his arms to carry on.

It is at this point that Moore strides forward, the only calm figure among 93,000 at Wembley, and the 400 million watching around the world. He carries the ball a few more yards, pauses to look up and then plays the same long, deliberate pass to Hurst that he has struck a thousand times.

For decades, the highlights reel has shown only Hurst taking possession of the bouncing ball, striding forward and lashing it left-footed into the top corner as Kenneth Wolstenholme remarks from the commentary box that some people are on the pitch. They think it's all over. Hurst's hat-trick goal, and those perfectly judged words to accompany it, have become the iconic refrain of England's World Cup triumph.

Hurst's finish is spectacular but, back in his own penalty

area, Charlton is in awe at the presence and composure of his unflappable captain, and the pass that no one ever sees. As Bobby Jones once said when Jack Nicklaus broke all records to win the 1965 Masters by nine shots: 'He plays a game with which I'm not familiar'. Charlton knew that same feeling of inferiority in the presence of greatness. Moore never did just get rid of it, even with ten seconds to play in the World Cup final.

Had it finished 3-2, the disputed, third England goal would have cast an eternal shadow over England's triumph. But that fourth goal settled any debate. 'Bobby felt it necessary to tidy up things: 3-2 and the Germans could argue till the cows came home but 4-2 and no argument, thanks very much, okay boys? That was Bobby,' Frank Keating wrote in the *Guardian*.

'In the final I just thought he was terrific,' Jimmy Armfield says. 'That was his moment really, his day in the sun. To set up that last goal that Geoff scored, to have that sort of composure at 3-2 in a World Cup final when he was tired, most of the players were tired. It was heavy going that day and to have that sort of composure to put that kind of pass in, that was the perfect way to remember Bob. That was what he was about; the temperament to pass the ball like that, two-footed, his reading of the game. He anticipated things and he was at his best then. 1966 was his best.'

Soon Moore was leading his team up the Wembley steps. For English football, they were a stairway to heaven. As Moore led his team up past back-slapping supporters, sun burst through the clouds. As he neared the top, Moore realised that his hands were sticky with orange juice and mud. And there was the Queen waiting for him wearing a yellow hat, yellow coat and a pair of lily-white gloves. He wiped his hands on his shirts and shorts to clean off the dirt. Still he was worried by the grubbiness. He leaned forward and wiped his palms on the velvet covering at the front of the Royal Box. Manners maketh the man.

Then England's hero walked along the reception line, stopping in front of the Queen and the Jules Rimet Trophy. On meeting Moore before the opening game against Uruguay, she had remarked on a red, white and blue floral display. 'The right colours,' she said. 'I hope they bring you luck.'

Now the Queen brought things full circle. 'They were the right colours after all,' she said. And then she gave Moore the golden, winged Jules Rimet Trophy. On he went down the line of dignitaries, shaking hands with the Prime Minister and the rest of the VIPs. There was protocol to be observed before he raised the trophy high in his left hand. England were world champions.

Moore brought the players down the stairs and on to the pitch to celebrate. Bobby Charlton looked fretful with tears. Stiles began to jig like a drunk at a wedding. Ramsey had to be coaxed into joining the photographs. Moore trotted around before being lifted on to the shoulders of his players in the indelible image of the day, and of the captain's life.

The delight is obvious though there was little extravagance in the celebrations. Even then – perhaps especially then – in the moment of ecstasy, Moore believed that there was a need for decorum. 'Everyone was elated, but most of us were trying to be correct,' Moore told Jeff Powell. 'Not get carried away by it all. Typically English. Perhaps that was me and Alf. Don't show people too much.'

Over in Barking, the same battle was being waged inside

Doss. She came into the house for the trophy presentation but fought back the tears, determined not to let her emotions flood out. She dabbed at her eyes and then said that there were jobs to do and she was off down to the shops.

Back at Wembley, Moore was interviewed on the pitch by Ken Wolstenholme and gave little away. 'I feel a little ruffled, Ken,' he said. 'I don't really realise what's happened at the moment. We're so overjoyed and so delighted that I don't really think our thoughts are with us just yet, still.

'For an hour or so I felt really marvellous, on top of the world. Everybody expressed the same feeling. All of a sudden everything seemed to drain from you and you felt as weak as a kitten. I don't know if it was the tension, you realised you were on the threshold of greatness. But we was all very, very tired – and then I think the Germans as much as anybody.'

As for the celebrations, Wolstenholme asked if there would be drink involved. 'As the evening wears on we'll have a few,' Moore replied. 'We just had a little drop out of the Cup. It's not a very big cup so you don't get too much.'

The players went on the coach back to Hendon Hall to change, then on to the Royal Garden Hotel, Kensington. Their journey took them through joyous crowds on the Edgware Road and past Paddington. All around London people jumped into cars and on to buses and trains to flock to Kensington High Street to hail the conquering heroes. The streets filled with thousands of well-wishers. When the players came out on the balcony, they had their taste of shrieking Beatlemania. Fans strained for a touch of Moore, as though just to brush against him could heal all their problems. Mothers held out babies for him to touch as if for a papal blessing.

The players went off in search of a good time, with Moore leading one group to the Playboy Club. 'There's something about that that just might attract me,' Jimmy Armfield told the captain. Many were happy to quietly soak up the sense of fulfilment, exhausted by the strains of the tournament and especially the final.

'I think for some of us it was almost a sense of relief at the end of it,' George Cohen says. 'I think people don't realise the pressure that you were under playing in your own crowd. With the tour before the World Cup, we'd been away for six, seven weeks. Nobby Stiles can look attractive after that long. It was a wonderful way to finish but it was a hard slog.'

To many in the wider world, the 1966 World Cup finals were a let-down. Too negative and destructive, including the brutalising of Pelé. The great Brazilian was scathing: 'In this atmosphere, football stopped being an art, stopped drawing the crowds by its skills, instead it became an actual war.'

There was also a feeling abroad that England had been given an easy ride, especially with the late switching of their semi-final to Wembley. A very good team had been given a helping hand. There is a modern revisionist argument that the triumph of 1966 was also the worst thing that happened to English football, emphasising the virtues of hard work over invention. It fooled English football into believing that everything was right with the domestic game when it needed to be continually reinventing itself by looking at continental advances.

Moore knew that England could not match other nations for flair. Winning the World Cup, he said, was based on 'superior teamwork, disciplined fitness and consistency', but he saw no reason to apologise for that. Ramsey's tactics had been vindicated and England, with at least a trio of world-class players in Banks, Moore and Charlton, had peaked with perfect timing.

The World Cup had made a prophet of Ramsey who had said so confidently, some thought ludicrously, back in 1963 that England would win the World Cup. And it made a superstar of Moore. Moore was voted the outstanding player of the World Cup finals and only Eusebio could make an argument of that award. Moore himself would say years later that he could not remember making a single mistake in the tournament.

It was Moore's year even at a time when Julie Christie was winning an Oscar, the Beatles releasing their masterpiece LP *Revolver*, the Rolling Stones big with 'Paint It Black' and Henry Cooper taking on Muhammad Ali for the heavyweight title.

The actor Michael Caine, who was starring in *Alfie* that year, marvelled at England's blond hero. 'It was his moment,' Caine said. 'It was that cometh the moment, cometh the man. It's a bit like a messiah. You know, out of the gloom of the fifties and the debt and everything and our sports history wasn't very great and he just came, like a gleam of light.'

12. Cashing in

Alan Ball drove home to Blackpool via the Knutsford service station on the M6, stopping off to eat egg and chips with his World Cup winner's medal tucked in his pocket. Likewise, Jack Charlton took a break on the A1 to feast on a fry-up in a greasy spoon.

Martin Peters went shopping for furniture for his new house. Geoff Hurst went home to wash his car and cut the front lawn which had grown unruly during his long absence with England.

This was the return to earth for the heroes of 1966 from the high of Wembley. They could have been forgiven for wondering what Bobby Charlton had been talking about on the pitch in the immediate giddiness of victory when he suggested that none of their lives would ever be the same again.

For Bobby Moore sitting in an armchair at home in Chigwell, snapping open a lager and contemplating what it meant to be a world champion, there was no such doubt. The captain's status, fame, earning power and celebrity soared like a Russian Sputnik.

For the skipper, much more than any other member of the

squad, World Cup victory was transformative and enriching; like stepping through a door into a different world where money grows on trees and it rains adulation.

All the players received invites and commercial offers and fan mail, but it was only Moore whose postman staggered up the drive with sacks bulging like Father Christmas.

Every one of them enjoyed a surge in fame and recognition, and queues of autograph hunters, but it was Moore who was anointed the nation's darling. At the end of the year, he was crowned BBC Sports Personality of the Year, a prize he accepted with a typically bashful and stilted speech. His victory was inevitable. What was truly extraordinary was Geoff Hurst, the hat-trick hero of the World Cup final, finishing in third place behind Barry Briggs, a speedway rider from New Zealand.

In the New Year's Honours list, Moore was awarded the OBE and Alf Ramsey received a knighthood. Reacquainted at Buckingham Palace for the investiture, the Queen told Moore that she had 'enjoyed the final very much'. There was also a CBE for Denis Follows, secretary of the FA, and an MBE for Ken Wilson, the head of the organising committee. The suits were looked after.

Yet there was nothing for Hurst for his goals or Ball for running himself into the ground. There was no recognition for the class and contribution of Bobby Charlton. No other player was honoured in a move of staggering oversight which, in the case of half the team, took the Establishment a shameful thirty-four years to put right.

The only parity was in their World Cup bonus. At Moore's admirable instigation, the England players had agreed to share an unexpected £22,000 World Cup windfall from the FA equally rather than follow Ramsey's proposal of £500 per man and the rest according to appearances (seven of the twenty-two-man squad had not played at all).

That much was fair but, mostly, it was a case of Moore, the captain and superstar – and then the rest. The whole team were world champions but it was Moore who was the new, stylish king of British sport, receiving invitations to celebrity parties, society events. When the first men on the moon were invited to drinks at Downing Street, it was Moore who was prominent on the list of great Britons who welcomed the astronauts.

As the man who had accepted the trophy from the Queen, perhaps it was inevitable that Moore would enjoy exalted status. He was undoubtedly a world-class presence, the rock of the team who had been at his very best throughout the World Cup finals. His popularity was also a tribute to his good looks, the muscular physique and the style with which he carried himself on and off the field.

Jack Charlton tells the story of the captain inviting him for a drink in the West End one day, and how Moore pulled up outside a swanky restaurant and tossed his keys to a valet. Charlton was dumbstruck. 'I never dreamt of doing anything like that in my life,' he said, feeling like a country bumpkin.

Bobby and Tina found themselves mixing in new company. 'A totally different life, everything first class, always the best seats,' Tina says. 'We'd be invited to all these parties with famous people.' But what was truly amazing was turning up to mix with lords and ladies, rock gods and artists, to discover that Bobby, the modest lad from Barking, was the unrivalled star.

He was mobbed, and not all the adulation was welcome – certainly from Tina's point of view. 'It could be very intrusive,' she says. 'People would push their girls and daughters up to him. Women would come on like they do with David Beckham no doubt. Bobby was very good and always included me but it must have been very difficult to be him. I think that's why he loved to be indoors sometimes, having big parties at home, Sunday lunches that would go on and on where it was private.'

Most Saturdays he was out, and quite a few other nights, too. Moore wanted to meet all the pop stars and they were desperate to meet him. The middle man more often than not was Stan Flashman who had a supply of front-row tickets.

Invitations came from unexpected places. The Earl of Suffolk wanted Moore to run out for his team against the local village so off Bobby and Tina went to mix with baronets for the weekend. A Greek shipping magnate who owned Olympiakos wanted Moore to play in an invitation game so off he flew, rewarded for his appearance with a trip round the Greek islands on a luxury yacht.

One night they took up an invitation to visit the home of Lionel Bart, the musicals composer, and clinked glasses with Joan Collins, Tom Jones and the Rolling Stones. There was a buzz when Moore walked in.

He was already familiar with the West End but now he was assured of a table at any nightspot; at the 21 Club, the White Elephant, Tramp, Danny La Rue's, Annabel's, The Valbonne. Bobby and Tina sampled the new Italian cuisine at La Trattoria Terrazza in Romilly Street, the height of Soho sophistication.

Moore ate and drank in them all and, after the World Cup, every door opened and new friends were waiting inside. He flitted between different worlds. He had his old pals from the East End like Terry Creasy, who was his minder and driver as well as the conduit who helped the West Ham players flog spare tickets.

He had his West Ham team-mates, other London players like Venables and Greaves, the growing celebrity crew of Jimmy Tarbuck and Kenny Lynch and new business associates – and Moore was able to cruise seamlessly between them all.

His colleagues became accustomed to watching Moore ready himself for a night out on the way back from away games. Fifteen minutes before they arrived in London, he would disappear to the toilet with his suit holder and wash bag. He never shaved before a game because the sweat would sting, and he hated memories of his teenage acne. He would emerge as the train pulled into Euston station with a fresh shirt, suit and tie, cleanly shaven, all dressed for a big night.

Sometimes Tina would be there waiting; other times his fellow players had no idea where the captain was heading. He liked to maintain a little bit of mystery. Geoff Hurst says it became a game among the players to find out where Moore was heading in his sharp suit. They would pepper him with questions and he would always reply that he had 'provisional arrangements'.

'Terry Venables tried to nail him on it once,' Hurst says. '"Come on, Bobby, what are all these provisional arrangements you're always talking about". We never did find out.'

He had more invites than he could ever accept. As one friend said: 'After the World Cup, I shouldn't think Tina's oven got used for a couple of years.'

When it came to money and not just celebrity, Moore was also in a different league from the rest of the heroes of 1966. For Bobby Moore Ltd, the tills were ringing like church bells on a Sunday.

Bobby Moore Sports Wear across the road from Upton Park

became just a tiny outpost in an expanding empire. Soon he added Bobby Moore Play-ball, Bobby Moore boots, a football, several books, TV and radio appearances, columns in the *Daily Mirror* and *Shoot!*.

One of his ghost writers was Michael Hart, a young agency reporter. When Hart turned up every week to meet Moore wearing the same school blazer, the England captain asked if he had anything else to wear. Hart said no.

The following week Moore turned up with a grey mohair suit on the back seat of his red Jaguar. 'Make sure you have it pressed regularly and get yourself a couple of light blue shirts to go with it,' Moore told the cub reporter.

'If I could have been anyone else in life it would have been Robert Moore,' Hart says. 'I never saw him play a bad game after that.'

Moore was never slow to put his hand in his pocket when he was out with his team-mates. Increasingly, he could afford to be generous. His income from playing – around £8,000 a year – was more than doubled by commercial earnings.

Jack Turner was a busy man sifting through all the opportunities. Bobby and Tina starred in a television advert for pubs, 'Look in at the Local', a commercial so wooden it should have been shot on mahogany. These were the days when an England captain could sell the virtues of a night down the boozer and get handsomely paid for it.

Tina enjoyed her own surge in recognition, caught in the first WAG snap by Terry O'Neill, one of the foremost photographers of the sixties who shot the pop stars, models and sports stars of the day. The picture shows Tina leaning back against a tree in Epping Forest wearing an elongated England shirt and knee high leather boots, Moore gazing on in slacks and polo-neck jumper trying to look like his hero Steve McQueen rather than a footballer from Barking.

It was the first time the England shirt had been 'sexed up', certainly by the wife of the skipper. 'I didn't realise what a big stir that picture would cause at the time,' O'Neill says. 'I didn't really know what I was doing, I was just following my nose when I got Tina to put the England shirt on. But it caused quite a hoo-hah.'

By 1970, Kellogg's paid £3,000 for a single commercial campaign (which was several months' worth of his basic wage) and Moore banked £20,000 from a testimonial that year sponsored by Esso. There was also a testimonial cabaret at the Park Lane Hilton where Kenny Lynch, Jimmy Tarbuck, Danny La Rue and Ronnie Corbett entertained more than 1,000 paying guests.

Moore was not above the odd job for cash in hand. He used to drag his friend Kenny Lynch along to open a shop or garage for £250, which was more than a week's wages for a few hours' work. 'Bobby never liked doing it alone because then he would have to make small talk,' Lynch says. 'With me along for the ride, he could take a back seat.'

Terry Creasy remembers driving England's World Cup winning captain to a garage in Weybridge where Moore had agreed to spend a couple of hours signing autographs and lending his name to a local business.

'I sat in the car while Bobby was out there on the forecourt signing for the kids, posing for photos,' Creasy recalls. 'He got back in the car and I asked him "did you get a little white envelope?" He'd pat his chest and smile. He had the cash and we'd head off to the pub.'

With the money flowing in for England's sporting icon, he

bought that cherished new Jaguar car and invested in a holiday home in Marbella where he counted Sean Connery among his neighbours. This was the glitzy life that Tina and Bobby had always dreamed of; eating in the best places, wearing the latest fashions and mixing with the stars.

For Moore, the World Cup changed something else significant, too – he was shackled to West Ham. How could they possibly sell him to Spurs now?

Moore knew it. Terry Venables secured his transfer to Spurs from Chelsea but the World Cup triumph effectively handcuffed Moore to Upton Park. As Venables says: 'There would have been no bubbles flying at West Ham for a long time if Bobby had been allowed to join another London club. It made it very difficult for him to go.'

Rather than continue to fight for a transfer, Moore asked for £150 a week, almost double his previous contract. For once, the club quickly buckled, giving him a three-year deal with an option for another three. They also gave him back the captain's armband which Greenwood had so testily removed in the spring.

Spurs bought Mike England as their new centre-half from Blackburn Rovers for £95,000, a record for a defender at the time. They did not quite enjoy the glories that Bill Nicholson had imagined, though they did win the FA Cup in 1967 before claiming the League Cup, twice, and the Uefa Cup at the start of the seventies. Perhaps Moore could have made a difference in pushing them towards a First Division title.

But the decision to stay was not overly difficult in an era when there was no risk of Moore's international place being jeopardised by playing for a middling club. He had hankered after Spurs but he knew that it would be almost impossible to engineer a transfer, and the summer away with England had allowed the tension with Greenwood to ease.

Moore was happy close to his roots, staying in the East End and near his rapidly expanding business interests. He was not prepared to go to war with West Ham and so, on a sunny day at Upton Park three weeks after the victory over West Germany, there was a rousing salute for the three World Cup winners before the first home game of the 1966–7 season. Moore led Hurst and Peters out into bright summer light to be saluted by an adoring crowd.

It took only ninety minutes for the good vibes to be washed away by a 2-1 defeat to Chelsea. The highlights show an agitated Moore waving his arms angrily at a badly positioned Jim Standen in goal when Charlie Cooke's shot beat him from the edge of the area. West Ham lost their first three matches that season and, even with their three world champions, finished sixteenth in the First Division.

After the high of the World Cup, there was professional frustration ahead with West Ham whose early promise under Greenwood was compromised by maddening inconsistency. There would be no trophies, no return to Wembley. Eddie Bovington is insistent that it would have been better for everyone if Moore had been allowed to go to Spurs.

'Bobby should never have stayed at West Ham. He should have gone to Tottenham, a bigger club, bigger crowds, trophies. West Ham weren't big enough for him. You've got the three of them, Moore, Hurst and Peters, and if you can't form your side around three World Cup winners there's something wrong.

'I know the World Cup came along but it might have been better for West Ham if he'd gone. It might have been better for

Greenwood. Really, there should have been a rapport with the coach and manager to make it work and they never had that.

'Bobby just saw his time out really after the World Cup. That was his pinnacle, he was at the peak of his playing career then, he was only twenty-five, and he just drifted along with West Ham after that and so did the team.'

The peak of 1966 was always going to be impossible to reclaim but, after three visits to Wembley in as many years, Moore cannot have envisaged the unsettled times that followed. The booze didn't help.

13. Win or Lose, On the Booze

He did well to get away with it so long. It was not until the day of his thirty-sixth birthday in April 1977 that Bobby Moore was arrested, for the first time, for drink-driving. After some enthusiastic celebrations, Moore drove his Daimler Sovereign into a bollard near his home in Chigwell, cutting his head as he veered off the road. Fortunately, nine-year-old Dean, who was also in the car, escaped unharmed.

Police sergeant Bryan Hicks told Stratford magistrates that Moore was more than three times the legal limit. Properly pissed, in other words. Moore was banned from driving for a year and fined £150. There would be another conviction some years later for the same offence but the real surprise was that Moore had not been caught before. The peaked chauffeur's cap must have worked as a cunning disguise.

No one ever knew where Moore found that cap, simply that it came in handy. If he was out on the beers and driving, he would wear the chauffeur's garb as he steered his red Jaguar XJ6 through the streets. He reasoned that the police were far less likely to pull over someone who looked like they drove for a living. Sometimes he would give the lads a lift home, hiding under his hat. England's impeccable hero concealing his identity to pull a fast one over the police? The West Ham players found that very amusing.

Knowing his way home to Chigwell was never a problem, however much Moore had drunk. According to Brian Dear, 'Bobby knew the West End better than a sewer rat.' Even if Moore was stopped after a heavy night, his reputation would often save him, with a friendly policeman ushering England's hero on his way or even offering to escort him back to Essex. Once when a policeman tried to flag him down out in the countryside, Moore simply sped off.

That Jaguar finally met a sticky end in 1969 when Moore agreed to take a group of the West Ham lads down to Margate for a midweek charity match organised by Jimmy Tarbuck. No one recalls if they had Greenwood's permission for half the first team to play a friendly kickaround in the middle of the season. They would probably have gone even if Greenwood had tried to block them.

Along with Tarbuck and Tommy Steele and other celebrities, they faced a Mayor's XI made up of amateurs from Ramsgate FC, Margate FC and the Kent Police – and a giggle it was, too, as well as raising thousands for the local coronary unit. Then it was on to watch Tarby perform on the seafront and to celebrate a brilliant day out.

One beer became half a dozen, and then it was time to drive home. Harry Redknapp remembers being in the car in front when he heard a mighty bang behind. Redknapp's car had taken the conventional route around a roundabout; a drunken Moore had gone straight across. 'There was a bit of a mess,' Redknapp recalls. 'Bobby ended up leaving his car on top of the roundabout. Someone had to come back and fetch it the next day. I think it was a write-off.'

Redknapp chuckles as he recalls those days when England's revered captain was king of the boozers, though it was not just Moore but half the West Ham team. Every football club had its drinking school but West Ham's would have been top of the table.

'When I look back now at some of the things we used to get away with, I think we all took advantage of Ron's nature,' Redknapp says. 'We'd get beat 4-0 at somewhere like Newcastle and we'd be on a train coming home when Mooro would order half a dozen cases of lager. The rest of us would be losing a week's wages on the cards.'

Jimmy Greaves was a latecomer to the Upton Park drinking club. Even as an experienced boozer, he was shocked at the insouciant attitude to alcohol he found when he arrived from Spurs in 1970. For a man fighting a worsening addiction, he said that he 'could not have gone to a worse club than West Ham'. And 'king of the bar stool' was the upstanding captain.

The tale is told of a young player who is about to sign for West Ham but is fretful about a lingering injury and whether he will fail the medical. In between negotiations, and as he awaits the results, he is taken down to the Black Lion pub, the regular hang-out for the West Ham players, where some of the senior pros are quenching their thirst.

Moore is at the bar.

'What's up?' he asks the worried player.

'It's my injury,' he says. 'I don't think they'll take me.'

'Can you put your foot on that rail?' Moore asks.

'Er, yes.'

'Can you put your elbow on this bar?'

'Can do,' says the mystified footballer.

'Can you lift that drink?' Moore persists.

The player takes a gulp of lager.

'So what's the problem?' Moore concludes. 'You've passed. Welcome to West Ham.'

Between the beginning of the sixties and the middle of that swinging decade, lager sales soared from a mere 3 per cent of the British beer market to almost 20 per cent. Moore cannot have been single-handedly responsible for that surge, though listening to the stories of his heroic drinking it sometimes sounds like he tried. He would explain his thirst with the analogy that 'a car needs petrol'.

Moore's motto was 'win or lose, on the booze', according to Harry Redknapp. 'Bobby would have been captain of the England drinking team,' he says. 'He'd love to drink, could drink for England, swallow it like he had no tonsils. If you had a night out with Bobby, you knew you'd had a night out.'

'I think he might just have been world champion lager drinker,' Jimmy Tarbuck adds.

Even George Best was inspired to praise Moore's prodigious drinking, noting that the England captain would down vast quantities yet always look fresh and immaculate the following morning. Typically, even when he was sinking lager and gin and tonics by the gallon, Moore was the world's smartest, neatest, tidiest drunk. Even when he staggered home barely capable of standing, he would remember to brush down his suit and fold his underpants.

His biggest excesses were saved for those evenings when he was away from prying eyes, surrounded by trustworthy friends like Alan Mullery who, after one England international in Vienna, gave the captain a fireman's lift up to bed when he was legless. At public gatherings, Moore would never be dishevelled. He had his own rules; drink in half-pints so it appears you are consuming less; never loosen your tie; always hide the empties under the table. Even when Moore was on a session, it paid to give the impression of looking immaculate.

There are endless tales of extraordinary consumption, and odd occasions of disreputable behaviour like urinating all over a garage forecourt, but his party piece sums up Moore's gentle humour. He would remove his trousers – folding them neatly over his arm – and walk into a pub or stand at the bar in his pants. Not exactly a prank to make Gazza blush.

Moore never saw his drinking as a problem because, unlike Best and Greaves – and later John Charles and one or two other West Ham team-mates, who fought difficult battles with alcohol – he was certain that he had the discipline and restraint to pick his moments. He was sure that it did not undermine his game.

He had the wit to recognise that there was a price to be paid for a night of boozing, and he would pay his dues on a Sunday morning. On a day when only the injured players would be expected to report for treatment at Upton Park, Moore would be there for his Sunday morning penance, a regular 10 a.m. appointment with his conscience.

'Sometimes he'd come in with his bow tie and dinner suit on where he'd come straight back from a function, been out all night somewhere,' Redknapp says. Off came the tuxedo, on would go a boiler suit, sweatshirt, bin liner. Moore would come out looking like the Michelin Man and start a long jog around Upton Park. Around the pitch was a perimeter track of red tarmac. Moore would trudge around for three-quarters of an hour, the booze seeping out.

The long run was not just for sobering up but for weight control, too. Conscious of his waistline to an obsessive degree, Moore would often spurn food completely on a night out. He very rarely ate breakfast before training. Particularly as he grew older, he could go a couple of days just on snacks.

After his run, he would have a bath, a shave, put on a smart shirt and nice jumper. Then he would head to the pub.

The Black Lion near Upton Park, the Retreat in Chigwell, the Bald Hind, his local in Chigwell, the Moby Dick on the A12, Slaters Arms at Chadwell Heath (conveniently near the training ground), the Tollgate, the Globe. Interview enough of Moore's friends and team-mates about his favourite drinking holes and the list becomes dizzying.

Far from being a problem, Moore saw a few lagers as an important part of relaxing and team-bonding, especially on those long train trips back from the north. He was always sure to reach into his pocket to buy a case for the lads.

As soon as the Pullman from Manchester pulled into Crewe station, the players would spring to action. The train door would snap open and someone would sprint to the shop on the platform. As the guard whistled, a couple of crates of lager would be hastily loaded onboard. The journey home could be resumed. Panic over. There was beer to be drunk.

While conscious of his responsibility to set an example, Moore believed it was down to the individual to know when he had consumed enough. 'I hope I didn't influence other players, particularly younger players, to drink,' he said. 'I always invited a young player into my company if he was feeling left out of things. If he didn't want to drink that was fine by me. Every individual knows what he's capable of and what's good for him.'

Frank Lampard was one young player Moore befriended over a lager. Lampard was only a kid with a couple of appearances behind him when Moore beckoned him over on the train. Lampard was so surprised that England's World Cup winning captain would show any interest that he initially thought Moore was waving at somebody else.

'I get up and walk over and Bobby tells me to sit down. "Well played. Now, do you want a beer?" It's a little thing but I'll never forget how good that made me feel, him showing an interest. I don't know if he took to me because I was from that way, living in Barking, but we sort of hit it off from that day. We'd go for a drink and that was when you would see Bobby start to relax.'

Alcohol consumption was by no means West Ham's only problem, or even the main one, as they tried in vain to become a consistent force in the First Division. When they were good they were sensational. Geoff Hurst enjoyed a few prolific seasons, buoyed by his Wembley heroics. Crowds swelled at Upton Park to watch Greenwood's stylish passing team. They were entertainers, with average gates rising from 26,000 to 32,000 by 1970.

They would enjoy great nights when everything clicked, thrashing a formidable Leeds United 7-0 in a classic League Cup fourth round match in November 1966. The team of Jack Charlton, Norman Hunter, Johnny Giles and Billy Bremner were swept aside. Moore was in majestic form and Bremner sought to harry and hassle, gnawing like a Scottish Terrier at the back of his legs and ankles.

Towards the end of the match Moore had tired of Bremner's irritating snapping. Upton Park held its breath as the England captain turned sharply to go face to face with his aggressor. In the post-match interview Moore was asked what he said to Bremner and whether he had threatened to give him a taste of his own medicine.

'Absolutely not,' he said. 'All I said to him was "Billy, have you not noticed that we are 7-0 up? There's no point in you kicking me around now is there".'

Chastened by Moore's manner, Bremner reputedly replied; 'Och, Bobby, you're absolutely right.'

There were occasional gluts of goals – 7-2 against Fulham in February 1968, 8-0 against Sunderland (when Hurst scored a hat-trick in each half) and 7-2 against Bolton Wanderers. But an image built up of a team of southern fancy dans, great in the sunshine on a nice pitch but easily bullied on a cold night at Stoke. It was not that simple but, as with all stereotypes, there was a kernel of truth. 'We lacked some toughness,' Brian Dear says, 'especially away from home.'

West Ham drew plaudits for their cultured game but they were not competing for honours. There was a sense of unful-filled ambitions after the high standards set with the cup triumphs of 1964 and 1965. They had been talked about then as a coming force in English football and the World Cup had only heightened expectations. But with finishes of 16th, 12th, 8th, 17th, 20th and 14th in the First Division between 1967 and 1972, it was easy for their critics to talk of insufficient substance to go with their bursts of style.

'Put it this way,' Redknapp says. 'We had Geoff Hurst, Martin Peters and the great Bobby Moore in the team and we'd still finish in the bottom half of the table. Doesn't say a lot for the rest of us, does it?'

Greenwood's footballing principles were admirable but

they began to grate with Moore. It was all well and good for the manager to believe that the growing obsession with results would be 'the ruination of English soccer' but there was a balance to be struck – and Greenwood did not get it right. 'Perhaps I was too idealistic,' he admitted. 'Certainly I was not ruthless enough. We had plenty of artists but not enough willing artisans. We were short of good job-men, men who upon losing the ball would win it back, men who could turn the tide.'

Moore urged Greenwood to sign some gnarly veterans like Maurice Setters, the former Manchester United defender, believing he would be a perfect addition to harden up the defence. In public, the captain aired his frustrations with typical diplomacy. 'I often wonder whether Mr Greenwood – in an effort to win a title or two – might not change tomorrow to the use of some strong-arm, tough players to achieve that object,' he said. 'But I doubt it. This is where our success lies, if any, by providing the customer with enjoyment and entertainment.' In private, he began to grow disenchanted by the reluctance to address obvious failings.

He wanted the club to sign a few big players to lift the place, and to energise him. Moore made a candid admission: 'I would have liked more powerful, more dominating people around me at West Ham. People like that inspired me to involve myself and to enjoy life. I needed to react to big personalities.'

But in the West Ham tradition, Greenwood looked whenever possible to the youth ranks. He turned to the promise of Redknapp, Lampard and Trevor Brooking, who were all in awe of the England captain. 'With Bobby, if you gave the ball away it was like you were letting the club down,' Lampard says. 'He'd never shout at you. He didn't need to. He'd give you a look or just say "don't do that".'

He did snap once at Trevor Brooking, something rare enough for the midfield player to recall it years later. Moore dribbled the ball out of defence, laid it off to Brooking and went for a return which never came. Brooking had tried a fancy turn and been caught in possession. 'I'm trying to think of the terminology he used but it was something like "fucking hell, give the ball back instead of poncing on it",' Brooking recalls. 'He didn't have to say much more than that to make an impression. It wasn't a mistake I was keen to make again.'

Brooking made his debut in 1967, a classy young midfielder and an observant member of the dressing room. Teetotal, he was too straight-laced to be part of the drinking club. He was never pally with Moore but could not fail to be struck by the captain's remarkable sang-froid, and his need for control.

'I can't think of any stage during a game, in a room, any situation or discussion where Bobby would look as if he was struggling or betray discomfort,' Brooking says. 'He never wanted to appear inadequate. But I think he had to work really hard at that. It takes mental strength to develop that aura.

'I can't say what he felt internally, but externally he would never look flustered or panicked. There were always two or three moments during every game where it looked as though he was going to get closed down or caught out, and suddenly he'd be out of danger, walking away as if "what's the problem?". He never looked at full stretch or under pressure. That made him a target for some teams to try to ruffle him up and unsettle him but I can't remember it ever working.'

The players loved Moore for his coolness, allied to a dry sense of humour. When West Ham flew to Houston Astrodome to play a friendly in April 1967 in the American indoors, Moore won the toss. 'We'll play with the air conditioning,' he said.

They loved it when, in a match against Wolverhampton Wanderers at Upton Park, he reacted with typical composure after his clearing header struck Gerrard Lewis, the referee, on the back of the head and momentarily seemed to have knocked the official unconscious. As the game continued, and tackles flew in, Moore calmly bent down, picked up the referee's whistle and brought the match to a halt. As Brooking says, 'typical Bob'.

They admired Moore even more when he stepped forward in the midst of one of football's most titanic cup ties, a four-legged League Cup semi-final against Stoke City in early 1972 when West Ham at last threatened to return to Wembley. Already an epic contest after home and away legs, plus one drawn replay at Hillsborough, the two teams faced each other again at Old Trafford. Not long had been played when West Ham's goalkeeper Bobby Ferguson had to retreat to the dressing room with concussion after he was kicked in the head diving to grab the ball in the mud.

Clyde Best was West Ham's emergency goalkeeper. 'He loved throwing himself around,' Brooking says, 'but, being a semi-final, Bestie just couldn't face it. He thought he was in over his head.' There was an awkward silence as Best refused to take the shirt and the rest of the players stared at the ground. Then Moore piped up: 'All right, I'll do it.' He was the only one brave enough.

He had played in goal once before, more than a decade earlier, for the last twenty-five minutes of a victory against Chelsea but this was in West Ham's biggest game of the season. Within minutes of pulling on Ferguson's shirt, West Ham conceded a penalty. 'Odds of hundred to one,' the commentator said of Moore's chances of denying Mike Bernard from twelve yards. Moore shuffled to his right and managed to parry away the penalty. Sadly, the heroic tale was spoilt when Bernard pounced for the rebound. Amid the mud and the rain, West Ham went on to lose 3-2. They never did secure a return to Wembley.

Greenwood's principles were also costing West Ham in the transfer market. His players still shake their heads in bewilderment at the failure to sign Gordon Banks from Leicester City in 1967 – declining to do so because he had already given his word to Malcolm McDonald, the Kilmarnock manager and an old friend, that he would buy Bobby Ferguson. Greenwood kept his honour but Ferguson was no Banks of England.

Moore was becoming increasingly disillusioned, feeling a growing detachment from his manager. Cynicism was taking hold. Greenwood pulled Moore into his office to accuse his captain of showing deliberate lack of interest in the team talks. Greenwood later wrote of his frustration in his autobiography: 'I felt he became very aloof, locked in a world of his own, and although his cold detachment was a strength on the field, it was an attitude which made things very difficult in the small, everyday world of a football club. Moore even started to give the impression that he was ignoring me at team-talks. He would glance around with a blasé look on his face, eyes glazed, in a way that suggested he had nothing to learn. "Who needs a manager?" he seemed to be saying. The danger was that other, less experienced players would believe what they saw.

'I called him into my office and told him: "Don't give the impression that you're not listening. You may be kidding some of the other players but it doesn't wash with me. Whenever I ask for something to be done on the field you're the first to do it. I know you are listening to every word. So why the act?" He did not argue.'

Moore was not the only player Greenwood was falling out with. After one defeat, he accused Peters of saving his best appearances for England, not West Ham. 'Why is that, Martin?' he demanded to know, in front of the team.

Eddie Bovington was always one of Greenwood's harshest critics and saw the problem as lying with the manager: 'If Ron was so good, why did West Ham never challenge for the title ever? Ron needed to be harder with people. It's all very well giving people responsibility but some people need to be told what to do.'

Greenwood was a great coach but he could not get his players to run through walls for him, like Bill Shankly or Brian Clough. Brooking says Greenwood would take the easy way out, dropping younger players if changes were needed. 'He didn't like confrontation with the senior ones.'

In the circumstances, it was probably inevitable that indiscipline would creep into the club, and a booze culture, too. Alan Ball was staying down in London once when Moore invited him to come to Upton Park on a Sunday morning to have some treatment before an England meeting. Ball almost fell off the table when, as he took ultrasound on his ankle, Rob Jenkins walked in carrying a crate of lager. Jenkins, of course, was the physio. 'Anything like that at Everton would have been impossible,' Ball said. 'It just couldn't have happened.'

Out came the beers, cans chucked around. Ball said it was like being in the pub – which is precisely where they went as soon as the treatment session was over, heading to the Black Lion.

Rob Jenkins still has his physiotherapy practice over the

road from Upton Park, a man full of colourful memories about the days when booze was common currency at West Ham and players could avoid double sessions of treatment by slipping him a few beers. This was the culture and even when Greenwood did try to crack down and impose a curfew, such as on the night after a shocking performance at Stoke City, his instructions were flagrantly ignored. Staggering back from a bar in Newcastle under Lyme, the players tried to sneak in through the hotel's back entrance but the gates were locked. As they clambered over a fence, Moore slipped. His leg was gashed by a protruding spike.

Jenkins had to patch up the injured captain the next morning as the players tried to keep their escapade secret from the manager. 'We had to keep Bobby out of Ron's sight on the journey back,' Redknapp says. 'Not easy because he had a limp.'

They had some famous piss-ups, with no story told more frequently than the Christmas when Moore was particularly thirsty. It was a ritual for the lads to go out on Christmas Eve having collected a turkey each as their present from the club.

Tina was waiting to cook the bird but her husband did not come home. She knew exactly where to find him, ringing up the Globe and asking him to get back so she could prepare the next day's dinner. The hours went by, Moore still had not left and Tina was growing exasperated. Despairing, Tina called Doss.

Redknapp takes up the tale. 'Next thing you know, Doss walks in. There's the captain of England in a crowded pub, full of girls from offices, men from the factories. "Come on Robert, we're going home," she says.

'I can still hear Bobby now. "But Mum, I'm twenty-nine".'

Redknapp laughs. 'On the way out, Bobby's staggering

a bit and his old mum was saying "someone must have put something in his drink. He's not quite himself today".'

Moore drove home where Tina was ready to explode with rage. She stormed out to find a pissed Moore grinning at the wheel of his car, with the turkey wearing a seatbelt in the passenger seat. 'I wasn't at all happy,' she says. 'But I had to laugh.'

14. Bogotá

There was no hint of the turbulence ahead when the England squad boarded a BOAC Boeing 707 at Heathrow bound for Mexico on 4 May 1970. No inkling of the storm to come.

The group that set off for the World Cup finals did so with rampant, and justified, optimism. They skipped up the steps in their new suits, stopping to smile for the press photographers, with tons of Findus food in the hold and hope in their hearts.

The captain voiced the collective confidence more boldly than anyone. 'England will win the World Cup,' Bobby Moore announced. 'In my opinion, England are more skilful than any other international side.'

In Moore's eyes he could easily set aside his frustrations with West Ham and look forward with hope when it came to the national team. England were not only defending champions but possessed a better squad than in 1966 thanks to the emergence of Brian Labone as his defensive partner, Alan Mullery in midfield and especially Francis Lee, Manchester City's dynamic, barrel-chested forward.

They had lost only four games in four years and though one of those defeats, in a brutal contest with Yugoslavia, had cost them the chance to win the 1968 European Championships, Ramsey's side had gone further than any previous England team in reaching the last four. It was a loss which featured the first dismissal of an England player when Mullery was sent off for retaliation, and also a rare lapse by Moore when he allowed the ball to float over his head for Dragan Džajić to score the only goal. But England had finished a respectable third after beating Russia in a play-off and Mullery remembers a trip of high spirits as he shared a room with the captain, putting up with his unusual sleeping rhythms.

'Bobby brought over a portable record player and he'd put on the latest hit LP by Engelbert Humperdinck morning, noon and night. That's what I remember from that trip, going to sleep with Engelbert and waking up to hear him again.'

Twelve months before the World Cup, Ramsey's side had lost narrowly to Brazil in the Maracanã, leading until a quick, late double from Tostão and Jairzinho. Mullery had subdued Pelé and, from that tour of South America, England had come away with the sense that the most they had to fear was from the baking heat and altitude in Mexico.

England's preparations were painstaking in the hope of overcoming these extreme conditions. By flying out a full month before their first match in Guadalajara, Ramsey was hopeful his players could acclimatise. The doctors had studied the science of dehydration and altitude. Food and bottled drinking water were taken out in vast quantities. The FA even arranged for a team bus to be driven from London to Mexico rather than rely on local suppliers.

Nothing had been left to chance and, by flying out so early, there was time not just for training but bonding. Ramsey's squad played golf and cricket, visited a rodeo and thrashed the travelling English journalists in a friendly game of football as they eased into their surroundings in Mexico City. Even the manager seemed to be softening, just a little.

Ramsey initially banned sunbathing but relented, allowing the players twenty minutes – ten on each side with Harold Shepherdson blowing his whistle when they had to turn over. How the Italian squad, who eventually joined England in the Hilton hotel, laughed at the comical sight of pasty English footballers trying to tan as if by military command.

They might have noticed, too, that Moore was already more bronzed than most. Scuttling off to snatch a few rays of his own on the hotel roof one day, Peter Thompson, the Liverpool winger, found Moore basking on a towel.

Hoping to guard against any cliques, Ramsey had broken up the usual rooming partnerships in those early weeks. Moore was paired with the taciturn Thompson. Chatting over a coffee, the former winger and publican, smiles wryly now at how that turned out.

'I was a little bit overawed because I was born in a council house in Carlisle and Bobby was living in a mansion in London,' Thompson says. 'I'd even heard he had butlers. When I was put with Bobby, Geoff Hurst laughed and said "that'll be interesting". I was quiet and Bobby was too. To be honest, we barely said a word to each other.'

Among the main gang, however, there was plenty of fun to be had. Ramsey arranged a social evening at the Reforma Club, a country club run by wealthy expats in Mexico City which was the main training base for the players.

It promised to be a stiff affair with the manager watching on, monitoring the alcohol consumption. Some of the players decided to liven up the evening by drawing lots to see which player would have to dance with the prettiest girl, the slimmest, fattest and ugliest. To his mortification, Moore drew the latter. 'And when I say we found an ugly one I mean it,' Mullery recalls. 'She was a monster.'

Less than thrilled at the prospect of exposing himself to public embarrassment, especially when sober, Moore initially refused. The rest of the squad weren't letting him out of it.

'Eventually Bobby walks over and asks this girl for a dance and you can see all the guests thinking "what on earth is going on?" We're all crying with laughter,' Mullery says. 'The deal was he had to dance three times so you can imagine what the girl is thinking by the end. "I've pulled the handsome England captain".

'Bobby was furious on the way back to the hotel. "I'm never doing that again!" Some of the other lads would love to play up to that, make a fool of themselves. Bobby wasn't happy.'

Gradually the training became more intense, and Ramsey had arranged practice matches against Colombia and Ecuador where they would play at altitude. If they could cope with Bogotá at 8,500 feet, the logic was that they would be far more comfortable playing matches at Guadalajara in Mexico which was more than 3,000 feet lower.

Ramsey and the FA doctors were sure it was worth the trip even if it did mean leaving Mexico, and the pleasant Reforma, to head to a 'sombre city of criminals and cripples', as Brian Glanville described Bogotá in the *Sunday Times* in 1970. En route, management warned the players that they were heading into a city rife with pickpockets and chancers; a place where there would be beggars and street hawkers trying to flog dubious wares.

Stick to the main hotel, the players were told. Don't stray too far. If you want to buy anything, purchase only from reputable shops. But even after following those instructions to the letter, Bobby Moore was entrapped in the scandal that hangs, unresolved, over him even now.

What happened to the bracelet? Who took it? What did it look like? These questions would pursue Moore for the rest of his days.

We know the mythic item is supposed to have been an 18-carat gold bracelet encrusted with twelve diamonds and twelve emeralds. We know it was reputedly worth £650 and that, possibly, it once lay in the glass case of a jeweller's shop in the Hotel Tequendama, the finest in Bogotá and England's base when they arrived around 4 p.m. on 18 May 1970.

In the foyer, England players loitered as they waited for their rooms to be arranged and the keys handed out. For most there was no rush. They played cards and mooched around. Some wandered in and out of the shops including the jeweller's, the Fuego Verde, or 'Green Fire', which was in the middle of the hotel lobby, glass-walled on three sides.

At around 6.30 p.m., Bobby Charlton decided to check out a ring he could see on display through the window. He thought his wife, Norma, might like it so he and Moore sauntered in. Peter Thompson also showed up before wandering off to see if there was any mail waiting for him at reception.

Charlton was shown the ring by the pretty young shop assistant but was put off by the price. He had been in the shop for a few minutes at most. He and Moore walked out. No one quite recalls who raised the alarm – Moore said a woman, Charlton a man – but, after they had joined the rest of the players on the sofas in the lobby, someone came over from the shop and said there was an item of jewellery missing.

There was a rummaging around the cushions where Moore and Charlton were sitting. The players were mystified. They walked back to the shop where the shop owner, Daniel Rojas, had appeared. Suddenly the charge became more specific. A bracelet, he said, had been stolen. Then the female shop assistant pointed at Moore. She said there were three players inside the shop but Moore was the only one she recognised for certain. He was the accused.

Alerted by Neil Phillips, the team doctor, Ramsey came over. Now there was a crowd, a kerfuffle. A policeman arrived. Still the England players could make no sense of the accusation. 'You can search us if you like,' Moore said. 'We've nothing to hide.'

Charlton and Moore gave a short statement to the policeman and rejoined the rest of their team-mates. They gossiped among themselves and told each other to be careful that nothing was planted in their bags. Charlton was agitated. He always was a worrier. Moore told him it would all blow over but even his composure would be strained by the web of accusations about to entrap him.

The first sign of an escalating crisis occurred in the office of Keith Morris, the chargé d'affaires in the British Embassy in Bogotá, the morning after the alleged theft. Detectives arrived with Rojas, the shop owner, and the assistant, Clara Padilla Salgado, who was sticking to her story. Two players had entered the shop, she insisted. They had stolen a bracelet.

Morris still recalls events with absolute clarity, saying that he could hardly forget the extraordinary developments as he held out a photograph of the England squad and asked Padilla to point out the men she believed guilty of theft. 'She pointed straight to Moore and Charlton,' Morris says. 'With their position and standing, two phenomenal figures, you can imagine my reaction. It couldn't have been worse.'

She had also mentioned a third man in the shop. When he heard, Thompson approached Ramsey to say it was him. Ramsey told him to stay out of it: 'Alf just looked at me and said "I'm not being funny, Peter, and please don't be offended but they're not interested in you". I said "smashing, that'll do me". They were trying to fit up Bobby from the start.'

Morris immediately went to speak to FA officials, and to Moore and Ramsey, to explain that the shopowner wanted to press charges. He was immediately struck by the contrast between the England manager and his captain. No lover of travel, or foreigners, Ramsey was apoplectic that anyone could dare make such an accusation.

'Ramsey's reaction was genuine fury, horror, outrage,' Morris says. 'Moore's reaction was completely deadpan. He didn't endear himself to one because he wasn't that kind of fellow, very restrained. But the qualities he had as a footballer emerged entirely through the whole episode. He never panicked.'

Moore was told to concentrate on his football, which he did with familiar assurance. On Wednesday 20 May he was part of a full-strength England XI that beat Colombia 4-0, one of England's finest performances for months.

The next morning, he made a fresh statement. A detective measured Moore's fist and said it was too large to have gone through the opening in the display case. With an assurance from the police that they were 'satisfied with Moore's account', the England captain prepared to fly out of Bogotá thinking it was the end of the matter.

Fleet Street hoped the same. The incident had garnered

minor publicity in Colombia, with no names mentioned, but it had not been reported back home. The travelling journalists had heard about the accusation but were loath to go to print.

'We never got in a touch with the offices because it didn't look like it was going anywhere,' Ken Jones recalls. 'Someone said that if you put it on telex that he could be charged and he isn't charged you'll be done for defamation of character. There was no story. But when the shit hit the fan, dear oh dear . . .'

The shit and the fan still did not come into contact for a few days. The problem seemed to have been left behind as England flew off, and upwards, to Quito at more than 9,000 feet for their final preparation match. On the 24th, after a couple of days' acclimatisation, the same England starting XI won 2-0.

They had just over a week until their first World Cup game and prepared to head back to Mexico. The pre-planned schedule took them back via a stopover in Bogotá, back to the scene of the 'crime'. Among the FA hierarchy they discussed whether it was wise to go through Bogotá but Moore and Ramsey said that there was nothing to fear, no case to answer.

Embassy officials were entirely supportive of the decision, noting that 'a sudden change of plan might be interpreted as an admission of guilt'. The squad landed back in Bogotá on Monday 25 May at 11 a.m. where they had a six-hour stay till the flight to Mexico. If only they had known the trouble that lay in wait, they might have diverted that plane anywhere else but Colombia.

During their brief trip to Quito, the case against Moore had been reopened. A new witness, a street hawker named Alvaro Suarez, was prepared to testify that he had seen Moore slip the bracelet into his jacket. Waiting at Bogotá airport were detectives with a warrant for Moore's arrest.

Had it not been for the intervention of the British Embassy, Moore would have suffered the embarrassment of being escorted straight off the plane by police in front of other passengers. Morris had hurried to the airport, having struck a deal that Moore would submit to more questioning later that day.

The squad headed back to the Tequendama Hotel where they settled down in a cinema in the hotel to watch *Shenandoah*, an American civil war movie featuring Jimmy Stewart. But the real drama was being played out elsewhere.

As the film reel rolled, Moore slipped out at an agreed time to meet two plain-clothes detectives. He had no idea as he stepped into their police car that, far from simply helping with inquiries down at the station, he was heading off to face a magistrate.

As the film finished, and the players grabbed their bags to head back to the airport, Moore was being sucked deeper into the plot of a *noir* thriller. Standing in a small, airless office, he was being babbled at in Spanish, unable to understand a word that was being said, never mind an accusation of theft he knew to be preposterous.

What he had expected to be a twenty-minute formality – a few questions and 'thank you, Mr Moore, do travel safely' – turned into a four-hour ordeal. He kept pointing out that he had a plane to catch, a World Cup to play in. But the hearing went on, and on, through tortuous legalese that Moore could make no sense of.

'I was completely bewildered by it,' Moore said, 'not being able to understand what was being said, no understanding of the procedure.' A criminal lawyer had been laid on by the British Embassy, and a student interpreter was on hand, but diplomats and FA officials were barred from the hearing. Dr Andrew Stephen, the FA chairman, and Denis Follows, the secretary, had to scurry around outside, trying to grasp the escalating seriousness of the accusations against their captain.

Suarez was insistent that he had seen Moore take the bracelet; Padilla, the shop assistant, was sticking to her story of a theft; Rojas, the owner, was adamant that a valuable item had gone missing. Moore, meanwhile, protested in vain that he had not even seen the bloody bracelet and the whole thing was too ludicrous for words.

Late on a hot evening, hours since he had eaten anything or even drunk a glass of water, and with his team-mates long departed for Mexico, the England captain was informed at around 10 p.m. that he was facing detention.

Colombian law gave the magistrate five days to decide whether Moore should face a full trial. He wanted to use that time to gather more evidence; in the meantime, Moore would be locked up as a common criminal.

As lawyers and officials continued to jabber at each other, forms were thrust in front of Moore to sign. Meanwhile, Morris and the rest of the diplomatic corps raced around frantically trying to seal a deal which would spare Moore from incarceration.

They had been using all their influence through government channels to try to make the examining magistrate aware of the public outcry if England's captain was put in a cell. Fortunately, Alfonso Senior, director of the Colombian Football Federation, suggested a compromise which allowed everyone to keep their dignity. Moore would be allowed to stay at Senior's home, effectively under house arrest. The magistrate agreed, provided that Moore was kept under armed guard.

Tom Rogers, who had started as British ambassador in Bogotá only that week in a post previously regarded as a diplomatic backwater, sent a message back to London that the Colombians had made 'a considerable concession' in freeing Moore.

Yet even Moore's composure had by now reached its limits, with his team-mates in a different country and the seriousness of his predicament now stark. It was, he later said, like finding himself in the pages of an Agatha Christie story, uncertain of the next twist but fearing the worst. 'My whole career stood to be ruined,' he said, and he wasn't a man given to melodrama.

In the *Observer*, Hugh McIlvanney drew on his own literary analogy to describe the trap in which Moore was ensnared. He wrote of 'the strain of an ordeal that had sufficient echoes of Graham Greene if not Kafka to push an ordinary man toward hysteria'. And he was not given to melodrama either.

The nightmare was only marginally less traumatic for Fleet Street's finest. As one of the biggest stories of their careers was unfolding, most were underground visiting the famous Cathedral of Zipaquirá, a church inside a salt mine an hour from Bogotá. They had nipped off on a sightseeing trip and were blissfully unaware that England's captain, and the World Cup campaign, was engulfed in an escalating crisis.

The reporters rushed back to the airport, climbed on the plane to Mexico with the England players and FA staff, clicked their seatbelts and settled down for a drink, a smoke and a chat. As the plane took off, they had no idea that Moore was in a courtroom accused of theft. 'Well, Vic Railton of the *Evening*

Standard later claimed he knew,' Ken Jones says. 'But he didn't bloody well do anything about it.' Even now, professional pride still burns at the memory of the story that got away.

As the plane made its way out of Bogotá, storm clouds were gathering. The pilot announced that appalling weather would necessitate a brief stop in Panama to check the fuel. It was as they were descending, tossed around in high winds, that one FA staff member mentioned to a journalist: 'haven't you noticed that the captain is not on board?'

'Eh?'

'He's been arrested. He's still in Bogotá.'

Hold the back page! Hold the front page! Except the reporters were on a plane somewhere high above Central America.

As the plane touched down in Panama, the press pack dashed around, hunting for morsels of information. The FA officials had slipped off into the first-class lounge and were saying little, not least because they were largely ignorant themselves. The press had only twenty minutes to find out what had happened to Moore before they were called for the onward flight to Mexico City. It was too little time to establish the facts and make contact with their desks back in London.

'We had to make a snap decision whether to get back on the plane with all the players and officials and find out what was really going on or to be stuck in Panama with nobody,' Brian James of the *Daily Mail* says. 'We couldn't win.' With heavy hearts, they boarded the plane.

James showed enterprise by trying to chat up a stewardess to see if the captain would make contact over the radio. 'Any chance he could call Fleet Street 270435 and ask for the news desk?' he asked.

No such luck. They eventually arrived in Mexico to a bedlam

of television crews. The world had woken up to the scandal while the travelling party were stuck 20,000 feet in the air. James eventually got through to the *Daily Mail*'s foreign editor who demanded that he was on the next plane back to Bogotá. When he explained that there was no flight till the following day, the order came back to get a taxi. 'I had to point out that it was two thousand miles away,' James says.

Back in Bogotá, Moore was adjusting to life as a suspect. Alfonso Senior's house made for more comfortable surroundings than a jail cell and at least he had company, albeit in the burly shape of two armed guards who did not speak a word of English. When Moore settled down for the night, he had one guard sleeping in his boots on a single bed in his room and another dozing in the hallway. He called them Pedro and José.

Desperate to make contact with Tina, and suffering from worse insomnia than usual, Moore placed a call at 3.39 a.m. local time – breakfast in England – in the hope of warning his wife of the breaking crisis. He had been beaten to it by a call from a newspaper in the middle of the night. Stirred from her bed, Tina assumed it was a wind-up or a ridiculous mistake. But she opened the curtains of Manor Road, Chigwell, that morning to find the press camped outside, cameras peering through the windows.

In Bogotá, Moore had seclusion. Tina could not leave the house. The police came to help control the media scrum but the only safe way out was via the back door, crawling on all fours across the garden and climbing over a fence to a waiting car. Hiding on the back seat under a blanket, she went off to see a stressed Doss and Bob in Barking as they picked up the papers to read on the front page that their son was being accused of theft. Tina went to stay with Geoff Hurst's wife, Judith, and waited anxiously for the next call from her husband or a government official.

In Bogotá, the British Embassy did all they could to put pressure on the Colombian judiciary to release Moore. They highlighted the embarrassment the story was bringing to the country when even the Colombian papers were sympathetic to the Englishman. *El Tiempo* pointed out that this was just one of several incidents involving foreign sportsmen accused of unsubstantiated theft.

'The Colombians immediately assumed it was a set-up,' Morris says. 'This sort of thing was common enough. The wildest rumour at the time was that the Brazilians were behind it in a plot to help win the World Cup, but I never believed that for a minute. Most Colombians were very sympathetic to Moore. There are many Anglophiles and they are football mad. The idea that they would be associated with buggering up the World Cup would have been very hard to take.'

A group of rich Colombians told the local media that they would club together to pay for the bracelet if that would make the problem disappear. Moore also had the sympathy of his playing rivals. The Italy captain, Giacinto Facchetti, told the newspapers: 'He is too big a man to stoop to petty thieving.' German captain Uwe Seeler summed up the general reaction to the news of Moore's arrest: 'We thought it was a joke.'

From UK government papers, still kept on file in the National Archives in Kew, we learn that the Colombian secret service believed in Moore's innocence from their initial investigations. They told British diplomats that Moore should be allowed to rejoin the England squad while inquiries were concluded, but the judiciary showed no inclination for a quick release.

Moore went out for a walk with his guards increasingly fearful that the World Cup would start without him. Denis Follows, the FA secretary, was particularly panicky and sent a telegram to Harold Wilson, the Prime Minister, via diplomatic channels: 'Delays in legal processes now becoming serious. Every minute's delay in securing Moore's release militates against England's World Cup chances. Request urgent action at highest level.'

As papers were prepared for Cabinet discussion, government lawyers examined the extradition treaties between the two nations. Number Ten replied to the Earl of Harewood, president of the FA, that the PM was 'greatly concerned', promising to apply diplomatic pressure for Moore's release through the president of Colombia if necessary.

Meanwhile, by an extraordinary quirk of the Colombian legal system, the next stage in Moore's ordeal involved a confrontation with his accusers back in the Fuego Verde shop that he hoped never to have to see again.

It was a frenzy, the vast lobby jam-packed with photographers and camera crews as Moore faced his three accusers – Padilla, Rojas and Suarez. The purpose was to re-enact the scene of the 'crime' in front of a judge to help establish who was telling the truth and who was lying.

Moore could have done without the circus, but it proved beneficial in at least one significant way. Padilla accused Moore of slipping the bracelet into the pocket of his England jacket. Moore asked her to show which pocket. She said the left side. There was no left pocket.

There were still two witnesses against one but Padilla was

rattled by this hole in her story, while Suarez was a shabby figure from the edge of the underworld whose miraculous appearance from nowhere, and his claim to have witnessed the whole incident, simply did not add up.

Yet still Judge Dorado, presiding over the case, demanded that everyone return to the courtroom. As the hours dragged on, Moore asked for food and drink, paying for sandwiches to be brought in and even shared among his accusers.

At the end of another long, wearying day, and a hearing which lasted until 7.45 p.m., there was still no ruling. Moore was told to return to Senior's house for his third night. At least he was being treated well. Senior invited some guests for dinner and it became a long evening, Moore well lubricated along with Pedro and José. Moore could not complain about his lodgings except for one pressing matter – the start of the World Cup was just four days away.

Moore woke up on the morning of Thursday 28 May and left his home for a jog at the Millonarios football club with his two guards. Senior had provided some kit and the chance to run and kick a ball at least kept him sane. It was not so much the charge hanging over him that upset him now as the difficulty of staying fit and the prospect of missing out on the World Cup, but this part of his ordeal was at last coming to an end.

Moore was summoned to another hearing with Judge Dorado. Perhaps political influence had worked because, after a twenty-minute session, Moore was told that he would be given conditional release. He could leave while another judge decided whether to drop the charge or to demand his return for a full criminal trial.

It had been a tough baptism for Tom Rogers but there was

something to celebrate. He wrote to the Foreign Office: 'Moore is free to play in the World Cup and I suspect that in practice the solid weight of Colombian opinion in his favour will protect him from further embarrassment.'

At lunchtime, Moore released a statement: 'I am very happy to be a free man once again and I am pleased that the accusations which have been made against me have been shown to be unfounded. Now all I want to do is to forget the incident and return to my job of playing football and help England retain the World Cup.'

Both men would prove to be overly optimistic in believing that the case was over but at least Moore was free. As diplomats praised him for his patience and calm through the storm, Moore boarded flight AR370 of Argentine Airlines from Bogotá to Mexico City in the company of Follows and Stephen. At last he was heading to rejoin his team-mates.

Geoffrey Green was on the tarmac in Mexico to greet him, describing the scenes for *The Times* with his familiar panache. 'Moore's return could not have been more spectacular had he stepped from the aeroplane holding the World Cup itself for the second successive time. From the moment he made landfall on Mexican soil, bedlam broke loose.'

As bulbs flashed and more than 200 cameramen jostled for the best picture and to hear Moore speak, Green wrote: 'He was carried along like a cork in a fast flowing river. Through it all, he presented a picture of unruffled, smiling dignity. It was a hero's return. No footballer, I would say, ever experienced a more frenetic reception anywhere. In spite of the atmosphere of suspicion which enveloped him in recent days, he has emerged from it all with his stature increased.'

In a gushing compliment to Moore's steely calm, Green

added: 'Here was a man sure of himself and of his ground. Somebody, I suspect, is going to pay for all this shortly on the field of play.'

The FA held a press conference where Stephen heaped praise on Moore for his steady nerve: 'I never knew Bobby very well before. But he has opened my eyes through all this sorry business. He has been splendid from first to last – calm, undismayed and always with a sense of humour. I am proud of him.'

Reporters wanted something stronger, asking whether it was all a Latin American plot against British football. The tone of the coverage back home was angry, with strident editorials attacking the 'conditional release'.

Irritated by an editorial in the *Sun* saying the government should still be doing more, Harold Wilson asked officials if he should intervene further. But at least one Foreign Office mandarin was already annoyed by his involvement according to government files: 'The PM took action on Moore's behalf for political reasons during a general election campaign and I see no reason why we should allow this somewhat dubious intervention to colour our attitude in the future,' the official recorded.

Free at last, Moore sent a telegram home: 'Feel in excellent health and no need to worry about anything. Lots of love to you and the children. Bobby'

With an overnight wait before he could fly from Mexico City on to Guadalajara to catch up with the team, he went off to relax, staying at the residence of Eric Vines, First Secretary at the British Embassy. It was while sitting there that he was amazed to see Jimmy Greaves saunter in.

Greaves was celebrating the end of the London to Mexico

World Cup rally, a marathon event in which he had been co-driver and navigator for Tony Fall, a professional driver. They had finished a respectable sixth.

Hearing that Moore was in town, Greaves had made his way to Vines's home and, seeing the media frenzy out front, climbed over a wall at the rear and walked in through the back door.

'What have you done with that bracelet, eh Mooro?' Greaves said, as he caught his old pal by surprise. Then, of course, they emptied the drinks cabinet.

15. Pelé

Bobby Moore arrived as if he had been briefly detained at the airport with some lost luggage. He had shed a few pounds. He was unshaven perhaps for the first time since puberty. For once, his clothes may have been less than immaculate after four days in the same suit.

But in the most important respect, his demeanour, Moore was so unruffled that the gathered hacks from Fleet Street marvelled at his unflappable calm. At the press conference in the team hotel in Guadalajara, after Moore stepped off the small business plane that carried him from Mexico City, to be met first by a visibly relieved Alf Ramsey and Harold Shepherdson, he apologised for 'looking like a tramp' (which, of course, he didn't). Meanwhile, everyone else in the room was gawping, once again, at his almost unnatural sang-froid.

The gathered media hoped to prise from Moore the full drama of his incarceration. They hoped to hear how furious he was that he had been detained. They wanted outrage that he had been accused of theft in the first place. They should have known better. There was no belligerence or bitterness, or much outward emotion at all aside from an unmistakeable determination from Moore to put the matter behind him and concentrate on the World Cup. Moore told the gathering: 'Once I had got over the shock of what had happened to me I decided I was not going to let this thing get me down. As the days went on it was not so much the psychological strain as the boredom.'

But surely he was seething at the imprisonment, the trumped-up charge, the blackening of his name and the ordeal on the eve of the biggest tournament? 'I have no anger about what has happened,' he replied. 'I suppose the people had to do their job and that is it.' Ken Jones turned to one of his colleagues and remarked on Moore's infinite capacity to rise above the melee: 'I wouldn't fancy playing against him next week.'

Jones still marvels at Moore's ability to shrug off the stress: 'Bobby Charlton would have been destroyed in those circumstances. It would have finished him, but Bob Moore had some inner strength. To this day I can't believe that he could be that strong. To be able to come through that, never knowing what would be the outcome and then step into a World Cup a few days later, you can't believe it.'

Moore was hiding one frustration. Deep down, he felt the team had been wrong to fly off without him, leaving him in Bogotá. He felt abandoned and later confided in one or two friends that he believed Ramsey, in particular, should have stayed. In the manager's defence, he was not to know that Moore would not make the plane until the moment it took off, but leaving the captain behind had troubled quite a few in the England camp. Bobby Charlton expressed his guilt to Ramsey, especially given that the accusations against him seemed to have vanished, leaving the captain to face the nightmare alone. Charlton consoled himself that at least Moore could cope better than anyone.

As usual, Moore kept his emotions hidden, even from his team-mates, breezing back into the England team hotel to be greeted by Alan Mullery holding a glass of champagne. Mullery remembers Moore heading up to his room, taking off his England jacket that he had been wearing nonstop for days and throwing it into the crowd of fans below.

'It was like he was saying that's the end of it. Finished. Let's move on,' Mullery says. 'He looked tired, no doubt about it, and he'd lost a bit of weight. He must have had all sorts of feelings but he completely blocked them out. It was an unbelievable attitude. I'm here to do a job, to be one of the greatest defenders in the world. There's no one else in the squad could have done that.'

There is no more heroic expression of Moore's ability to lock away his troubles than his resumption of duties after his incarceration in Colombia, and the brilliance with which he played at the 1970 World Cup. Even though he was sure of his innocence all along, he was not to know how this saga would play out, how long it would last, whether he would face a full criminal charge. Just from the practical point of view of missing all that training the week before a World Cup, lesser men would have been thrown completely out of step.

'The point it raises about Bobby is whether he had done something or hadn't, that he was still the same man is remarkable,' Hugh McIlvanney says. 'Part of the mystery of Moore, that enigmatic nature, is could he have played brilliantly even if he was guilty? Moore is a mysterious guy. Even if you were falsely accused, you would be going "Jesus Christ, what state am I in?". Not Bobby Moore. He came off the plane and was better. Can you imagine that? Put yourself in that position. If you were falsely accused, you

Ramsey put his players through a gruelling pre-World Cup boot camp at what became known as 'Stalag Lilleshall'. By 1966 Jack Charlton had established himself as Moore's defensive partner.

Bobby Charlton scores his second goal against Portugal with a typically fierce shot, sending England through to the World Cup final.

England had never lost against West Germany when they lined up at Wembley on 30 July 1966 on the most momentous afternoon in English sport.

In the biggest match of his life, Moore was his usual unflappable self as he proved himself the outstanding defender in the tournament.

They think it's all over…it is now. Hurst lashes in England's fourth. Few recall that it was Moore's composure which set up that late goal.

Having wiped his hands on his shorts and the velvet balustrade to avoid sullying Her Majesty's lilywhite gloves, Moore accepted the Jules Rimet trophy from Queen Elizabeth II.

The celebrated image of Moore being held aloft by teammates was turned into a statue which stands near Upton Park.

Restrained even in the moment of glory, Ramsey had to be persuaded by his joyous players to join in the celebrations.

The first WAG photo was shot by Terry O'Neill in Epping Forest. The photographer recalls that Tina's sexing up of the England shirt 'caused quite a hoo-hah.'

Moore was increasingly at home among movie and music stars, joining Jimmy Greaves, Sean Connery and Yul Brynner for a chat on a visit to Pinewood Studios.

Dressed as a Pearly King, Moore drops his usual fashion standards to pose with Tina, Roberta and Dean.

Trudging around the perimeter track at Upton Park in his tracksuit was a familiar Sunday morning ritual as Moore sweated off the previous night's excesses.

Jimmy Greaves was already a heavy drinker when he moved from Spurs to West Ham in March 1970 but even he was shocked at the extent of boozing at Upton Park.

Moore was inundated with commercial opportunities, posing with model Kate Howard who was wearing Norlyn Niknax, tights which supposedly removed the need for underwear.

Moore felt like he was trapped in a noir thriller when he was arrested for allegedly stealing a bracelet in Bogota, days before the 1970 World Cup.

Ramsey had restricted sunbathing in Mexico so the players found alternative pursuits. Alan Ball and Jeff Astle enjoy a game of cards, while Moore and Nobby Stiles look on.

That tackle by Moore... Bobby gets to grips with a rampaging Jairzinho in one of the iconic moments of English football.

It is a famous image not of sport but of sportsmanship as Pelé and Moore exchange shirts following Brazil's 1-0 victory in Guadalajara.

The decision to withdraw Bobby Charlton with England leading West Germany 2-1 in the World Cup quarter-final would cause Ramsey lasting regret after the champions lost 3-2.

Moore poses with ninety-nine children from a primary school near Upton Park on the eve of his 100th England appearance. Some caps had to be borrowed from other players because the FA did not issue one for every match.

After all the glories, Moore's last game for West Ham came for the reserves against Plymouth Argyle in March 1974.

would be all over the place. "For fuck's sake, I am meant to be playing in the World Cup, a red-carpet occasion". This is a very strange man.'

Moore arrived in Guadalajara on Friday 29 May, only three days before England's opening match against Romania. Yet all the frustrations, the strains of Bogotá, were locked away in some cupboard of his mind and Moore stepped out again as the supreme defender and the reassuring captain. He played as well as he ever did.

England's 1-0 victory, thanks to a goal from Geoff Hurst, was steady rather than spectacular but they overcame the altitude, the heat of the afternoon sun and the antipathy of the local crowd who had taken against them. The revelation in the Mexican media that England had imported fishfingers, water and that team bus created an impression of xenophobia. And Ramsey did little to make friends.

Through the shrill whistles of the fans, the steadiest player of all was Moore. Later that night, Denis Follows wrote once more to Harold Wilson, thanking the Prime Minister for his support through Moore's difficulties. 'Had you seen him play this afternoon, you would have realised that the detention had no deleterious effect upon him,' Follows wrote.

The stage was set for England's second game, the confrontation with Brazil. The reigning champions against the favourites; the winners of the last three World Cups pitched against each other. The best defence against the best attack. Northern European mettle against South American flair. Different worlds, different philosophies. 'It was almost as if whoever won this match could go on and win the tournament,' Bobby Charlton said, 'and the Brazilians felt the same, I think.'

Mario Zagallo, the Brazil coach, would subsequently call it 'a game for adults'. An intense, sometimes bruising contest, with neither side giving quarter played under blistering sun and temperatures close to 100 degrees. As Ramsey told his players before the game: 'Would you give gold away? Well, the ball is gold today. Don't give it away and you will defeat these Brazilians. If you give it away in this heat you might not get it back.'

In one hard passage in the Jalisco Stadium, Francis Lee accidentally kicks Felix, the Brazil goalkeeper, in the head; Carlos Alberto takes brutal revenge; Alan Ball goes in hard to show that England will not retreat. The refusal to cede an inch adds intensity to a compelling contest, as England fight so hard to prove themselves equals with perhaps the greatest international side – certainly one of the greatest attacks – of all time.

Even more than forty years on, it is a gripping match. Is that really a blatant dive from Pelé? Could only a tank, or Bobby Moore, have stopped the rampaging Jairzinho? Through it all is the familiar, unflappable bearing of Moore leading England's resistance – at times like Lieutenant Chard at Rorke's Drift – against the threat from Rivelino, Tostão, Pelé, and especially those powerful surges by Jairzinho.

Commentating on ITV, Hugh Johns keeps being drawn back to the magnetic presence of Moore. 'What a tremendous influence this man Moore has had on England sides since the 1962 series . . . What an inspiration the wonderful captain Bobby Moore is to the side . . . Tostão, Tostão, and again Moore there to stop him. What a superb bloke to have in your side . . . Nobody back there except Bobby Moore, of course, as he invariably is . . . And Moore snuffs it. What a player this fellow is.' His voice rises, as if in rapture, every time Moore enters the fray.

Geoff Hurst believes it to be Moore's best game, if not his most flawless. Moore is nutmegged by Tostão in the build-up to the only goal which Jairzinho thumps past Gordon Banks after a beautiful sleight of foot by Pelé. Later, there is an unseemly grab of Jairzinho's shirt by Moore to stop the great Brazilian racing clear, which was not seen by the referee.

It was not a game when Moore was going to be able to influence England's attacking play as he would have liked. Playing between Brian Labone and Terry Cooper, all his energies had to be put into defence, one minute doubling up on Jairzinho and the next stopping Pelé and Tostão combining through the middle.

But Hurst argues, and no one will disagree, that 'if you are talking about character and his willpower, being under house arrest and then coming out and playing against Brazil and arguably the best forward line in World Cup history, Mooro was absolutely stunning. Look at the concentration, how alert he is every second.

'There's a great montage of Mooro tackling and playing Brazil at their own game, holding the ball up against the greatest side at 12 noon, 100 degrees, 5,000 feet above sea level. It's an England team on a par with arguably the best Brazilian team ever. If you played in a league game, Mooro could be one level. If you played in an international he'd be this level, if you play against the world he'd be this level and if the world played Mars he'd raise his game again. He wanted to be the best and he came pretty close that day. I would put the Brazil game above 1966 for Mooro.'

Gordon Banks has his immortal moment with his brilliant

save from Pelé, diving down to his right – and, no, Moore did not say 'come on, Gordon, catch those' though it sounds like his bone-dry humour – but it was the captain who was truly outstanding. There is a thunderous block on Pelé, a full-stop of a challenge on Tostão on the edge of the area and the moment just before half-time when the Brazilians are awarded a free-kick. Rivelino comes across to hit an inswinger round the wall with his left foot. As if clairvoyant, Moore moves himself a couple of yards in the nanosecond before the kick is taken. McIlvanney described the moment: 'As Rivelino's shot raged through, Moore killed it as coolly as he would have taken a lobbed tennis ball and strode upfield. The word "majestic" might have been invented for him.'

Putting Moore's performance in the context of his arrest in Bogotá, he went on: 'The impression was of a nature so comfortable with challenge that it needed crisis to show its true strength. Of the supreme sports performers I have seen in action, perhaps only Muhammad Ali was a more conspicuous example of grace under pressure.' From a sportswriter who has witnessed all the greats across every discipline, that is some acclamation.

To crown it all, of course, is 'that tackle by Moore' celebrated in song by Baddiel and Skinner and replayed a million times since. One hundred years from now when anyone asks what made Moore special, it will be the first piece of evidence – and perhaps the only one needed. Jairzinho has his tail up, which is a scary sight for any defender. He has scored Brazil's goal, is playing with zest and now he has the momentum of a forty-yard run at England's penalty area. In the commentary booth, Johns senses the danger. 'Carlos Alberto hacks it away. It's broken for Jairzinho,' he shouts. 'We've only got two defenders back! Jairzinho going all the way to goal!'

Moore backpedals into the penalty area and Jairzinho cuts to go outside on the right. But just as the Brazilian's speed seems certain to carry him past Moore, out comes the right leg. It's like Superman stopping a runaway train.

It's not a textbook tackle at all. A coach would tell a young child he is using the wrong leg. Moore has stuck out the right rather than sweeping through with his left. But somehow it makes the tackle more elegant, more idiosyncratically Moore. He has not slid in, as most defenders would have done, but stopped the ball dead while on one knee. Jairzinho's momentum takes him tumbling to the floor and Moore stands up and strolls out of the box as though no other outcome was possible.

That tackle is rightly renowned but it would be even more celebrated if it had led directly to an England goal – as it should have done. With four passes – Moore to Terry Cooper, to Colin Bell, back to Terry Cooper and into the Brazil penalty area – the ball broke for Jeff Astle. The substitute striker swung and missed, his shot flashing wide. England's best chance had come and gone.

England were beaten but at the final whistle came the embrace with Pelé which is one of the iconic images, not of sport but sportsmanship. Not a huge fuss was made out of it at the time. It took a little while for the still images to bring lasting resonance, but it is celebrated with good reason. As Moore smiles and Pelé pats him on the cheek, you cannot tell that there has been a winner and a loser.

It is not a photograph that needs a caption though, speaking to Pelé on a trip to London, it seemed necessary to ask what had been exchanged between the two men, aside from shirts. Some reports claim that Pelé said to Moore 'You no thief' in relation to the Bogotá incident but that is not how the Brazilian remembers it.

'I told him "listen, I want to be your friend after football, outside the field. I want to have your shirt",' Pelé says. 'Normally everyone asks Pelé to change shirts but this time I ask Bobby Moore for his shirt. That is the respect I had for him.' Moore himself recounted that he had said to Pelé 'see you in the final'. 'Yes, I think we will,' Pelé supposedly replied.

One might also see that moment as the symbolic handing over of the World Cup given what would happen over the next few weeks. It had been a close game – Francis Lee almost scoring with a header, Astle pulling his glorious chance wide, Alan Ball striking the bar – but Brazil had dazzled even when, by their own bold standards, adopting a relatively cautious strategy against the reigning world champions. England's hold on the World Cup had been loosened, though the captain's reputation had been spectacularly enhanced.

'The best defenders don't get the credit they deserve,' Pelé told me. 'It's always the attackers. That's one reason when anybody asked me my favourite England player, I always say "Bobby Moore". Bobby used to play clean. Very tough. Intelligent. Very good positioning. To dribble past him was very difficult. He was very strong but clean to play against. Always clean. I played a lot of other players but they fouled all the time, they kicked me. It would be ninety minutes of kicking. But Bobby was a great technical player.'

As Pelé once said of Moore: 'Of all the defenders I have challenged, Bobby Moore was the fairest, the best and the most honourable.' There have undoubtedly been better defenders; Franco Baresi, the brick wall of the great AC Milan team of the late eighties and early nineties, was surely the master of them all, the man you would want to defend the goal for your life. 'Baresi had everything,' Hugh McIlvanney says. 'He had pace. He was spiteful. He was sensational. Baresi was so quick that he could make a mistake and get back. Bobby couldn't do that which is maybe why he didn't make too many.'

Franz Beckenbauer was also quicker than Moore with a rare ability to play every position across midfield as well as sweeper. Daniel Passarella, the powerful Argentine, was more dominant in the air; Marcel Desailly, the rock for France's World Cup-winning team in 1998, much quicker to the tackle.

The Moore of his 1970 prime would perhaps struggle to make it into the all-time world XI to play Mars. But Pelé rated him the best he came across, especially after Guadalajara.

As the strains of Bogotá receded and he proved his form, Moore began to enjoy himself. He always did on England duty, training hard but also ensuring life never became too dull off the pitch. Back in the camp, he set about slipping under Ramsey's radar.

There had been a little tension months before the England party had even left for Mexico when Ramsey discovered that four wives were coming out for the duration of the tournament. We can record this as the first WAGs trip, paid for by sponsors including the *Daily Sketch* for whom Tina Moore contributed a diary. The wives of Peter Bonetti, Geoff Hurst and Martin Peters made up the quartet.

Ramsey was uncomfortable with the arrangement, rightly mindful of the potential distraction and the likelihood of envy among the vast majority whose partners were not present. But he could hardly complain given that his own wife, Vickie, also travelled out to Mexico. He tried to ration the conjugal visits, stationing Les Cocker and Shepherdson as guards on the ninth floor of the Hilton to monitor movements. But, ever resourceful, Moore managed to escape.

Francis Lee was recruited as his accomplice. 'Bobby said to me, "what are you doing this afternoon? Do you fancy a walk out? Tina's over and I need a bit of cover". So I said "all right, you lucky bugger".' Off they went in a taxi to the hotel where the wives, and some of the FA dignitaries, were staying. Moore sneaked off to Tina's room while Lee stretched out on a sun-lounger and lit up a cigarette, enjoying the peace and quiet.

'I'm thinking "this is the life",' Lee recalls. 'I had just stretched out when Denis Follows and two or three of the FA selection committee were walking along the lawn in their blazers. I'm there and Bob is up in the room with Tina. I rolled over and put my hand over my face, my sunglasses on and they walked straight past me. They wouldn't have known me undressed. I'd have to have a shirt on with a number on for the FA to recognise me.

'That was a near one because that would have been a severe penalty. One, he shouldn't have been there; two, I shouldn't have been helping him; three, I shouldn't even have been sunbathing. Even knowing the wives were over, Alf only wanted them to meet up after a game for a bit of dinner.'

Lee was relaxed about the presence of the wives but, as Leo McKinstry reports in his biography *Sir Alf*, their presence would have a destabilising effect on the England camp. Bonetti was rattled by wind-ups among fellow players about what the wives were getting up to in their hotel. Other players might have laughed it off but the insecure Bonetti is said by his team-mates to have become a bag of nerves.

That would not have been a problem had the Chelsea goalkeeper remained as deputy to Banks. But after victory over Czechoslovakia in the final group game set up a quarter-final against West Germany in León, disaster struck when England's number one went down with a bad stomach. He travelled on the bus journey from Guadalajara to León but suffered all the way with a fever and stomach cramps. On the day of the game, it was clear that he was in no condition to play. Given the stakes, the excellence of the opposition and Bonetti's nerves, this was a bad blow. There was speculation that it could have been foul play, though Banks later admitted that he might have drunk some unclean water.

There seemed no danger when England went 2-0 up through Mullery and Peters against West Germany. Ramsey's England had never lost from this position. Alan Ball was running around the pitch cockily chirping 'Auf Wiedersehen' to every passing German. The game had seemingly been won, but with twenty minutes left, Franz Beckenbauer surged past Mullery into a yard of space and attempted a shot that he can never have expected to go in. Nor did anyone else, until Bonetti dived over the ball, giving the Germans a glimmer of hope.

It was a couple of minutes later that Ramsey fatefully brought off Bobby Charlton, replacing him with Colin Bell. He had done the same against Brazil to save legs in the heat but that had not been in a knock-out game, or facing an accomplished German side who were gathering momentum. Then Ramsey sent on Norman Hunter for Martin Peters in the hope of seeing out the last ten minutes. His strategy was undone within a minute when Uwe Seeler equalised with an exceptional, looping header to make it 2-2.

Extra-time shows a tired England repeatedly clearing the ball only as far as the nearest German. The template was being set for countless future encounters, with England surrendering possession cheaply. The defence was stretched and, when the ball was knocked across England's goal face once more, Gerd Müller was there to volley from close range past Bonetti.

A squad that many regarded as better than 1966, with Lee offering more penetration, Hurst in his prime – and the quality of Stiles, Hunter, Jack Charlton, Osgood and Bell on the bench – had suffered England's first competitive defeat to West Germany. It was the first time England had lost from 2-0 up in seven years under Ramsey. The holders had surrendered the World Cup.

Ramsey needed a drink in the hotel afterwards and he knew where to find one. He went and knocked on the captain's door where Moore and Ball were drowning their sorrows. 'May I join you?' he asked.

Ramsey would be pilloried for his substitutions and caution. Moore, like most of the players, felt that it would have been different if only Banks had been fit to play rather than Bonetti. Lee reflects the majority view when he says: 'With Banksy in goal we would have won 2-0. The substitutions? It was 110 degrees, boiling hot, Bobby Charlton getting sunstroke on his head. And we didn't get a drink on the field, no bottles at the side of the pitch. You went from 11st 7 to 10st 10 in a game.

'So taking Bobby off made sense. Colin Bell was the fittest guy in the squad. It was the soft goal, the first goal, that put them back in it. They were out of it till then, finished. That's what changed the game.'

McIlvanney disagrees: 'Alf made an arse of himself. He

should never have taken Bobby off. Beckenbauer would never come forward if Bobby was there. Beckenbauer was very conscious of being in control. He didn't like to be embarrassed, more than most, and if Bobby went past you there was no catching him. Schoen wanted to play Franz further forward but Franz wanted to play where he could see everyone. That changed when Bobby went off. Jack Charlton walked out of the ground when Alf took Bobby off. He went up the road for a beer in a bar. He thought it was a disastrous move.'

From a distance, it seems a bit of both. Bonetti's dismal failure for the first goal undoubtedly had a significant psychological effect on both teams, while the substitutions were dangerously defensive, making no allowance for a German recovery. Peters says that many years later, when he made a social visit to see Ramsey in Ipswich, the manager was still castigating himself for the changes. But while Ramsey faced questions, Moore was lauded for his displays. Brian Glanville wrote that Moore played 'with as much, if not more, authority and influence as he had when voted best player of the previous World Cup.'

'Bobby was magnificent,' Lee says. 'It was as though he'd said "look, I've been wrongly accused of this felony, I'm now going to show the world how good a player I am". And it was amazing. From where he'd been and what he'd had to go through, to what he did on the pitch against Brazil and in the German match when he was immaculate, he was truly, truly tremendous.'

His stock as one of the world's great defenders was higher than ever, but Moore still did not know if his reputation was about to be blackened by that business in Bogotá.

*

Legally speaking, the case hung over Moore for another five years thanks to the complexities and inadequacies of the Colombian legal system. It has never been solved satisfactorily.

Perhaps the definitive answer lies hidden in dusty files somewhere on a shelf in a state archive in Colombia – but no one can find the paperwork, and not for want of trying. If you want to send someone mad, ask them to find old dossiers held by the Colombian government. Requests over months were passed from one department to another, and then back where they started. The Colombian ambassador to London lent his official weight to trying to resolve this saga once and for all, but still no files could be traced. A freelance journalist spent months trying to unearth the documents without success. A private investigator attempted to trace Padilla to the United States, where she is believed to have fled soon after the scandal, but the trail went dead.

For Moore, the case dragged on interminably. He had stayed on to commentate on the climactic matches of the World Cup, and then enjoy a holiday in Acapulco paid for by sponsors, but the case remained open even after he returned home from Mexico.

British diplomats pushed for confirmation that Moore was no longer a suspect; official recognition that the England captain was not a thief. They warned that relations had been strained between the two nations by such a sorry episode, and even brought trade deals to bear. In the government files, Tom Rogers says that in an audience with the president of Colombia, he reminded the president that Britain was still looking to offload a submarine and a Canberra aircraft – and that if Colombia went through with the purchase then British public opinion so outraged by the treatment of Moore might soften. 'The president appeared to think the point a reasonable one and said he would bear it in mind,' Rogers noted.

But still no one would confirm Moore's innocence. While the World Cup was taking place, the Colombian police reported that they had traced the bracelet. They said it was being hawked around the underworld and had established the identity of a female thief. But there was no arrest.

There were reports that Moore's accusers would be prosecuted for fraud. In August, the investigating officer, Captain Jaime Ramires of Colombian CID, once again told the British Embassy in Bogotá that he was certain Moore was completely innocent. Ramires had uncovered a copy of an agreement between Danilo Rojas and Alvaro Suarez, signed by both, with Rojas offering to pay Suarez for his support. No sum was mentioned but the media reported that Rojas offered Suarez 5,000 pesos (about £100) and that Rojas, Suarez and Padilla met at Padilla's house to agree on their evidence. Rojas countered that any payment for Suarez was purely compensation for the strain of the case, but the reports backed up the idea that Moore had been set up from the start. The Fuego Verde shop was closed down, the hotel terminating its lease because of the bad publicity.

In August, a panel of judges met to decide if Moore should be rearrested. Two voted in favour of rearrest, one against. The case was passed back to an investigating magistrate who demanded fresh evidence; new statements from Moore and Charlton, fingerprints and further investigation into the mystery 'third player' who had been mentioned by Padilla as hanging around the shop. In a sign that the highest levels of government were still involved trying to clear Moore's name, Sir Alec Douglas-Home, the Foreign Secretary, noted that

'Moore is naturally upset by these developments but taking them philosophically'.

The English newspapers remained staunchly behind Moore through all these developments. The *Sunday Mirror* carried an open letter to the Colombian ambassador in the UK under the headline 'End This Farce'. They wrote of the 'mental torture inflicted on Bobby Moore'. But the ordeal continued for months. On 17 December, Moore and Charlton reported to Bow Street magistrates to give their fresh statements, repeating everything they had said all along. 'I am still under suspicion,' an exasperated Moore told the papers.

And, at the heart of it all, the most extraordinary thing is that no one even knows if the bracelet ever existed – not even Moore, it seems. 'There never was a bracelet', Moore wrote in the first version of his authorised biography published in 1976. But, intriguingly, the line was not in the revised edition which was issued after his death.

To deepen the mystery, other quotes from Moore were also slightly altered in the later edition and the idea introduced that 'perhaps' someone took a bracelet when messing about – a notion which had been aired but dismissed completely in the original version. In the updated version, Jeff Powell wrote that Moore had told him, late into the night and no doubt after a lager or three, that perhaps one of the younger England players had done something daft.

Powell wrote then that he was never given a name 'not even in privacy'. Yet in a BBC documentary in 2002, Powell said that he *had* been told the culprit but had sworn to take the name to the grave. He said the secrecy reflected Moore's London East End upbringing in which it was a matter of honour 'not to grass'.

The prank-gone-wrong line has gathered momentum over the years. Names have been mentioned, including Jeff Astle but most commonly Peter Osgood though neither is around to refute the allegation or help solve the mystery. Monte Fresco, the renowned Fleet Street photographer, was in the hotel at the time of the supposed theft and hinted in conversation that there was more to the story – but he did not want to say exactly what because the England players had held a whip-round to replace some stolen money and he preferred not to blacken anyone's name. Fresco is no longer with us.

Stephanie Moore, Bobby's second wife, wondered momentarily if there had been an English player involved when, at the 1990 World Cup finals, she bumped into an inebriated Sir Bert Millichip, chairman of the FA. Millichip told her that she should not have any concerns that Moore had taken the bracelet because he knew the identity of the real thief. Stephanie mentioned it to Moore who shrugged and changed the subject.

By far the most likely explanation remains the initial assumption that this was a scam by the shop, targeting rich, high-profile clientele in the hope of forcing them to pay damages. The vast majority of players, journalists and FA officials I spoke to, and both Moore's wives, all stuck to the line that this was a set-up.

'I think she [Padilla] was paid a quite substantial amount of money though I think if you found her today she still wouldn't admit to it,' Stephanie says. 'I don't think there was anything else to tell. I think Bobby had this absolute disbelief that it was happening to him and that he'd been set up this way.'

Peter Thompson summed up the views of the squad members I spoke to: 'Footballers are stupid, but I don't think it was a prank that went wrong. It's more than forty years on, I was there and there was nothing said among the lads to make you think that so I can't see it being true. I think it was a set-up from the start.'

Francis Lee said much the same: 'It's unthinkable that anyone in the squad would have done it. You might have one or two scallywags here and there but even they wouldn't do that, not if you're playing for your country in a situation like that. Let's face it, it's beyond belief really. I'd tell you if I'd heard one of the lads took it, and I haven't. If someone took anything, it must have been an inside job.'

Geoff Hurst is equally insistent: 'The idea of anyone stealing it, that's a load of bollocks. No way. It wasn't unusual for this type of thing to happen, with an accusation, a set-up. It had happened before.'

Keith Morris, the diplomat whose recollections remain sharp, was certain that it was a sting, either because a bracelet had gone missing and Padilla panicked or because she was put up to it by her boss because the business was struggling.

'A Colombian senator in the nineties once chatted to me about it and said there was a great story, a considerable conspiracy that had never emerged,' Morris says. 'Of course he didn't tell me what. People rather like doing that, as if they are in the know. My belief at the time, and now, is that it was a very low-level scam.'

Tina Moore is certain that Moore would have told her if there was a different explanation. 'If Bobby didn't say anything to me, and he obviously was very close to Stephanie and didn't say to her, then I don't see how anyone could know unless they are lying,' she says. 'I find it very hard to believe he kept a secret like that unless I didn't know the man at all. I really truly don't believe that anyone else was involved. I'm sure Bobby would have told me. We were really tight then.'

In 1998, one English newspaper tracked down Alvaro Suarez, who was still sticking to his story, claiming that he had looked through a window and seen Moore slip the bracelet into his jacket pocket. 'The people in England have to listen to me because I am telling the truth. An idol is an idol, but he still commits errors. We all like gold, jewels, precious things. I would have gone to jail if I had been lying; I didn't go to jail.'

Suarez was not prosecuted, and nor was Padilla. The case against Moore was dropped, too. The bracelet, assuming it did once sit in that glass case, was never discovered. Perhaps all we can state with certainty is that Moore did not steal any jewellery. He was the last man on earth who would have acted so recklessly. He liked the good things in life but he was no thief.

'Maybe it was Lee Harvey Oswald,' Alan Ball quipped when asked shortly before his death if he knew whodunit. He, like everyone else, knew it could not have been Moore, though that certainty did not stop the innuendo lasting a lifetime.

16. Read All About It

Fame has always been a double-edged sword but it was only in the wake of Bogotá that Bobby Moore began to feel its capacity to wound. Until then he had been a man with such a squeaky clean image that the only danger was in appearing dull.

'Perhaps everything has gone too smoothly in my career – no sensational transfers, no brawls, no scandals,' he noted, before Bogotá. 'My best friends sometimes tell me that whatever publicity I get tends to make me sound "goody-goody", a sort of super Boy Scout.'

For years he had enjoyed exposure on his own terms, keeping his cancer secret, his boozing out of the papers and any other indiscretions, too. Moore had not put a foot wrong or, if he had, no one had noticed or thought to make an exposé out of it.

Moore had laboured painstakingly not to cause upset. When he filled out a questionnaire for *Shoot!* magazine, he dealt even with the gentlest probing as though it was a minefield of diplomacy. Toughest opponent? 'They are all difficult.' Best country visited? 'I like many countries.' Best friend? 'I have many friends.' When he revealed that his favourite meal was liver and bacon, onions, mushroom and spinach, he probably worried that it would cause offence to shepherd's pie.

For a man used to such control over his public image, to be dragged into a scandal of Bogotá proportions was a nightmare. Moore was being given the benefit of any doubt by the world's newspapers but it was hurtful enough just to see his name in the headlines. Even if no one thought he was capable of theft, inevitably there were still nudge-nudge rumours and unwelcome reminders.

When Moore played at Anfield for the first time after the World Cup finals, the Kop burst gleefully into a chant of 'we know you've got the bracelet, we know you've got the bracelet, na naaa naaa na . . .'. As Moore travelled around the country, the Scousers were not the only crowd to delight in his discomfort.

There had always been opposition players trying to wind him up, hoping to shatter that cool façade. Moore had put up with it for years but now the stick came with added relish. One of the worst cases involved Billy Meadows when West Ham played Hereford in the FA Cup. The non-league striker saw his chance for fifteen minutes of fame, and a good story to tell his mates in the bar, if he could rattle England's captain. Meadows drew on any ammunition he could, about Moore's wife, family and Bogotá.

'Bobby had always had players trying to wind him up but this was really diabolical stuff,' Harry Redknapp recalls. 'It was driving Bobby mad. It went to a replay and Meadows did the same again. You could see Bobby seething but he wouldn't bite. Afterwards in the bar Meadows comes up to Bobby, 'all right, Mooro?' like nothing has happened. Anyone else would have wanted to flatten him. Bobby still wouldn't bite.'

At times Moore used humour to laugh off the rumours. At a testimonial dinner, he told the banqueting hall of guests: 'I know it's customary to give gifts for the ladies, but I had enough trouble trying to get one bracelet never mind five hundred.' They loved that one.

In public he tried to rise above the furore and dismissed any suggestions that it was wearing him down. 'Actually it did not affect me as a player, whatever people might have thought at the time,' he said. 'The reason is simple. I felt no real involvement in the stupid, wretched business.'

That was his public stance. Privately, the case was taking its toll. Understandably, he was desperate to be exonerated yet the Colombian authorities were still pursuing him. Moore was so agitated by the refusal to drop the case that he considered legal action against the shop owners and witnesses, including Padilla. According to government papers, one Foreign Office official rang Moore to speak to him in August 1970 about the ongoing case. The official says that Moore was 'very emotional'.

There was an additional reason for his tension: Moore had returned from Acapulco straight into a kidnap plot against his family and a death threat. For a man who worked so adroitly to keep his reputation clean, Moore was spending a lot of time on the front pages. He was 'news', whether he liked it or not.

Moore had been back from his holidays only a few weeks when a handwritten, three-page letter dated 9 August arrived at the offices of the *Evening Standard* in London. The envelope had been posted in Birmingham.

The message inside was alarming: 'WITHIN THE NEXT FEW DAYS FIVE MEN (TWO OF THEM ARE ARMED) ARE

GOING AHEAD WITH THEIR PLANS TO KIDNAP MRS TINA MOORE (WIFE OF FOOTBALLER BOBBY MOORE). THEY WILL RELEASE HER ONLY IF MR MOORE PAYS THEM TEN THOUSAND POUNDS RANSOM MONEY.'

The writer claimed that he was 100 per cent reliable but could not reveal his identity because he was wanted by police for questioning over a bank raid. Explaining his motivation, the anonymous informant wrote: 'I think Bobby has suffered enough after all the trouble in Colombia.' Was the letter-writer a bank robber with a kind heart, or a crank?

The *Evening Standard* immediately informed the police and sent Michael Hart, one of the newspaper's football reporters who was friendly with Moore, down to Upton Park to talk to him. Moore was just about to climb on the team bus heading for a friendly at Bournemouth. 'As if I haven't enough worries already,' a troubled Moore told Hart.

On police advice, Moore did not get on the bus but dashed home to his family who were already under constant guard. Nine detectives, working in threes on eight-hour shifts, kept watch twenty-four hours a day. The Moores could not go anywhere without a minder for a fortnight.

When Moore drove to training in his white Cadillac, he was accompanied by a policeman. When Tina woke up to give the kids breakfast, there was a policeman standing by. When the Moores went to watch a charity game in Chichester, CID men mingled in the crowd.

It was a claustrophobic existence, alleviated only by the Moores' love of entertaining. Bobby would go to his bar, fetch a crate of lagers and crack them open with the officers. There was one happy spin-off when one of the policemen ended up marrying the Moores' family nanny. Those were the lighter moments in a period of inevitable anxiety. The police were taking the threat seriously so the Moores did too. They became paranoid anytime the children, Roberta and Dean, were not in sight.

Just when it seemed the danger had passed, there was a call to Moore's shop across the street from Upton Park. West Ham were playing and the caller said that Bobby was going to be shot. It sounded like a hoax but, in the circumstances, the police did not dare take any risks.

Police arrived at the ground, observed from the sidelines as the game continued and then, at the final whistle, marched out to surround Moore as he walked off. He could not resist a one-liner as the officers approached him. 'I know I played badly,' he said, 'but I didn't think Ron would have me arrested.'

Greenwood did not want Moore arrested, but, within a few months, he did want him sacked. As the kidnapping story faded away, the final act of Moore's tabloid trilogy was the Blackpool Nightclub Incident. Or, as Jimmy Greaves preferred to call it, 'The Day Fleet Street Went Mad'.

Blackpool was a scandal that even managed to rival the meltdown in George Best's career. Manchester United's wild genius was in the midst of a personal crisis, missing training, skipping matches, disappearing for a lost weekend in London.

On Monday 4 January 1971, Best kept an FA disciplinary commission – and a wearied Sir Matt Busby – waiting ninety minutes at Lancaster Gate because he had missed the train with a hangover. The papers were full of stories of Best's terrible behaviour and United's growing exasperation. Of all the men to knock Best off the top of the news agenda, who would have guessed that it would be the impeccable Bobby Moore?

Blackpool was a scandal which had a certain inevitability given West Ham's relish for boozing, and sinking morale at the club. The mood was low, form wretched. A 2-0 defeat at home to Newcastle United in mid-September 1970 left West Ham in twentieth place after five draws and four defeats in their opening nine league matches.

The board had signed up for a money-spinning friendly against Pelé's club, Santos, in New York the following week but, as the squad departed across the Atlantic for what should have been a jolly, the camp was suffused with tensions. The plane was barely off the ground when Greaves, Moore and Freddie Harrison, his business partner who had come along for the ride, were propping up the bar.

To pass the time, Greenwood joined the group, ordering a Coke. Harrison, to the suppressed giggles of the two players, slipped a Bacardi into the manager's drink. When Greenwood ordered another Coke, Harrison added another shot. Then the same again. Greenwood later claimed he knew what was happening and said nothing because he 'didn't want to spoil their little prank', but that is not how the players remember it. Moore and Greaves were laughing inside as Reverend Ron unwittingly became pie-eyed.

As the drinks flowed, tongues loosened and the chat became confessional. According to Greenwood's version, a sombre Greaves candidly admitted that he had started to freeze in front of goal. The brilliantly instinctive striker, only recently signed from Spurs in a deal that took Martin Peters to White Hart Lane, was now mired in self-doubt.

Greenwood topped that troubled confession by saying that he was considering resigning from West Ham, given their early season difficulties. It was honesty which did little for his authority with two senior players, certainly not with Moore, who took it as another sign of the manager's failing leadership.

Woozy after his spiked drinks, Greenwood tottered back down the aisle, slumped into his seat and was soon snoring loudly. As word spread that Reverend Ron was in a state, the players gathered around like naughty schoolboys. One player leaned over his comatose manager, pulling faces and making rude gestures. The giggles of West Ham's players at Greenwood's expense said everything about an undisciplined club.

The players had been pushing their luck for years and it was bound to catch up with them sooner or later. It took only a few more months. The seeds of trouble were sown in the bad weather forecasts that threatened many fixtures for the third round of the FA Cup due to take place on 2 January 1971.

West Ham had been drawn to face Blackpool but they travelled on the eve of the game with dwindling expectations that the game would go ahead because of the cold snap. Even before the train left Euston station on New Year's Day, some of the drinkers, like the thirsty Brian Dear, had already sunk a couple of pints.

Rumours about a postponement swirled, like the snow, as the team had an early dinner at Blackpool's Imperial Hotel. Then came free time which, under Greenwood's trusting regime, meant the players could go off to the cinema or take a stroll. The hard core, fatefully, plotted something a little livelier.

Rather undermining the subsequent claims by those who went out boozing that it was all perfectly harmless, other players already sensed danger. As Dear, Rob Jenkins and some of the players talked about wandering out into the night, Frank Lampard decided to avoid trouble.

'It was a Friday night so I said "no". I was only a kid. I was worried about playing my game. Me and another younger player, I can't remember who, slipped upstairs. I left the others, thank God. I bottled it really, but it was a lucky escape. What happened was totally unprofessional.'

By now the crew was Jenkins, Moore, Greaves, Dear and Clyde Best, the big, teetotal Bermudan forward. They got chatting to a couple of television staff in the hotel lobby who were heading out to see Blackpool's attractions. There was a spare taxi.

'The 007,' Moore told the driver. It was the name of a nightclub owned by Brian London, the heavyweight boxer from Blackpool. He had invited Moore to pop in when they had met at an event in the capital.

Dear would later claim that they had only a few halves of lager. Greaves admitted that he drank about a dozen, adding 'it says much about my alcohol consumption at the time that I wasn't drunk'. Who was counting?

After a couple of hours at the bar in the 007, the gang headed back to the Imperial Hotel at around 1.45 a.m. They ordered coffee and sandwiches and went to bed (Jenkins – the club physio – says he had forgotten Moore's sleeping pill that night but the captain had already downed a hefty nightcap).

Perhaps they would have got away with it had they won the match. But they didn't. On an icy pitch, West Ham were thrashed by the worst team in the top flight. It was exactly the sort of game that conformed to the stereotype of soft Londoners being outfought on a cold day up north; complacent West Ham beaten by inferior opponents.

Bob Stokoe, newly appointed as Blackpool manager, pushed Tony Green high up on Moore, and the forward gave the England captain a rare chasing. 'Bob didn't like players who were right up on top of him with pace,' says Jimmy Armfield, right-back for Blackpool. 'Bob had a problem with Green who was very quick and clever with the ball. We gave them a pasting.' It finished 4-0. West Ham were nineteenth in the First Division and now out of the FA Cup.

Monday morning's papers had some truly appalling news to cope with from the football world. That weekend, sixty-six fans had died in the Ibrox disaster, crushed in a stampede. In every paper there was anguish about the complacency of authorities, lack of safety standards, cries for government intervention (recommendations that went scandalously and tragically unheeded for those who would flock to Hillsborough decades later).

This was tragedy on a vast scale. At West Ham they were dealing only with fan fury following a particularly bad defeat, but the anger came with a troubling whiff of scandal.

Losing at Blackpool was bad enough, another cup run ended before it had begun, but what gave the complaints a harsh edge were the allegations about players drinking on the eve of the game. Moore, Greaves and the rest of the crew had been seen in the 007. Information was passed to Reg Pratt, the chairman. He, in turn, told Greenwood.

Fleet Street buzzed with the story. West Ham were said to be 'probing' a boozing session. Within forty-eight hours, it was front- and back-page news that Moore had been involved 'in a 2 a.m. party' in Blackpool. 'Lights out for Bobby Moore?' asked the headline in the *Sun*.

Moore's fall from grace even made news on the austere

front page of *The Times*. In the *Mirror*, Ken Jones told of 'an astonishing indiscretion' from the 'impeccably discreet' Moore. He wrote: 'It remains no less than extraordinary that Moore, with his calculated ambition and immense experience, could be drawn into a situation where the odds had to favour ultimate exposure.'

In the *Sun*, Peter Batt wrote, '[I] cannot comprehend how experienced men like them can have been so irresponsible', though he added: 'From a purely subjective viewpoint, the most sickening aspect of having to write this condemnation is that I happen to think Bobby Moore and Jimmy Greaves are about two of the nicest guys on or off the soccer pitch.'

Moore later argued that 'this incident got more space than the Vietnam War and was nearly as big as the Great Train Robbery in some people's eyes'. But Brian James of the *Daily Mail* insists that the Fleet Street reaction was far from hysterical.

'They got a bashing and one or two of the players did complain about the coverage afterwards, saying it was over the top. But I said "no, no, that's the reaction. That's the reaction of ordinary people who felt the team had let them down. When people started ringing the papers and saying 'we saw your players falling about drunk at 2 a.m. the night before a game', what do you expect us to do?" It couldn't be any other way. I didn't feel too much sympathy with them. My feeling was even if they thought the game was going to be off, you're probably going to have to play it soon. It wasn't a good idea to get smashed.'

At Upton Park, Greenwood did not need to read the papers. He had made his own inquiries. Furious, he pulled the players in one by one. All apologised, but the manager was incensed when Moore said that the club should have denied everything to the newspapers and tried to kill the story.

'Let *you* down?!' Greenwood fumed. 'You're the one who was in a nightclub.'

Greenwood's action was drastic. He went to the board and demanded that all except the teetotal Best should be sacked immediately. Not even Fleet Street's most outraged columnist had called for that.

The manager was urging the club to sack the England captain who, only weeks earlier, had finished runner-up in the poll for European Footballer of the Year. Moore's performances in the 1970 World Cup had left him trailing only Gerd Müller, the prolific West German striker who had scored ten goals in five games in Mexico. Six months earlier Moore had embraced Pelé, a man at the top of the world game. Now Greenwood wanted him thrown out.

An overreaction? However irresponsible the players had been, to sack three of them, including the England captain, for one drinking session was draconian. But, of course, this was not Greenwood responding to one lapse. It was an outpouring of accumulated frustration; a belated realisation that he had been too indulgent and a sign that his relationship with Moore was broken.

'I think Bobby was bigger than the club by then,' Frank Lampard says. 'Ron was, well, not a control freak but he wanted it done his way and Bobby was in a different step to him. It had suited Bobby staying at West Ham because he was king of the castle but I can understand from a manager's point of view, there must have been times when it got frustrating for Ron. Now Ron had the chance to do something about it.'

Geoff Hurst was another who had turned down the chance

to go out in Blackpool that night, telling his room-mate Dear 'absolutely no way'. He recalls: 'You don't go out Friday night even for a Coke. You're asking for trouble, even in those days. I remember feeling strongly it was a really stupid thing to do and they couldn't moan if they got nailed for it. A big cup tie, out the night before – I think Ron's reaction was understandable.'

After considering Greenwood's demand for heads to roll, the board came to an outrageously self-interested decision. They did not want to sack Moore or Greaves but they would dismiss Dear. He had been given a second chance after a spell away and now he had let them down. They felt he was dispensable.

Greenwood pointed out that they could hardly punish one player. The board relented. The compromise was a one-week fine and short suspension, though Greenwood extended the latter simply by not selecting the players – in Dear's case, never again.

It was the end for the amiable Dear who would slip disconsolately into retirement; a sad milestone in the descent of Greaves who would retire at the end of the season aged just thirty-one and plunge headlong into lost years of addiction; and a cause of deep dismay for Greenwood.

'He was very close to tears when I spoke to him about it a week or so after the whole affair,' Brian James says. 'I think he felt terribly let down by Bobby. He thought "I built my team around this young man and he knows I'll do anything to assist his career". But the relationship was purely professional, nothing personal, certainly by then.'

Greaves bumped into Moore in the car park at Upton Park after the disciplinary measures had been confirmed. Moore, he said, was 'shattered' by the furore and the blows to his standing and reputation. The captain could handle any internal punishment by Greenwood; it was the exposure he hated. As Moore explained in a crestfallen moment, 'it was goodwill all the way from 1966 through to Mexico and that rotten trouble in Bogotá. It took only one drink to undo it all.'

His club suspension cost Moore an England cap against Malta. Alf Ramsey would not pick a player banned by his club so Roy McFarland made his debut in central defence. At Upton Park, Moore's exile lasted five weeks, as Greenwood kept him on the sidelines even after he had served his punishment.

Omitting Moore was a test of the manager's nerve as Greenwood, too, came in for stick from the terraces. Results were terrible, the captain had been axed and fans were reading in the newspapers that the team was full of boozers. A 'GREENWOOD OUT' banner appeared at Upton Park. Others read, sarcastically, 'YET ANOTHER GREAT SEASON' and 'HAMMERS HOLIDAY CAMP'.

In Moore's absence, Hurst and Billy Bonds shared captaincy duties, and there was a surprisingly harsh tone from Jeff Powell, in the *Daily Mail*, who noted that they would 'bring inspirational qualities to a job in which Moore appeared insular and aloof'.

Moore and Greaves finally returned against Coventry City on 8 February, having each missed three matches. By that time, Greenwood needed them back as West Ham fought to avoid relegation. Eventually they crawled to safety but only just, finishing one place above the drop.

It was a dire period at Upton Park, and not just because of one late night. There was a piece by Brian James in the *Daily Mail* on the Monday after Blackpool, which is particularly noteworthy because it was written even before the boozing scandal had erupted. It was not coloured by the subsequent media storm.

James highlighted the roles of Moore and Greenwood in the club's malaise, and his strident and prophetic pieces provide a revealing snapshot of a dysfunctional club. He talked of Greenwood's idealism coming apart on and off the pitch, and how the trust and honour system at West Ham was crumbling. He wrote about how the manager's theory of treating players like adults and expecting them to respond was scornfully regarded as a weakness by 'a significant number of players' and how 'irresponsible behaviour' had destroyed West Ham.

Remarking that Moore had not actually played any worse at Blackpool than anyone else – despite the laughable post-match claim from Jimmy Meadows, Blackpool's coach, that the England captain was 'the worst defender in the world' – James also focused on failings in Moore's leadership.

He wrote: 'Moore, as a captain, must share blame for West Ham's plight. The lack of fire in their bellies on the pitch is his responsibility.'

He went on: 'You can see the weakness in Moore as a captain when you see him at moments of enormous success. He can score a magnificent goal and walk unmoved back to his place; he can wreck a brilliant rival move with a shuffle and interception and stand stone-faced as the crowds' cheers pour about him.

'In a successful team such monumental assurance is a blessing. In a struggling side this lack of apparent emotion is a burden. When West Ham concede a sloppy goal, Moore stands looking at the debris of his defence as though he doesn't care. When West Ham fail to score an easy goal the captain shrugs as though he expected nothing better.

'When a teammate fails he is slow to commiserate; when another succeeds he is among the last to congratulate. In such instances, Moore's calm can be taken for contempt. This may be unfair, but some West Ham players – below his status in the game – are overawed by his presence, and may take his silence as criticism.'

It was all well and good for Moore to embody Rudyard Kipling's 'If' – to treat triumph and disaster both the same, to keep his head while all around might be losing theirs – but this was the famous Moore coolness exposed as a weakness. James went as far as to say that West Ham would need to consider their captain's position. James added: 'With England such bland composure is unimportant. There are other extroverts around to do the shouting and the raving for him. West Ham particularly need to be inspired or coaxed to a courage and a physical output that does not come naturally.

'If he can't unbend, then West Ham must find a less lofty, more committed and demonstrative man to lead their battle to survive.'

It was an unforgiving assessment but not one written lightly by a journalist with impeccable contacts at Upton Park. There were numerous reasons for West Ham's travails, from Greenwood's failings in the transfer market to his refusal to compromise his tactical principles, and Moore could hardly be scapegoated given that he remained the outstanding world-class talent.

But the captain was part of the problem. There was a slackness about West Ham which had been eroding team discipline for some time, and Blackpool had confirmed that neither Greenwood nor his skipper were addressing the issue.

All the youthful ambition of the mid-sixties had turned to complacency, as Greaves confirmed in his own memoirs.

When he had arrived at Upton Park in March 1970, the striker had expected to be reinvigorated at the famous Academy; to find a coaching centre of brilliant young players, an exciting centre of innovation.

Instead, he wrote: 'I have to be honest and say it never struck me as being that way. Compared to what I had been used to at Spurs under Bill Nicholson and Eddie Baily, I found training at West Ham and the general running of team affairs to be lax, at times disorganised and occasionally shambolic. Fertile ground for a disenchanted footballer who had begun to drink more heavily than was good for him.'

Greaves was pissed even on the eve of his West Ham debut at Manchester City. At breakfast on the day of the match, Rob Jenkins told him: 'Jim, do yourself a favour, don't go anywhere near Greenwood.'

'What are you talking about? Why?'

'Because you fucking stink of booze,' Jenkins replied.

Greaves had been out until the early hours, though reeking of alcohol did not dull his talent that day. He scored twice.

As if the drinking was not trouble enough, the Blackpool gang also had to cope with at least one newspaper mentioning that girls had been at the 007 club and had accompanied the group back to the hotel. All the players strenuously denied it but Greaves had a row with his wife, Irene, and was in tears when he spoke to Greenwood.

In the Moore household there was also disharmony. Bobby had rung Tina to warn her: 'There's going to be something in the papers, and you're not going to like it.' They rowed even though Tina did not believe the flimsy suggestion that girls had come back to the Imperial Hotel.

Moore told Jeff Powell, quite categorically, that he was not a womaniser: 'Even when the girls were chasing young footballers my game was a few lagers with the lads at the bar. What the others got up to was up to them but it wasn't for me.'

It is a claim to fidelity which is not entirely confirmed by discreet conversations with Moore's friends. None want to be quoted on any rumoured lapses and risk damaging his reputation but one name, that of a glamorous television personality, was mentioned by three different sources as a possible affair dating back to the sixties. The woman in question declined to comment. At least one other alleged incident was alluded to by friends but they chose not to embellish.

Rumours that Moore may have been unfaithful are perhaps not surprising even if they do fly in the face of his unblemished image and his own denials. Perhaps an affair could have been a way of proving his manhood after the operation to remove a testicle. Also, Moore could be a charmer, and his fame and looks were bound to make him a magnet for women. He did not chase women with the relish of some of his team-mates but he was never short of admiring glances.

Whatever the truth behind the rumours, Moore's marriage to Tina at that time was becoming increasingly erratic. They had always been a combination of fire and ice. 'There are some classic stories,' Geoff Hurst says. 'I'm afraid some are off-limits. But, yes, fire and ice sums it up nicely.'

They had their arguments, often fuelled by drink. Usually Moore would keep his cool in the face of provocation, and that only wound Tina up even more. Enraged by her husband's behaviour at a party when he danced with another woman with a little more gusto than she found appropriate, Tina flew into a fit of jealous rage. She marched up and threw a drink in Moore's face, the contents dribbling down his jacket lapels. Moore dabbed gently. 'I think it needs a touch more tonic, love,' he said, to the immense amusement of his friends.

Moore would look with cool disdain on the occasional dramas and bursts of high emotion from his wife. He abhorred histrionics, especially in public. You can imagine him asking what was the point of wasting emotional energy on marital rows.

When one spectacular argument erupted while they were driving around the North Circular on their way back from a night out, Tina ripped off her jewellery, including her wedding ring, and hurled it out of the window. Moore went back the next day, the England captain hunting around the central reservation on his hands and knees looking for the precious rings. Whenever he was giving friends a lift, he loved to point to the spot where he had scrabbled around for Tina's jewellery. 'I was a bit fiery I'm afraid,' Tina says. 'I was always a bit feisty.'

Moore could bear an argument – he would simply turn on his cold front, his protective shield – but what he hated was a scene, and Tina had a tendency to emotional eruptions. Bobby would smile sweetly whenever Tina raged, take his wife aside and tell her in no uncertain terms not to play out their difficulties in front of other people.

It was unfortunate timing, then, that Moore was due to be featured on *This Is Your Life* in the same week as the Blackpool scandal. Tina had been running around setting up all sorts of surprises for her husband just as trouble was brewing.

No wonder Moore looks particularly bashful when Eamonn Andrews suddenly surprises him with his big red book, emerging from the shadows after Moore had been set up to receive an award in his testimonial year.

Moore blushes when Andrews says: 'We could have chosen a better week. It's not the happiest in West Ham's history.'

'You can say that again, Eamonn,' Moore deadpans.

Moore's old friends and colleagues roll out to pay their respects and there is a short message played from Ramsey. But Greenwood is notable by his absence. The Blackpool episode was by far the worst strain on a relationship which had endured, but only because neither man was given to explosive confrontations which could have shattered it completely.

In the bitter aftermath of Blackpool, Greaves was convinced that Moore would not see out another season at a club where 'what little collective spirit existed amongst the West Ham players evaporated'. Greaves was insistent that Moore had suffered an appalling character assassination, a 'public execution' at the hands of the press.

He wrote: 'What the critics and commentators did to him was as sickening a case of kicking a man while he is down that I can recall. It's probably the only incident in my career that I felt deeply bitter about.'

Perhaps the furore said something about a changing world where anyone was becoming fair game for the tabloids, even England's heroic captain. But it also spoke of the disintegrating relationship between Moore and Greenwood.

'It was hard sometimes to get to the bottom of that relationship between Ron and Bobby,' Rob Jenkins says. 'He was a funny guy, Greenwood. Although he was a wonderful manager with his football, he didn't impose himself with certain players and that's where the problems came in. Some players became slight enemies. That's what Bobby did.

'But for Ron, he could also see what Bobby was like. I mean everybody loves Bobby and they think they know him, but he wasn't quite the angel that some people like to portray. I loved Bobby, but all this putting him on a pedestal . . .'

17. Death in Poland

Even when relations were at their worst with Ron and West Ham were middling along in the First Division, or, worse still, fighting to avoid relegation, Bobby Moore always had England. Even when the inquest into a wretched season at Upton Park was casting doubt over the skipper's role, Moore knew that he remained the stalwart of the national team's defence and Alf Ramsey's redoubtable leader. Yet, one day, even that certainty was bound to crumble.

Moore could not go on for ever but it was the nature of his decline that hurt, clutching vainly for his old majesty. He lived as a ball-playing defender and this is how he died in international football; resolutely refusing to hoof the ball to safety. Where Moore had once turned elegantly away from danger, he found himself lurching perilously into trouble.

The story of his decline is wrapped up in England's collective demise, a slow but unmistakeable slide from the moment they had been knocked out of the 1970 World Cup finals by West Germany. Even in defeat in León, Ramsey and his men could imagine that they were still among the elite. Hadn't they given Brazil, the champions, a worthy battle? Moore and his team-mates remained convinced that but for the manager's mistaken substitutions and Banks's illness against West Germany, they would have proved themselves superior.

The delusion of English supremacy lasted for almost two unbeaten years after Mexico – but when reality bit it stripped away the emperor's clothes, destroying any notion about Ramsey's team being among the best in the world. The humbling came against West Germany in the 1972 European Championships quarter-final played over home and away legs. This time there could be no debate about which side was superior. It was then, too, that the first signs of Moore's mortality on the international stage surfaced.

Ahead of the first leg at Wembley, Ron Greenwood sought to help his country by resting Moore and Geoff Hurst from West Ham's trip to Arsenal. Imagine that. A club manager going out of his way, and weakening his own side, to do the national side a favour – though do not imagine that Greenwood's gesture told of a more selfless age.

While one club manager was helping the national cause, another was very much looking after his own interests. For most of the previous eighteen months, Moore had been establishing a partnership with Roy McFarland, the Derby County defender. Ramsey was furious when McFarland was withdrawn by Brian Clough shortly before the clash with West Germany on grounds of injury yet played in a critical title match against Liverpool forty-eight hours later. Ramsey seethed at Clough's duplicity.

Larry Lloyd was available to play as stopping centre-back but Ramsey decided that the Liverpool defender was lacking international experience and instead gave the number five shirt to Moore, to the captain's surprise. In this pairing with Norman

Hunter, Moore was expected to pick up Germany's potent goalscorer Gerd Müller, with Hunter sweeping around him.

From the start, Moore was ill at ease. Hunter, too. They were two fine players but accustomed to playing very similar roles for their clubs. Even in training, there was confusion about their movement as they duplicated each other.

Their shared uncertainty was compounded by Moore's belief that a midfield of Alan Ball, Colin Bell and Martin Peters lacked defensive bite, though it is questionable whether Alan Mullery or Peter Storey would have made much difference given West Germany's domination.

On a slick Wembley pitch, dampened by evening showers, the visitors seemed to be playing at a different pace: quicker, uncatchable. England looked leaden and predictable, with a barrage of long balls from deep up to Hurst. Günter Netzer ran the game for Germany, running behind the England midfield. 'We were murdered,' Moore later remarked. The captain was the most notable casualty.

The first German goal stemmed from Moore's over-elaboration. Determined to play out of defence, he put his team in deep trouble. Intercepting a cross inside England's penalty area, Moore shaped to turn past Siggi Held. No sooner had he done that than Herbert Wimmer rushed to close him down.

Moore should have whacked the ball away but turned again, this time straight across his own penalty area. The instincts were admirable, the outcome disastrous. The ball was clumsily scooped across the box straight to the feet of Müller. A quick interchange – ping, ping, ping – from Müller to Held and a first-time shot by Hoeness put the Germans 1-0 up. Moore's greatest strength – his determination to keep possession – had been turned against him.

Rodney Marsh eventually appeared in place of Hurst but too late for many of a disgruntled Wembley crowd. Even when Francis Lee equalised there was a sense of gloom. In the eighty-fifth minute, England fell behind for the second time and Moore was again at fault.

Marsh lost the ball on the edge of the German penalty area, leaving England immediately vulnerable to the speed of the counter-attack. Held accelerated down the left past Paul Madeley. Moore chased back and tried to make a sliding tackle outside the area. He just caught the ball with his studs, but Held still had momentum and, as both players tangled in the area, Moore hooked the German's leg. Penalty.

'Frankly I thought that decision was a bit harsh,' Moore claimed. 'I made contact with the ball when I tackled. I didn't chop Held down.' But it was a challenge made out of desperation. Moore must have known the risk he was taking in going to ground.

Gordon Banks could not keep out the penalty from Netzer and Müller added a third in the final moments. It was not just the defeat but how comprehensively England had been outplayed by a Germany team which had advanced so far since 1966, with Netzer roving freely between midfield and attack.

England did not know how to handle him, and one intriguing insight comes from Ken Jones who recalls that, as England's plan unravelled, Hunter pleaded with Moore to change roles.

'Netzer was tearing them to pieces, dropping off in front of the defence and Norman said to Bob, "come on, you come here and I'll play there and I'll murder the bastard". Bob said "oh no, this is the way Alf wants us to play and until we get off at half-time this is the way we'll play". A lot was said about how much influence Bob had on Alf but that completely distorts the idea that Bobby could take responsibility for making changes on the field.'

The evidence was damning about England's stagnation. As Hugh McIlvanney wrote in the *Observer*: 'Cautious, joyless football was scarcely bearable even while it was bringing victories. When it brings defeat there can only be one reaction.'

A negative England kicked their way to a goalless draw in the second leg in Berlin, Netzer complaining bitterly about the brutal treatment he received from Storey and Hunter. England were on the slide, the heroes of 1966 fading out.

Hurst had played his last international in the first leg, Banks would play only twice more for England, leaving Moore, Ball and Peters left of the world champions. Loyalty to his players had always been central to the Ramsey ethos but the Germany defeat fuelled a debate about whether he had relied too much on the old guard.

Peter Osgood, the England striker, was among those who believed that even that small group of stalwarts had been kept around too long, Moore included. Osgood said: 'He [Ramsey] should have started to rebuild right away [after 1970] because if we qualified for 1974 it was obvious that Bobby would be too old and Mullery, Hurst, Lee weren't going to be around. If he'd done that, with the talent we had and the likes of Channon, Keegan, McFarland and Todd, we would have qualified in 1974, but he left it too late to bring them in. Mooro played until 1973, which was too long.'

Francis Lee says that the problem was less about culling individuals than changing tactics to keep pace with an evolving world game. Ramsey, Lee argues, was far too wedded to the straight lines of 4-4-2. Variation was required.

'I thought that after the World Cup in the seventies that Alf should have changed it because we got exposed playing four at the back,' Lee says. 'Even before Mexico, we had played against Holland at Wembley and Johann Cruyff started up front as the second striker, but after ten minutes he dropped off into midfield. Well, you can't give him space and nobody picked him up. A good player like that, he just ran the game. Then Günter Netzer did the same for Germany at Wembley, playing free and wandering all over the place. We didn't adapt to solve that problem.'

There was some truth in both arguments. Ramsey was undoubtedly too mistrustful of new players coming through. Talents like Marsh were regarded as too individual, too maverick compared to the solid pros he had turned into champions.

He was still stuck in the old ways but it was also understandable that he wanted to keep a spine of his world-beaters. Moore certainly believed that he still had plenty left to give. He was sure that he could play on until the 1974 finals.

Moore did carry on, chalking up personal milestones including his 100th cap on a frozen pitch at Hampden Park, Glasgow, in February 1973. Presented with a silver salver by the FA, engraved with the flags of all the countries he had played against, Moore became the third centurion after Billy Wright and Bobby Charlton. It was the night of the three Cs in attack – Allan Clarke, Martin Chivers and Mick Channon – and a 5-0 thrashing of the old enemy.

But the vultures were circling around Ramsey. A month earlier, England had been fiercely criticised for drawing 1-1 against Wales at Wembley in a qualifier for the 1974 World Cup. It was a result which left little margin for error in matches against Poland, with only one team to qualify from the group. England could ill afford to lose when they flew out to Chorzow.

On the eve of England's critical qualifier in Poland, Alan Ball sat with the travelling English reporters at a local bar where he treated them to a glowing appreciation of Moore, the captain and his good pal. He talked of Moore's ability to play for West Ham, where he had not won a trophy for years, and then step up to England.

'He's amazing,' said Ball. 'Season after season he plays for West Ham, a family club just happy to be in the First Division, yet he always manages to raise his game for England.' As David Lacey wrote in the *Guardian*, fate, once tempted, rarely fails to oblige.

What followed the next evening is a hard sight to bear – and not just because England were clad in yellow shirts, blue shorts and yellow socks; an abominable, short-lived diversion from the country's traditional colours.

England were unrecognisable and Moore was a diminished version of the once imperious defender. Always sturdy, his thighs had started to thicken out a little into his thirties. He was carrying a little more flesh and even less speed. He was culpable for the first goal after just seven minutes, straining for a free-kick at the near post and deflecting it past Peter Shilton. But it was the second goal soon after half-time which was the momentous blunder. The nature of it told of a great career turning to rust.

Roy McFarland nods the ball back to Moore who has time and space. But instead of a back pass, which he will have thought too negative from high in his own half, or a hurried clearance, which was beneath him, Moore obeys the ball-playing instincts of a lifetime and tries to play his way out. Brian Glanville called it Moore's 'moment of hubris'.

Moore's first touch is unusually clumsy, the ball bouncing off his right foot a yard or so behind him. Suddenly the onrushing Włodzimierz Lubański is on top of him. Moore still has the chance to play safe, to whack the ball clear, but he tries to turn back on himself past Lubański. The move is clumsy, leaden, obvious. Lubańksi pounces. The ball is stolen, the king deposed.

Even in his prime, Moore hadn't been quick enough to retrieve a mistake and he was never going to catch the Poland striker, his country's greatest goalscorer, as he sprinted away to thump the crucial goal inside Shilton's near post (and if we are going to pity poor Moore, spare a thought for the brilliant Lubański whose cruciate ligament was snapped in a bad tackle by McFarland in the second half. He missed the World Cup, too).

For Moore, and for England, it was a calamitous blunder. At 1-0 England had hopes of recovery. At 2-0, they were beaten. 'A tragic error by England's sheet-anchor captain' was how Geoffrey Green put it in *The Times*. The shock was all the more profound because, as Bobby Robson once pronounced, 'Bobby Moore made fewer mistakes than any defender I've seen in my life'.

The significance of the moment was not lost on anyone. 'If Bobby Moore had wept, we would have all wept with him,' Ramsey said, as though at a funeral. And it was, of sorts. At thirty-two, Moore's international career was effectively laid to rest in the coalfields of Chorzow.

For Moore, there was only one way to find relief and that was in a beer can. In his bedroom at the end of the corridor in the

Hotel Silesia, lager in hand, Moore faced up to his footballing mortality. He paced around his bedroom reliving the worst night of his professional life.

He was rooming with Ball, himself smarting after a late red card, and poured out his torments. Mike Summerbee was called and instructed to join them. Other players wandered down for a drink. In the commiseration party was also Nigel Clarke, who needed to coax a column out of Moore for the *Daily Mirror*. Clarke found Moore as he had never seen him before.

'He was absolutely bereft,' Clarke recalls. 'He was walking up and down saying "I should have done that. Did I cover that? Did I not notice? Am I getting too slow? Did I not pick this up quick enough?" I sat there and my heart went out to him because you saw a guy, as cold and immaculate and organised as Bobby, and he was bleeding.'

Moore's mistake had put England's participation in the World Cup in jeopardy. From champions in 1966, and contenders in 1970 until the implosion against West Germany, defeat in Poland meant they might not even make it to the 1974 finals.

As the players drank away their sorrows, there was a knock on the door. Ramsey had instructed his players to have an early night because they were flying to Moscow first thing the next morning. The England manager walked in and the players looked up, ready for the familiar stern rebuke and an order to go to bed.

'I thought I told you boys not to have a drink and to have an early night,' Ramsey said. 'But I'll have a large gin and tonic, thank you, Bobby.'

*

Clarke had to compose a column from Moore, which appeared under the headline 'I Let England Down'. Mixed in with the self-flagellation – 'I never knew I could feel so bad about anything' – was a more revealing remark about the captain's state of mind.

Moore sensed that many were now glorying in his mistakes and revelling in evidence that he was over the hill. 'I know this gives extra ammunition to the band of critics who feel I should be out of the England team,' he said. 'They were after me in 1965 – again just before the World Cup – and I had to prove I could rise above it. A similar campaign is getting into its stride now, and again I must prove people wrong.'

Those critics were hardly a deafening chorus. Moore had far too much credit in the bank for that. But his sombre mood showed the pressure he was under and his weariness after a decade of constant scrutiny. That same year he had put his name to an unusually introspective article in the *Daily Mirror*. The headline set the tone: 'The problem of being me'.

'It's always being said – behind my back – that I'm cold, aloof and sometimes insincere,' Moore began. He went on to say that his life was not all money, hero-worship and the good times. He talked about a daily barrage of rudeness, insults, snide comments; of being 'pestered and bothered by bores'; of casual acquaintances 'trying to make you their own and force friendship on you'.

He complained that 'rarely can I say what I feel in public or in the press.' He said that he spent his life biting his tongue. 'There is always someone who wants to tell me what is wrong with my game, West Ham's, England's – and with Sir Alf Ramsey. Some tell me I'm useless . . . I always agree.'

Moore had always avoided confrontation when he was out

in the pubs. If anyone came up looking for trouble, which was not infrequent, he would ask politely to be left alone. But years of keeping up the wall of politeness was bound to take its toll. As Harry Redknapp noted: 'Sadly, the more famous he became, the more difficult it was to even switch off as he used to. There was nowhere he wasn't known, and he felt he always had to be on his best behaviour.' As Moore's form had slipped, and Ramsey's regime had started to be questioned, there were more bores than ever seeking to tell the England captain where he was going wrong.

At West Ham, they had enjoyed one of their more promising seasons, finishing a respectable sixth in the First Division, but Moore's year was defined by that nightmare against Poland which was the last significant act of his international career.

The squad travelled on to a friendly in Russia in downbeat mood. Moore's insomnia was worsened by the summer heat in Moscow and memories of that mistake in Poland. In the early hours, Moore left the Metropole hotel for a walk 'trying to restore some of my hurt pride'. He strolled for a while but, still restless, found a bench to lie on for a doze.

Unable to sleep, Mike Summerbee had also left his sweltering room for some fresh air. 'It was a lovely park, lilac trees hanging down, a lovely smell. I headed over to a bench and who was fast asleep over there but Mooro. We stayed there from about half past two till six in the morning.

'We headed straight to Lenin's Tomb on Red Square. On the hour, two jack-booted soldiers would march up to replace the others, the clock chiming just as their rifles touched the ground. Mooro loved the precision. I remember him watching it admiringly, saying "takes some planning that".'

England went on to Italy for the last match of the summer

tour. In Turin, Moore set a new caps record, overtaking Bobby Charlton. He had appeared in 107 of the last 116 internationals, all starts. The press gave Moore a Capo di Monte porcelain ornament in recognition of his achievement but England lost 2-0 and Moore felt Ramsey was being a little distant.

Moore had too much pride to accept that his England career was nearing its end but the signs were ominous. After the Italy match, Moore got steaming drunk with Alan Ball and stayed on boozing at the airport in London once the team landed, before staggering home and collapsing in an armchair. The hangover lasted some time.

The night before England faced Austria in September 1973, preparation for the decisive return against Poland the following month, Moore went with the rest of the squad to see the new Bond film *Live and Let Die*. 'In the circumstances it was the appropriate choice,' Moore noted.

His humour hid the deep hurt he felt when Ramsey took him aside on the team bus heading back from training to say he was being dropped for the first time in his England career. For so long he had been an automatic choice, whatever his form, but Ramsey told him that Hunter deserved to play in the number six shirt. Ramsey had made plenty of tough calls in his time as England manager, and done so without a flicker of emotion, but he admitted that dropping Moore was one of the most difficult: 'It was a bad moment for me. Bobby was shattered.'

Moore would say he was 'stunned by disappointment', and retreated to his hotel room where the telephone began to ring incessantly with journalists seeking a reaction. There was nothing positive to be said. The team picked by Ramsey was clearly the one the manager had in mind to face Poland. As he sat and wondered whether his England career was over, Moore could find only one trickle of consolation: 'Maybe the knockers will pick on somebody else now I'm out of the side.'

He still had his defenders. 'MOORE OUT – What the hell is Alf up to?' the back page of the *Daily Mirror* demanded to know. But a 7-0 thrashing of Austria silenced Ramsey's critics, if only temporarily. As Currie, Channon, Chivers and Clarke all claimed goals for England, it was inevitable that Ramsey was not going to break up a winning team, including the pairing of McFarland and Hunter, when Poland came to Wembley with a place in the World Cup on the line.

It was a calamitous night; the match when Hunter mistimed a crucial challenge and a Polish goalkeeper, derided as a clown by Brian Clough in a TV studio, defied England. With the game stuck at 1-1, Moore sat on the bench urging Ramsey to send on Kevin Hector to give England more attacking threat, but Ramsey delayed the decision until the final seconds. The captain had been ousted and the manager had lost his touch.

As ever, Moore was dignified at the end. When the final whistle blew, he sought out Hunter and wrapped a consoling arm around his shoulder, telling the Leeds man not to blame himself. There had been many contributors to England's downfall, not least Moore, as well as a fine Poland team that would go on to finish third in the tournament the following summer.

After three World Cups, starring in two of them as one of the game's outstanding defenders, and a record number of England appearances, Moore won his 108th, and last, cap when Italy came to Wembley in November 1973. He led out England for one final time.

A goal from Fabio Capello was not in the script, giving the *Azzurri* their first ever victory over England and confirming that changes to a declining side were long overdue. Nobody said anything to Moore but he knew his England days were over. Within six months, Ramsey had also gone. That glorious day in 1966 belonged to a sepia past.

18. Fulham

Just when it seemed Bobby Moore's career was ebbing away, Brian Clough stormed into his life like a tornado, sweeping him off his feet. It was an exhilarating feeling, a surge of energy, passion and vitality that Moore had not felt for a long while at West Ham.

Here was Clough, the most dynamic manager in the country, offering to revitalise Moore's career the way he had done with the veteran Dave Mackay. Hadn't Mackay won the First Division championship under Clough at Derby County in his thirties? Even if Moore's international career was fading, perhaps it was not too late to win that elusive league title and enjoy a glorious finale. Perhaps he might play in the European Cup for the first time.

Moore could feel the old hunger flowing when he took a call at home from Clough in the summer of 1973 asking if he was interested in meeting up. The contact was all highly dubious, of course, but when did Clough ever listen to the rules. For Moore, that rebelliousness only enhanced the attraction.

As Moore nursed the wounds of Chorzow, Clough had set the move in motion on, of all places, the genteel lawns of

Wimbledon. Nigel Clarke, Moore's ghost writer at the *Daily Mirror*, was walking through the All England Club when he heard a distinctly nasal, North East voice barking at him. He turned to see Clough walking among the Pimm's drinkers wearing football shorts and a blue England top, tennis shoes and no socks. 'I need to speak to you,' Clough said. 'I want to sign your mate. But I don't want you writing about it.' Clarke duly passed on Moore's home number.

Clough invited Moore to meet him at the Churchill Hotel in Portman Square. From the outset, Clough lived up to his reputation for brashness. When the maître d' said that Moore was dressed too casually to come into the dining room, Clough replied that if they were not allowed in he would never bring his team to stay in the hotel again. They were shown to their table.

They had barely sat down when Clough got to the point. 'I hear you want to win a championship medal,' he said. Then he started dangling other temptations. He said that he would pay Moore a fortune, almost doubling his wages. He told Moore that he could commute from Chigwell and stay in Derby one or two nights a week.

For every question Moore asked, Clough had an answer. Moore had reservations about how he would fit into the Derby team which had won the First Division in 1972 and just reached the European Cup semi-finals. Clough already had Roy McFarland, Moore's defensive partner with England, plus the most expensive defender in the country, Colin Todd. Still Clough would not give up.

When Moore hesitated, he was invited up to Derby, according to Kenny Lynch who says that he acted as chauffeur: 'Bobby rang me and said "Cloughie wants to see me tomorrow".

As soon as he said it I knew what was gonna come next – "will you come with me?" Bobby knew I was a really big friend of Cloughie. We used to go to the cricket together all the time. So we drove up to Derby and there was a practice match going on at the old ground. I told them to talk business but Cloughie insisted I stay.'

According to Lynch, Moore again expressed his doubts about how he would fit into the team. 'I'm glad you've invited me, Brian, but you've got McFarland and Todd. What are you going to do with me?'

Clough responded with persuasive flattery. 'I tell you what I'll do. I'll put you on the pitch and I'll get those two to come up here and watch and learn.'

'I looked at Bobby and he physically grew a foot,' Lynch recalls. 'I realised why Cloughie was such a great manager.' After all those years of Greenwood's reserve, it was not hard to see why Moore fell for Clough's passionate seduction.

Clough's next move was equally bold. Without warning, a few weeks into the 1973–4 season, he turned up at Upton Park with one of the Derby directors and demanded to speak to Greenwood. Shown to the manager's office, he pulled up a chair as if he owned the place. When Greenwood, a little taken aback, asked what he could do to help, Clough replied: 'Have you got any whisky?'

Uncomfortable with the tone of his visitor, but too diplomatic to protest, Greenwood poured a measure. Clough asked for some water. Greenwood told him there was some in the kitchen just outside. Clough disappeared and did not come back for another twenty minutes. 'I've been looking around the place,' Clough said. 'Isn't it lovely.' Greenwood subsequently discovered that Clough had sweet-talked one of the receptionists into opening up the directors' box so that he could have a snoop.

Taking his seat, whisky in hand, Clough got down to the business. 'I want to sign Bobby Moore and Trevor Brooking.'

'Impossible,' Greenwood replied.

Clough started throwing numbers. £100,000? 'Not for sale, Brian.' £200,000? 'We're not selling, Brian.' Clough would later leak that he had offered £400,000 for the pair.

Greenwood said he would take it up with the board, if only to get Clough out of his office. Then he made a few inquiries and discovered that not only had Moore been tapped up by Clough but the captain was eager to leave West Ham.

The good news for Moore was that the directors were tempted to sell an ageing player, especially for that money. The bad news was that Greenwood told them that he would resign if they did. It had been a woeful start to the season – West Ham would not win any of their first twelve games – and Greenwood feared a long, hard relegation battle if he let Moore and Brooking leave without securing replacements. Greenwood instructed the board to turn down the offer, but Clough was not going to give up that easily.

Willing to employ any method, however underhand, Clough raised the stakes by leaking the deal to the papers. The headlines screamed that a move was in the offing: 'MOORE WANTS A TRANSFER!'; 'BOBBY LOOKS FOR A GLORY CLUB!'; 'MOORE WILL GO TODAY!' It was typically bold by Clough but it backfired. When the papers dropped on 15 September suggesting that Moore's move to Derby was as good as done, Greenwood thought it a disgraceful attempt at manipulation. He promptly dropped his captain for the game that day at Manchester United, selecting nineteen-year-old

Kevin Lock in his place. There was also a public rebuke for Moore from Greenwood: 'I thought it would be better for the team if I left Bobby out following the unexpected adverse publicity this morning, which I thought was bad for morale.'

Attitudes hardened on the West Ham board. Selling Moore made business sense but Clough's brash methods had caused upset. Reg Pratt, the chairman, was scathing: 'We are not prepared to be pushed around by outside pressure. We like to think at West Ham that we are a club of principles, but you wonder how you can keep them in this day and age.'

Moore was stuck. He did not want to ask for a transfer – the penalty for that was losing an entitlement to 5 per cent of the transfer fee – and now West Ham were determined not to give him one. Worse still, all the publicity had proved counterproductive with Hammers fans disgruntled by his apparent eagerness to escape Upton Park.

When Moore returned to the team, it was to the grumbles of the fans in the Chicken Run. Moore's fan mail contained a mix of those begging him to stay and others expressing disappointment that their hero longed to get away.

Their dismay was nothing compared to Moore's own frustration. He would still be talking years later about his regrets that he never played for Clough, describing it in a newspaper column as 'one of the biggest disappointments of my life . . . I'm still haunted by dreams of Cloughie and what might have been'.

Clough was regretful, too. Long after the deal had collapsed, he bumped into Nigel Clarke: 'We'd have conquered the world if I'd signed your mate.' When, as manager of Nottingham Forest, Clough encountered Moore some years later, he confirmed his eccentric appeal by giving Moore a package. 'Just a little something for Tina,' he said. Inside was a tablecloth made of Nottingham lace and a handwritten note with a heartfelt message: 'It was a tragedy we could never get together.'

Except it was and it wasn't. Just a few weeks after the proposed transfer collapsed in September 1973, Clough left Derby County, resigning after the umpteenth bust-up with the chairman. Moore's time working under Clough would have been very brief. He might have won that elusive championship medal given that Derby were champions under Dave Mackay, Clough's successor, in 1974–5. We will never know. By then, Moore had managed to secure his move away from West Ham but he would not be chasing a league title.

Inevitably there was one last squabble over money before Greenwood and Moore finally went their separate ways. The two men would part with a handshake but Moore's good manners masked a burning sense of betrayal.

When Greenwood called the captain into his office at the end of February 1974 to say that he could leave before the end of the transfer window the following month, he added that there would be a fee of £50,000 for the buying club. 'That's £25,000 for West Ham and £25,000 to you. Not a bad handshake,' Greenwood reasoned.

Yet Moore was adamant that he had been promised that he could leave for nothing, maximising his own chances to make money. He demanded a free transfer. The club refused. Moore seethed. After all the years of toil at a club which had not won an honour in nine seasons, Moore regarded it as the final insult. Six months earlier, Clough had been ready to pay a six-figure sum for the England captain. Now West Ham were trying to deprive him of a windfall so they could scrape some cash out of the deal.

West Ham could have made much more by accepting Derby's offer but Greenwood had wanted to keep his squad intact at the time. By early 1974 relegation was no longer such a danger. It sounds like sacrilege but West Ham had started to move on without their captain. Injured against Hereford in an FA Cup tie on 5 January, twisting his knee ligaments and forced to come off after thirty minutes, Moore had been missing for a couple of months and the team had moved up the table with Mick McGiven in the number six shirt.

Trevor Brooking does not want to say that West Ham were better off without Moore, but it sounds rather close to that conclusion when he remarks: 'This sounds terrible but, those latter days with Bobby in the team, we never had the balance of the players. Goalkeeping and centre-half was a big problem because Bobby wasn't great in the air and we never really had the dominant centre-half or keeper that came for the ball. We lacked an aerial presence.'

When Moore returned to fitness, he was kept in the reserves by Greenwood. On 9 March he pulled on the claret and blue to face Plymouth Argyle reserves in front of a tiny crowd at Upton Park in the Football Combination. That cup tie against Hereford proved Moore's 642nd and last first-team match for West Ham.

As word spread that Moore was up for sale, Stoke and Leicester expressed interest from the First Division. Norwich City, where John Bond was manager, inquired but Moore's pay demands were too high. Moore hoped that Malcolm Allison might make a move as manager of Crystal Palace, reuniting old friends, but the call never came.

He was close at one point to signing for Portsmouth, and had agreed terms. They would allow Moore to commute from

Essex, with Moore insistent that he wanted to operate from a London base because of his business interests and particularly because he had just built a new mansion.

For the Moores to build their own dream house was a giant leap for a footballer. This was the original Beckingham Palace. The neo-Georgian Moorlands still stands as one of the more tasteful on Stradbroke Drive, a street of conspicuous consumption in Chigwell. If you were to imagine a row of footballers' houses, it would be something like this leafy avenue of garish mansions with high walls, security gates and fleets of expensive cars on every drive.

Moore's new home inevitably attracted media fascination. The *Daily Mail* ran a feature on the 'super pad for superstar Bobby Moore'. Tina had designed it down to the spiral staircase and the drive-in porch so that she and Bobby could glide from car to house without their hair or immaculate clothes getting damp. 'It was so tidy you were afraid of sitting down,' one friend says. Coffee-table books were always fanned out in perfect symmetry, cushions always plumped, kids' toys stacked away. Moore would practically follow guests around, fastidiously tidying the ring-pulls into beer cans.

It was here where the Moores hosted long Sunday lunches when Bobby would offer to fetch guests a drink and bring back a crate. The bar in one corner of the living room was his pride and joy, as well stocked as any pub. In Moore's latter days at West Ham, Terry Creasy and a friend ended up at Moorlands on what became a mammoth bender. Moore rang Creasy the next day, not with a hangover but in high excitement. 'I had to do it. I've just counted up how many cans we got through,' Moore said. 'Go on, have a guess.' Creasy didn't get close to the answer of 150. They had drunk almost twenty pints per man.

A framed photograph hung on the wall above the bar signed 'to my dear friend Bobby Moore, Francis Albert Sinatra'. The house was built at a cost of more than £80,000, and that was one good reason why Moore had railed against West Ham for what he believed were broken promises over his transfer. He had an expensive lifestyle.

In the end, it was Fulham who stepped in. The chance to stay in London clinched the deal. It would mean dropping down a division so Alec Stock, the Fulham manager, despatched Alan Mullery, Moore's England team-mate over many years, to sell the delights of Craven Cottage. Mullery arrived at West Ham in a taxi and told his friend: 'If you want to spend the next two or three years having fun then come to Fulham. If you don't then I'm buggering off.'

The deal was done and, before West Ham's home game against Coventry City, Moore walked out on to the pitch at Upton Park not in kit but in casual garb, a dazzlingly patterned V-neck jumper and lengthening curly hair, to wave goodbye to the fans. With a handshake on the pitch and a smile for the cameras, he showed a warmth to Greenwood that he certainly did not feel inside. Moore's respect for his manager, and the club he had served for so long, had been shaken by that last contractual wrangle.

Eight years after he had come so close to joining Spurs, and only months after his dreams of playing for Clough had been dashed, Moore drove away from Upton Park for the last time and headed west to Fulham. 'Bobby didn't take much persuading,' Mullery says. 'I think he'd always had a soft spot for Fulham.'

Moore had grown up admiring Johnny Haynes and revelled in playing with Fulham's most legendary player in the 1962

World Cup finals. Like West Ham, Fulham had the reputation as a traditional family club. 'He was up for the move,' Mullery says, 'though after the first game I think he wanted to change his mind.'

The crowd swelled to 18,114, more than double the usual number. At homely Craven Cottage there was a buzz at the prospect of watching the great Bobby Moore. The streets were crammed, the queues at the turnstiles forming long snakes as, just a few days after leaving West Ham, Moore pulled on the white of Fulham for the first time.

Moore felt his own tingle of anticipation, the thrill of a new beginning as he ran out to face Middlesbrough, though the good vibes did not last long. Managed by Moore's old defensive partner Jack Charlton, Middlesbrough were tough opponents. With a young Graeme Souness in midfield and Alan Foggon up front chasing long balls over the top, Moore's debut was a nightmare. After the fourth Middlesbrough goal had gone in, he turned ruefully to Mullery. 'Does the goalkeeper ever use his hands?'

'Bobby was a great reader of the game, that's what he relied on, but in the Second Division, they were hammering balls up to centre-forwards over the top to chase. And he was never good in the air,' Mullery says. It was a sobering start but Moore's three and a bit seasons at Fulham mostly proved a joy.

He came closer to a trophy than he had managed in a long while at West Ham. In the 1974–5 season, Fulham embarked on a giddy FA Cup run which took in a record eleven matches, including an epic fourth-round tie against Clough's Nottingham Forest. The scorelines read like binary code – 0-0, 1-1, 1-1 – as the two sides met four times in fourteen gruelling days. Eventually a 2-1 victory for Fulham in the fourth encounter propelled them on to a fifth-round tie at Everton where a giant was slain in front of 45,233 fans. Viv Busby scored the late winner for Fulham, a brilliant shot on the turn. He was dancing around in ecstasy when a familiar East End voice barked at him to stop and concentrate.

Carlisle United were beaten in the quarter-final and then Birmingham City knocked out in the semi-finals after a replay at Maine Road. John Mitchell scored deep into extra-time and legend has it that even Moore celebrated that one.

Fulham were going all the way to Wembley and, as fates would have it, the opponents were West Ham. 'You couldn't write as fiction his part in this one and hope to get it past a comic-book editor,' Frank McGhee wrote in the *Daily Mirror* of Moore's Wembley date with his former club.

The final pitched a distinctly mediocre West Ham against a lowly club in Fulham in the showpiece match of the season, but the country was gripped by the prospect of a fairytale as Moore returned to a Wembley final for the first time since 1966. 'England will be a deserted place this afternoon when thousands who couldn't buy tickets at any price switch on and pull the ring-pull of the first can of beer. The presence of one player perhaps explains why – Bobby Moore,' McGhee wrote.

It did prove a romantic tale, though the hero was not Moore but Alan Taylor. The twenty-one-year-old West Ham striker scored the game's two goals only months after signing from Rochdale. It was a good story, but not the one most of Fleet Street had hoped to write.

Moore still saw the bright side, all smiles as he went to collect his losers' medal. He gave Mullery a consoling hug as they walked down to the dressing room.

'All right, Al?' he said. 'It's been a good day.'

'But we lost,' Mullery replied.

'It's still been a good day,' Moore said. 'We were there.'

It would become even more enjoyable for Moore at Fulham when he was joined by Rodney Marsh and George Best in the summer of 1976, with Craven Cottage thrilled by the arrival of two of football's showmen. 'Pure showbiz,' Marsh recalls. 'The first dozen games we beat everybody, playing brilliant football.' The facts do not quite support the recollections but who was worrying about boring stuff like results?

For a time, Fulham were the country's glamour side, on and off the pitch. A 4-1 victory over Hereford Town is still a YouTube classic, featuring glorious showboating from Best and Marsh who, at one point, start tackling each other near the halfway line. For a free-kick on the edge of the box, Best scooped the ball up to Marsh to attempt a spectacular volley. In a time notable for worsening hooliganism and clogging defenders, Fulham managed to treat the game as though, above all, it was fun.

Marsh remembers less about the games than the race to have a shower and be first to the bar at the Duke of Wellington in Chelsea. He describes a scene, repeated on many evenings, of Best in one corner surrounded by women and Bobby Moore propping up one end of the bar, watching all the entertainment unfold with a wry smile, half a lager and a Campari chaser on the side. 'Just imagine, George Best at one end and Bobby Moore at the other and so much crumpet around,' Marsh says. 'It was like a showbiz tent. Wonderful times.

'On a Sunday morning we'd go to a little pub in Hampstead. In those days it didn't open till midday but the guv'nor would always open it early for Bobby. Smashing days. Proper drinking and all sorts of silly stuff.'

For Moore it was an enjoyable way to wind down a career, and his team-mates learned to chuckle at his little idiosyncrasies. Travelling down to an away game at Bristol City, Fulham had their own carriage. The players saw Moore having a chat with the steward and slipping him some cash. 'What's that about,' they asked. 'Never you mind,' he replied. They found out when they boarded the same train for the journey home. Moore reached down under his seat and pulled out a cold can of beer. There were another half dozen in his private supply.

Next morning, the sweatsuit was back on for his run though Moore was slowing down as the rest of the Fulham players discovered on a pre-season slog around Richmond Park. Never one for long distance, Moore dropped off the back of the squad and went missing. Alec Stock eventually found him walking in the wrong direction among the deer in the Royal Park.

In the midst of his Fulham adventure, Moore took up an offer to join the burgeoning football scene in America. Pelé and other big names were seeing out their careers in the well-paid, slow-paced comfort of the NASL (North American Soccer League). In the summer of 1976 Moore was tempted out for a long summer at the San Antonio Thunder where he played twenty-four matches, and also his final 'international' matches.

Recruited to play for Team America in the USA Bicentennial Cup – a tournament featuring Brazil, Italy, England and the hosts to celebrate 200 years of Independence – Moore pulled on the red of the United States in what Fifa would call unofficial games even though Brazil and Italy gave full caps. In front of 16,000 supporters in Philadelphia's JFK Stadium, Moore lined up against England but the presence of Pelé could not save Team America from a 3-1 defeat to two goals from Kevin Keegan and one from Gerry Francis.

Moore was tempted to stay on in America but Fulham wanted him back for one last season in England. It was notable for little other than the second dismissal of Moore's career in the most unlikely circumstances, sent off for dissent. Captaining Fulham in a League Cup tie against Bolton Wanderers, Moore exploded with uncharacteristic fury when Bolton equalised six minutes into injury time. Moore felt the referee, Kevin McNally had played far too long and said so, forcefully, to the official.

McNally dismissed Moore, a decision that sparked amazing scenes when the rest of the Fulham team followed Moore into the dressing room and refused to come out for extra-time. Only after pleas from the referee and two policemen, and Moore urging his team-mates to get on with the game, did they re-emerge to play out a scoreless additional half-hour.

The party was losing its fizz. Stock left as manager late in 1976, replaced by Bobby Campbell. The crowds electrified by Best and Marsh and Moore in the early months had started to dwindle. Best had become frustrated that the club had reneged on promises including a luxury flat to live in, and he was sent off in the midst of a kicking match at Southampton.

It was fun while it had lasted but, at thirty-six, Moore had seen enough. The final match of his career came on 14 May 1977 at Blackburn Rovers. Fulham took a big travelling army to watch Moore in his last game, with friends and family including Doss swelling the numbers. A special train left Euston bound for the north.

Moore ran out to a guard of honour from the players from

both clubs to be presented with a cut-glass memento. With neat symmetry, it was his 1,000th first-class game. A nice round number before he faced up to the rest of his life.

Retirement for sportsmen is said to feel a little like death; all that buzz of attention, fame, adrenalin giving way to a great void of nothingness. Moore did not dread it. He knew the end was coming and, psychologically, was well prepared. What he had not anticipated was that he would conclude his long and glorious career mired in debt.

19. The Worst Businessman

To reach the site of the old Woolston Hall, you turn off the A113 just outside Chigwell and follow the signs to the gym club and the driving range. There, at the end of a tree-lined drive, you come to Mooro's restaurant. The place is billed as 'a homage to former owners of the original Woolston Manor House, Bobby Moore & Sir Sean Connery', but you suspect Moore might weep at what his grand vision has become.

Inside is an American-style diner where, on a quiet weekday, a solitary family sits in a booth munching buffalo wings and chicken burgers. There are a few replica football shirts on the wall. That familiar photograph of Bobby Moore clutching the Jules Rimet Trophy fills the lobby.

It feels like a theme restaurant with no theme, but then the association of Woolston Hall and Moore always was disastrous. The property was twice set on fire, the flamingos were eaten alive and two of Moore's business partners were shot at. Moore escaped with his limbs intact but he lost his fortune, and a lot more besides.

Woolston Hall was the reason that Moore concluded his football career fretting about how to pay the bills, apologising to Tina that he could not afford champagne dinners, even wondering whether to sell the personalised splendour of Moorlands in Stradbroke Drive.

It seems unfathomable that he should end up in such dire straits. No English footballer had been more intent on ensuring that he would be made for life in retirement; no footballer of the era had more opportunity to give himself that luxury. Moore had always preached that football was a short career and, when it ended, he wanted to make sure that he was financially independent. He wanted to be set for life.

Cruising along in his Daimler, he would listen to his hero Frank Sinatra on the tape recorder, singing along to the soundtrack of the musical *High Society*. 'The song says "Who wants to be a millionaire?" Well I do,' Moore said.

It should have been a realistic ambition for the country's greatest sporting icon. The problem is summed up bluntly by Jimmy Tarbuck as he sits in a golf club in slacks and patterned jumper talking about his old friend: 'Bobby was so very honourable but he was so naïve and the worst businessman.' And there is emphasis on 'worst'.

It was not just the bad ventures that Moore locked himself into but the one he turned down. It is no exaggeration to say that Moore's life might have taken a different course had he made a better business decision in the heady months after the 1966 final. The day he spurned an offer to join the IMG stable cost him an inestimable amount of money and a luxurious retirement.

The invitation was from Mark McCormack, an American lawyer who was quick to spot the endorsement potential for leading sports stars in the television age. Founded in 1960, his company, IMG, had quickly become the leader in the field in turning sports stars into money-making corporations. You take a top golfer and you make him Arnold Palmer Inc. The American businessman was offering to do the same for England's World Cup-winning skipper.

IMG was looking to move into football and Moore – revered, handsome Moore – was the obvious target as the captain, the golden boy, the marketing man's dream. IMG said they would take Moore global, and make him a face of big business.

They also approached Geoff Hurst, the hat-trick hero of Wembley. Hurst was flattered but turned down the chance. 'It didn't appeal to me because they wanted 20 per cent of my income before they started making money for you,' Hurst says. 'I wasn't earning fortunes at West Ham and that seemed a lot to be handing over.' But it was Moore that IMG really wanted.

Tarbuck was consulted by Moore over the approach. He instantly saw the long-term potential and a whole new world far bigger than running a sports shop or penning a column in *Shoot!*. Tarbuck told Moore to grab the chance with both hands.

'I know they wanted to take his earnings, 15 per cent or whatever it was, but they promised "we'll promote you",' Tarbuck says. 'And Mooro was already as big as anybody in the footballing world, Pelé, Beckenbauer, you name it.

'Bobby listened to the wrong people. It was Freddie Harrison. I'll name him and take the flak for that. Freddie Harrison said "what do you want to be giving away 15 per cent of everything?". So they did a leather business, beautiful gear, but it earned two bob.

'One of his biggest mistakes was not going with McCormack

and that's the God's honest truth. It could have changed his life, put him on a different level. He had the fame and everything else but he ended up a comparatively poor man considering his status.'

Morris Keston, another friend of Moore's who briefly became a business partner, was also a strong advocate of going with IMG. He spent a night at Annabel's in the West End trying to persuade Moore to drop Jack Turner, the Mr Ten Per Cent who could bring in a *Titbits* column, in favour of the American giant.

'This is Mark McCormack, not some fly-by-night,' Keston told Moore. 'He'll make you so much money you won't even care what West Ham pay you.'

Moore was resolute, saying that Turner took only 10 per cent of commercial deals. IMG wanted a bigger slice of everything. 'I don't mind McCormack having a large chunk of what he brings in but I can't let him have a percentage of my West Ham salary,' Moore insisted.

And so the invitation to join Palmer, Nicklaus, Björn Borg and countless other global stars in the IMG stable was rejected. And instead Moore decided to chance his arm as a fashion designer, running a country club and peddling bespoke shirts. As Hunter Davies wrote in his magnificent book *The Glory Game* in 1972, 'Everyone seemed to be a business partner of Bobby Moore.' But not one of them seemed to be making any money out of it. Moore's rejection of IMG and the chance to build a corporate profile became more short-sighted with each business failure. And there were quite a few.

Typical was the leather coats business set up with Freddie Harrison and Keston, two friends who had experience in the rag trade. Moore fancied himself as a fashion guru, making his own sketches of coat designs. By 1969, they were knocking out eighty garments a week, £60 each to high-end clientele and selling through Austin Reed, Liberty, Harrods, Selfridges and a showroom in Percy Street off the Tottenham Court Road. Half the First Division seemed to be clad in Bobby Moore suede leather.

But Keston pulled out because of conflicts with Harrison and soon circumstances turned against Moore. Harrison's ambitions led him to set up a bigger plant in Essex just as the government declared the three-day week to conserve electricity. As production stalled, Harrison took the manufacturing to Cyprus only for that to coincide with Turkey's invasion of the northern part of the island, with hundreds of leather coats stuck in the factory.

Moore had a lovely coat to show for it, but he was also £5,000 worse off by the time the business crashed. Bobby Moore Jewellery? That was another flop. Bobby Moore Shirts and Ties? Thousands of pounds were lost as the business failed to keep up with orders.

But it was the failure of Woolston Hall which dwarfed them all.

The best that can be said is that it must have seemed like a good idea at the time. A country club with Moore and Sean Connery as two of the owners; England's World Cup icon and 007 himself. You can see the attraction.

Moore imagined a luxurious venue just down the road from his new home in Stradbroke Drive. He could swing down for a round of golf, a few beers with the chaps and perhaps a sauna and manicure on weekends. Business and pleasure could combine in a world of luxury and affluence.

The upmarket club in a restored old manor house would feature a swimming pool, tennis courts, hairdresser, sauna, golf driving range and cocktail bars. With Chigwell home to an expanding set of nouveau riches, there seemed a sound business logic.

The old manor house was bought using a £125,000 loan with the Dunbar Bank arranged by Connery, who was one of the bank's founders, but the venture was unravelling before it had even started. One of six initial investors, an Essex publican called Kenny Bird, was ousted after a row. That removed the only director who knew anything about the catering and licensing industry.

Then matters turned sinister. In early March 1972, when Woolston Hall was being developed, a small fire had to be extinguished. An empty paraffin can was found nearby. A few weeks later, just a month before the scheduled grand opening, the arsonist returned and the ancient hall, and some of its lavish fittings, went up in flames. The damage was not devastating, but more money had to be poured in for repairs. The opening had to be delayed.

This was just the start of an unfolding nightmare. Del Simmons, a car dealer, was an associate of Connery's through golf tournaments. He was also involved in a number of nightclubs including the Capabana in Ilford where, according to one biography 'he enterprisingly employed a bogus French accent in his time as a croupier'.

Michael Wade was the son of Lou Wade, a rich and flamboyant purveyor of women's clothes who owned a large home on Stradbroke Drive. Lou was the type of garrulous, larger than life character so beloved by Moore, and accompanied West Ham and England on many trips, spending plenty of time with the captain at the bar. Lou and Michael Wade were partners in the Woolston Hall business, as was Simmons – all well known to each other in Chigwell.

When Michael Wade sat in Simmons's lounge one evening in Manor Road watching a western, a car pulled up outside. A shotgun blast shattered the front window, pellets striking the chandelier and shattering glass across the lounge. Simmons and Wade dived for cover.

The story would take some prising out of Simmons but it appeared that he, or one of his cars, had been caught up in an armed robbery. He had given evidence against some bad men. They had gone to prison. Now they were out of jail and seeking vengeance. 'Del was a grass,' as one of Moore's friends puts it, bluntly.

The directors debated Simmons's role and decided that he brought too much notoriety, perhaps even outright danger. Simmons went, but the gangsters didn't. Threatening phone calls were made to several of the directors warning that Simmons's association with Woolston Hall could mean reprisals for all of them.

Gossip swept through the Chigwell set and the £100 annual memberships became harder to shift. The grand opening kept being put back, causing some members to withdraw. When eventually they cut the ribbon, Moore and Connery were the star attractions as guests quaffed free champagne and feasted on caviar. 'It was the land of plenty on the opening night,' Tina Moore says. 'I'm not sure it ever recovered.'

The founders had been so extravagant that the business never stood a chance. It was a palace of luxury. They had pumped in thousands to fill it with the best silver service bought from Bond Street. Someone had the bright idea that the lake should contain flamingos, imported at vast expense. A diving board for the pool was shipped over from the United States.

Within weeks, the silver had vanished into the night, reputedly pilfered; the flamingos were decimated by local foxes; the diving board turned out to be too long and was declared a health hazard. The restaurant had more waiters than diners.

The grand project did not take long to collapse in ruin. By the time it folded, the damage was mindboggling; trading losses of £242,000, a total debt estimated at £533,527.

Quite how this became Moore's problem more than any of the other directors' remains hard to trace. He, along with Connery, had resigned as a director in 1973 but continued to be a shareholder. The problem, Tina says, was not the initial investment of £5,000 but a complicated system of guarantees and liabilities. Moore was ensnared in a complex web of agreements and became the big loser in subsequent litigation as creditors chased after their money. 'One by one they all pulled out and left Bobby to cope with it,' Tina says.

She paints the picture of a man who enjoyed setting up the business, with his taste for finery, but never had a proper idea what he was getting into. He certainly would not have read the small print on any undertakings.

In business dealings, particularly if there was a need for confrontation, Moore used to ask Tina to intervene. 'You're better at handling these things than me,' he would say. All his worldliness seemed to evaporate when it came to commerce.

Unsure how Moore came to be left with the worst of the liabilities, Tina is certain that extracting himself from the horrors of Woolston Hall cost the best part of £100,000. Even for the wealthy captain of England, that was a fortune. 'It felt like millions in those days,' Tina says. 'He was the only one who had to pay and I don't know why. I just know it was a terrible thing. It took years by the time he finished paying it back.'

The collapse forced Moore to sell his holiday home in Marbella where he enjoyed hanging out with Tarbuck and other celebrity friends. He even countenanced selling Moorlands. He discussed it with Tina but, in the end, his pride could not bear it and they muddled on. Tina went back to work, taking a job in the beauty department at Harrods, but the financial worries put a strain on their marriage.

Moore took Tina for dinner one night and told her that he could not pay for the luxuries they both loved so much. 'He bought a bottle of champagne and said that's what you should drink all your life but I can't afford it any more,' Tina says. 'I think it all had an impact on us as a couple. It would when you think about it.'

You might think the disaster of Woolston Hall would put Moore off business but he kept on speculating, losing – and finding trouble.

He went into the pub game, investing in five, including the Black Bull in Stratford, which was reopened as Mooro's. But either someone had it in for Moore or he was cursed with terrible luck.

Four days before Mooro's was due to open in November 1976, someone broke through the back door, poured petrol over the seats and chucked a match on their way out. Damage was limited to furniture and fittings thanks to the hard, sweaty graft of twenty firemen, but Moore told the *Daily Mirror* that he was 'sickened' to have been targeted again.

'I suppose that's the price you pay for being in the public eye.

Some people love you, but others want to get at you,' he said. But if Woolston's problems could be put down to Simmons' dubious past, what was the explanation for this attack? Why target England's hero? Why, as Jeff Powell wrote, did Moore appear to have his own 'personal arsonist'?

'I guess I must be jinxed,' Moore reflected, also noting that his clothing warehouse in Plaistow had been broken into, and set alight, and his clothing shop in Marylebone was also ransacked. Unlucky? Or bad connections? 'Perhaps I'm naïve but Bobby was beyond reproach as far as I know,' Tina says. 'I would lay my life on that. Bobby was never involved in anything seedy at all and he certainly didn't do any dirty deeds. That would be beyond his mental capacity. I don't know, possibly it was a case of the wrong people, wrong time.'

For a man who was so image-conscious, Moore had made some strange choices. Many footballers bought pubs – but of all the pubs in all the world, one of those in the Moore portfolio was the Blind Beggar in Whitechapel.

It was the notorious boozer where, on the evening of 9 March 1966, as Moore chased around in defence for West Ham in the first leg of the League Cup final against West Bromwich Albion, Ronnie Kray entered holding a Luger 9mm automatic, his favourite pistol. He used it to shoot George Cornell, a member of the rival Richardson Gang, in the forehead.

As Kray walked out leaving Cornell dead on the floor, legend has it that the record player stuck on constant loop playing the Walker Brothers' 'The Sun Ain't Gonna Shine Anymore'. It is a macabre scene that still endures in gangster folklore.

One of the witnesses to the killing was Patsy Quill, the landlord. Questioned by police, he was adamant that he hadn't seen anything. For many months, the barmaid said the same after she and Quill had received a visit from 'Red-faced' Tommy Plumley, a Kray hoodlum, who advised that if they knew what was good for them they would keep very quiet.

The police knew who the killer was within hours but it took three years to bring Kray to justice. With astonishing bravery, the barmaid changed her story to testify that she had, indeed, seen Kray walk into the pub that night with a gun in his hand. The moment she took to the witness stand was when Kray knew that he would spend the rest of his life behind bars.

It seems a strange choice by Moore to have followed the Woolston Hall debacle by taking a stake in the pub where they joked for years that the house drink was a Luger and lime. He took a share with Jimmy Quill, Patsy's brother.

The pair also took over the Three Horseshoes in Spellbrook, Woody's in Chigwell and the Hope in Southend. The Salmon and Ball was reopened as Tipples, a bold attempt to give Bethnal Green its first cocktail bar, and then there was Mooro's which did open once they had repaired the fire damage.

Moore's business partnerships have inevitably raised questions about links with East End criminality. His friends insist that any connections with gangsters were, like the Simmons shooting, by extension or forced upon him by fame.

As West Ham and England captain, a man of such high profile who never strayed far from his East End roots, everyone wanted a little piece of Moore, and that included the gangster crew he would occasionally see at boxing nights and in the pubs and clubs. He met the Krays on the social scene because the brothers wanted to be seen in his company.

Kenny Lynch knew all the faces from his long years as an entertainer. 'Oh yeah, proper East End boys would come over to see him, when he came down to my club. The [Kray] twins would come in all the time. Bobby was idolised by all sorts. He was such a good-looking bastard.'

Moore never sought to distance himself from his background. His partnership with Quill only strengthened his East End connections. 'We used to go to all sorts of places you'd never expect to find the England captain,' Nigel Clarke, his ghost writer on the *Daily Mirror*, says. 'Bob loved hanging around his own kind like at the Globe in Bethnal Green. Or we'd go to a pub owned by Terry Creasy in Plaistow, the Britannia.'

Clarke tells of going to meet Bobby in the East End one day to write a column and being ushered into the sort of boozer where the music stops when a stranger walks in. Bobby Ramsey, a fully-fledged associate of the Krays, was in there. 'Just keep your head down, Nige,' Moore said. 'You'll be fine.'

Moore's associations never seem to have gone beyond the social, but the arson attack on Mooro's remains unexplained. Someone who did not like Moore? Turf war? An enemy of Quill's? Jimmy Quill, sadly, declined to talk.

Tina says that Quill was frustrated that Moore did not put more into the running of the pubs than the very occasional appearance. He hated the aggravation and the confrontation involved. The certainty he had taken into those pay negotiations as a player did not transfer into the business world.

Moore's interest was purely in standing on the customers' side of the bar. Harry Redknapp used to drink with Moore in the Blind Beggar and knew the Quills well. Most of the West Ham footballers did. 'Jimmy and Patsy Quill were good friends,' Redknapp says. 'Patsy's gone, sadly, but Jimmy is a great guy, really. An East End boy but smart. Bobby loved Jimmy's company, his group of mates. We had some nights in those pubs, I can tell you.

'We went in one night, me, Frank Lampard senior and Bobby into the Blind Beggar after an away game somewhere. Bobby said "do you fancy a quick lager?" before we met our wives. We're in the Blind Beggar, I went to the toilet and this guy followed me in. If you could draw a villain, it was him. Big geezer, black coat, scar down his face, jet black hair. He went "tell your mate Bobby Moore, I'll cut him from here to here." And he drew his finger across his throat.

'What for? "Because he thinks he's a film star". I said "he ain't done nothing, what's he done?" This big guy just says "I don't like him". We left the pub and next morning I rang Jimmy up and told him what had gone on. Jimmy says "oh, yeah, I know him, Mickey something or other". Mickey went in that night, Jimmy had a chat out the back of the place – and he never went in that pub again.

'In them days in the Blind Beggar on a Saturday night, all young girls and fellas, music going, a great East End pub, I've seen a fight break out and Jimmy come over the bar like Superman. Jimmy could handle himself, a real straight-up guy. Jimmy was the guv'nor. Bobby loved him.'

But the pubs did not fare too well either. Tina can't recall if they lost money but she knows that the profits did not add up to much. With those crushing debts from Woolston Hall, Moore could not afford to put his feet up and lounge around in the splendour of Stradbroke Drive in retirement.

20. Elton

The England striker Frank Worthington once said 'footballers are frustrated pop stars and pop stars are all frustrated footballers'. The remark certainly had a ring of truth in the case of Elton John.

Music made him but football was in the blood through his uncle Roy Dwight, best known for a broken leg while playing for Nottingham Forest in the 1959 FA Cup final. Young Reg Dwight inherited a passion for the game. In the seventies, as Elton John, he had taken to accompanying the England team on foreign trips, enjoying the chance to mix with his heroes. The players were thrilled as the piano man treated them to private, late-night gigs in the bars of various European hotels.

In the summer of 1976, as 'Don't Go Breaking My Heart', his duet with Kiki Dee, topped both the American and British charts, John bought Watford FC. As a boy from Pinner, he had stood on the terraces, marvelling at the goalscoring exploits of Cliff Holton. Now, as the club's owner, he wanted to live the dream.

He had ambitions to take Watford flying up the league from the Fourth Division and he just needed a manager to do it. As an England fan, he could imagine no better candidate than Bobby Moore.

In the Hollywood version of the story, our hero would become a bright young manager, so successful at club level that he would go on to lead England, three lions on his blazer, like his mentors, Greenwood and Ramsey. His understanding of the game, so complete as a player, would underpin a brilliant coaching career, making him a statesman of the dugout as he had been on the pitch.

That was what John envisaged and Moore thought he had found his own saviour in the pop star. He needed work to stabilise his finances and John was willing to pay him extremely well to take over at Watford. The timing seemed perfect with John seeking a new manager just as Moore was finishing his playing career.

During Moore's final weeks at Fulham, the two men had met for a productive lunch and were on the brink of a deal. Jeff Powell splashed the story on the back page of the *Daily Mail* on 11 May 1977. It takes a juicy exclusive to give a Fourth Division club such prominence in a national newspaper but, as Powell wrote, this scoop featured 'the giant of international football' and 'the show business colossus'.

With unusual bullishness, Moore proclaimed that little Watford were bound for greatness: 'We are talking about emulating what Bill Shankly did at Liverpool and what Don Revie did at Leeds, building a great club from scratch. It is the biggest and most exciting challenge in football.'

Never mind that Watford were ranked seventy-fifth of England's ninety-two professional clubs. John had already shown his seriousness by offering a contract which would make Moore one of football's best-paid managers on £15,000 a year.

The story broke three days before Moore's farewell match at Blackburn. With typical neatness, Moore could retire after his 1,000th game and start a new career, a new life, the following week. There was just one problem. In all the giddiness of luring Moore, John had not told any of the other Watford directors about these clandestine talks. The first they knew about their prospective new manager was when they read it in the *Daily Mail*. And while John might have been the money behind Watford since his takeover a year earlier, the club was not a dictatorship.

Two directors, Muir Stratford and Geoff Smith, spoke as soon as the newspaper dropped and shared their mutual concerns. Then they contacted John, certain that Moore did not represent Watford's best hopes, and definitely not at that cost.

'When the story broke, we both got hold of Elton and said "are you sure that Bobby Moore is the man who will watch a reserve game on a freezing night in February?"' Stratford recalls. 'We were in the Fourth Division and we felt it was a job for someone with experience. Bobby Moore had never been a manager.

'I have no idea how Elton came to the idea other than Bobby was a past England captain and a big name. Elton didn't know much about football at the time. He had great enthusiasm but little knowledge about football in general. His inclination was to go to the top, a famous name, but Bobby would have been a personality manager. We felt strongly that we needed something different.'

John was taken aback by the opposition but agreed to seek further advice, and to consider the claims of the young manager being pushed by Stratford and Smith – a chap he had never heard of called Graham Taylor. Just thirty-two, the former Grimsby Town full-back had already achieved an impressive promotion with Lincoln City. He was no Bobby Moore in stature or global renown, but he had knowledge of lower leagues, a reputation as a highly organised coach. He also had admirers in high places.

When John sought the advice of his friend Don Revie, the England manager immediately threw Taylor's name at him. 'When Don Revie said "go for young Graham Taylor", that was an important moment for Watford and for us as directors,' Stratford says. 'It showed we knew what we were talking about.'

So as Moore waited for the phone to ring with confirmation of his new job, instead it was a home in Lincoln which was fielding calls. First Revie left a message for Taylor to say that he had just recommended him to Watford. Then John made contact to persuade Taylor that by dropping down a division he was really making an exciting leap forward. Taylor liked the pop star's ambition, just as Moore had done.

Taylor took the job and Watford never looked back. Their journey to the top was even more direct than some of their football. It was an extraordinary success story under Taylor, from the lowest tier to second place in the First Division, nestled between Liverpool and Manchester United. They went to Wembley and into Europe.

Meanwhile, Moore waited – and waited – for the call that never came. On holiday in Majorca in late May, he went for a run down the beach, picking up the English papers to read on his sun lounger. It was several weeks since he had shaken hands with John. When he turned to the sports pages, he stopped dead in shock.

There, in black and white, was a story that Watford had a

new manager. And it was not him. Tina saw the colour drain from her husband. 'He came back in with the paper and he looked grey,' she says. 'Bobby was lost for words.'

It was a blow to Moore on many levels; the shock of finding out through the media; the hole in his income; the broken promise. He had talked publicly about the Watford job, about his dreams and ambitions, so there was embarrassment, too.

When Moore spoke to friends, even years later, it was one of the few setbacks about which he would express dismay though he never once let out a public word of bitterness. When asked, he said only that Watford had a bright young manager whom he wished all the best.

'Bobby was always forgiving and accepting, in a way that I wasn't,' Tina says. 'Bobby liked Elton and he didn't like confrontation so he put on a brave face.' Even when John pulled up in a black limousine as Moore walked through London one day, Moore was full of pleasantries. He never brought up his sense of deep disappointment.

One version of the story features John sending Moore a £10,000 cheque to ease his conscience. 'Knowing Elton's generosity, that would not surprise me one iota,' Stratford says.

Either way, Moore was cut deep. The smooth transition that he had envisaged from one phase of life to another had been blown to smithereens, and in embarrassingly public circumstances. It would be another two and a half years before he would enter management and even then he would do so as tentatively as a man climbing into a steaming bath.

And so began the next life for Bobby Moore. It was harder than he can ever have imagined – though perhaps that is the problem. Perhaps he never did imagine it. Perhaps he simply believed that it would fall into place, and that management offers like Watford, or better, would fall into his lap.

It must have been a confusing period. On the one hand, he was still the legendary Bobby Moore. In October 1977, he flew first-class to New York as a personal guest of Pelé at the Brazilian icon's final match, when 75,000 crammed inside Giants Stadium. Moore rubbed shoulders with Muhammad Ali and Robert Redford at the post-match banquet, a star in a glittering galaxy, yet he returned to unemployment, and the enduring financial damage caused by Woolston Hall. He had the flash cars and the kids at private schools, but he was out of savings and the job offers were notable only for being so few.

Moore needed work. He needed football but football did not seem to want him. Moore had his own theory about that: 'There were one or two business things I wanted to do and maybe a lot of people felt that was turning your back on the game or might have been signs of disinterest.'

Those reservations that Watford's directors had expressed – was Moore, the World Cup winner, likely to watch a reserve game on a cold Friday night? – raised further doubts among hiring clubs. Ken Jones believes that Moore's stature was the biggest problem: 'I suspect people were afraid of him because he was such a big name in football. Directors were afraid of him. They didn't think they could deal with him. That was the main reason.'

There was also Moore's own reluctance to push himself. If the rest of football, like Watford, thought he was too grand for scouting trips, or too distracted by business interests, then he had to go and convince them otherwise. But he was never good at self-promotion. Polite charm, yes. He had endless supplies of that. But not actively selling himself.

Moore was not the only one of the World Cup winners to discover that a medal from 1966 brought no short cuts in management. Bobby Charlton remarked on a meritocracy at work, 'one which could leave you on the outside, however much fame you had won on the field'.

Geoff Hurst saw it, too. 'I let it be known that I wanted to stay in the game as a coach or manager. Sadly, this prospect didn't excite the game as much as I thought it would,' he wrote. Hurst began managerial life down at non-league Telford where his menial tasks included clambering up a ladder to paint the stand. His rapport with Greenwood did, however, bring coaching work with England, and ultimately led to a managerial stint at Chelsea. When Greenwood wanted an assistant, he turned to Hurst not Moore.

Jack Charlton fared the best, beginning a substantial career in the Second Division at Middlesbrough. But, unlike brother Bobby who fell into management almost reluctantly with Preston North End, Jack had made it clear among his many contacts that he was determined to stay in the game. He had a head buzzing with ideas after taking his coaching badges. He had been to Lilleshall on courses and circulated his name around the leagues.

Moore told friends that he wrote the only job application of his life in 1977 when he applied for the England vacancy following Don Revie's resignation. The FA did not bother to acknowledge his interest, or that of Jack Charlton who had also applied.

Moore had been ready to take on the challenge at Watford but, having lost that chance, football looked at him with suspicion. His fame raised questions about his desire and motivation. His numerous business interests sent out mixed messages.

Late in 1977, he sought to drum up interest via the media: 'This is a frustrating period in my life. I'm open to offers as a manager or a coach. That's what I want to do and that's where I feel I have something to offer. But I can't sit and wait forever. I must start earning again.'

With his financial troubles, he was prey to any idea that would make good money. He was even willing to pull his boots on at thirty-six if he could make a quick buck – or krone, as it turned out.

Even in Denmark they regard Herning as the boring back of beyond. A town of textiles and clothing factories, with a population of 30,000, it sits in the middle of the dreary flatlands of Jutland.

If Herning has a claim to fame it is that Bobby Moore finished his career in European football there, playing among the postmen and butchers of the Danish third division. It is a story told in the yellowing pages of the scrapbook in the refurbished clubhouse, a remarkable time when Moore came into their midst, a world champion among part-timers, a Gulliver in Lilliput.

In Herning, they tell fondly of the day that Moore tried a crossbar challenge and succeeded with ten in a row from the edge of the penalty area. How they gawped at his enduring quality on the ball. They reminisce affectionately about a man of modesty, a world champion who never acted as though little old Herning was beneath him. But mostly they marvel that Moore came there at all.

Of all the strange diversions in Moore's life, this was undoubtedly the most bizarre. Recruiting big-name English stars to make a splash is a long-established formula for overseas leagues, but whereas David Beckham got the LA Galaxy, a squillion-dollar contract, a home in West Hollywood and dinner parties with Tom Cruise, Moore was a freak show in Denmark's bottom division – and he even got the sack from that.

Helge Mølsted Sander reflects with pride that he tempted Moore out there in the first place. A businessman who became an MP and cabinet minister in Denmark, in 1978 Sander ran the little amateur football club Herning Fremad. He saw it as a vehicle to revolutionise Danish football.

The game was run by a national association which regarded professionalism as the root of all evil. Sander was determined to drag Danish football out of amateurism. What better way than to hire a foreign player. He needed a mercenary. He needed a star.

Sander knew he could not persuade a current international so he set his heart on someone just over the hill. 'I wanted Peter Lorimer but he was too expensive,' Sander recalls from Denmark. 'Then I had contact with Bobby Charlton. We had telephone contact twice but it wasn't possible.'

Then a journalist said that he knew a friend who knew a friend who could provide a number for Bobby Moore. Contact was made and Sander came to London. Naturally, he met Moore in a pub.

They talked and in February 1978 Moore flew to Denmark to conclude negotiations. The Danish newspapers got hold of the story and ran a big picture of Moore with Sander. Moore's smile hid many misgivings. To put Herning in perspective, the first team had played a pre-season friendly against a local butcher's company, with sausages as the prize.

Moore bought himself more time to think, but there were

no better alternatives, no jobs in management. Decent cash was on offer, though reports that Moore received £24,000 for his stay are wildly exaggerated. He was due 5,000 Danish kroner (just under £500 in 1978) per match and all expenses paid. There would be win bonuses of 800Kr and Moore also had a cut of sponsorship, though it was hardly enough to fill the Woolston-sized hole in his bank account.

Travelling by two flights, stopping off in Copenhagen, Moore arrived in April 1978, five days before his thirty-seventh birthday. Newspapers flocked to see the world champion in their midst. In terms of publicity, Sander got exactly what he wanted. The usual crowd of 500 swelled to 4,000 for Moore's debut. This was a national story being played out in little old Herning.

His first game finished with a 1-0 defeat to Holstebro, though Moore was exempt from criticism in the local paper. The scrapbook contains the report in *BT*: 'His debut ended in defeat but Bobby Moore was worth his weight in gold'.

Ekstra Bladet reported: 'He's a lot slower than when he was at his peak but in the Danish third division that does not matter. He has his vision and his technique is above perfect.'

If there was dissent, it echoed the famous story about the New York Cosmos executive who said of Franz Beckenbauer: 'Tell the Kraut to get his ass up front. We don't pay a million bucks for a guy to hang around in defence.'

In the same vein, Moore was asked why he wasn't playing further upfield to give full value for money. 'I'm a sweeper, I have played there all my life,' Moore said, doing his damnedest to retain his dignity in trying circumstances.

Off the pitch, Moore was popular enough. Ole Nielsen, general manager of Herning in Moore's time, happily recounts tales of picking up their new star from Billund airport where Moore would arrive with a pair of boots and a few gifts. He would bring pop records over for the other players because they were cheaper in London.

'He did not act like a star at all,' Nielsen says. 'We would speak about football and his achievements but he could talk about playing in the World Cup in the same way that he'd order a coffee. He was down to earth like that.'

But little problems soon developed off the pitch when the other players discovered that Moore would commute from Essex and join only one of the thrice-weekly training sessions. 'There was jealousy,' Nielsen says.

The biggest issue, hardly Moore's fault, was that the rest of the team were paralysed by his aura. Sander says: 'All the Herning players became 10 per cent worse and the team we played raised their level 10 per cent because everyone wanted to beat Herning and Bobby Moore. Our players were so nervous. Bobby tried to speak to them and to organise them. But they were worried about playing badly in front of him.'

What little enthusiasm Moore had for the project evaporated when his third match took him to Bornholm Island, in the Baltic Sea, to face Ronne. The pitch was a recreation ground with the crowd held back by rope. For Moore, the average crowd of 100 swelled to 900.

Now he was not even coming to one training session per week. 'Moore disappoints' was the headline after his fourth game, a defeat to Aabenraa. 'Herning Har Fiasko' reported *Jyll Posten* after a home defeat to Glostrup.

By the time Moore faced his ninth, and what would prove his final, game in Denmark, Herning were second bottom and his team-mates were blaming their world champion – not for bad play but for unbalancing the dressing room by being too damn famous.

The experiment was floundering and the final blow came against Aalborg Freja on 20 May. Herning were humiliated, a 5-0 defeat. As Moore changed afterwards in a silent dressing room, Sander approached him. 'It's over,' the owner said. Moore was being given the shove.

'I think that must have been the first time he was fired in his whole career,' Sander says. 'I felt really bad but the team was struggling and we couldn't afford him anymore.'

Moore rushed to catch the plane back to Copenhagen and then home to London, never to return. *Herning Folkeblad* reported on the break-up: 'It's been sad to watch Bobby Moore in his short stay in Danish football. From being a star, he's ended as a fiasco here. It's not his fault but you are better off playing among your equals and he was far too good.'

The end came as a relief to everyone. As soon as Moore departed, Herning won three games in succession and would only just miss promotion. The politics had been banished from the dressing room. But the business with Moore was not over.

There was an ugly fight over compensation, with Moore convinced that he had a contract until the middle of June and was owed 15,000Kr (around £1,500). Sander insisted that the deal was match by match.

No one can recall now how the squabble was settled, and it is a sign of Moore's financial troubles that he was considering legal action at all. Sander prefers to remember a decent man and an experiment that had worked as a 'publikumsmagnet' but little else.

'I still feel sad remembering how it finished,' he says. 'What is really sad is that after that short talk in Aalborg Stadium, we never spoke again. Of course Bobby was disappointed we had to let him go. But he could see that it didn't work. He had a feeling that it was his fault. It wasn't his fault. You can't change the world in a month or two.'

In Herning, they still have that scrapbook and the memories of when Bobby Moore came to play for their little club. They remain proud that they can claim a world champion, an icon, as one of their own. Moore's reflections on life in the Danish third division are unrecorded. He preferred to brush over this bizarre Scandinavian swansong as though it never happened.

21. Barely Managing

Bobby Moore once described management as a rat race best avoided. He talked of great players reduced to quivering bags of nerves, their health ruined by the strain as soon as they went into the dugout. 'Would I be a manager? There are times when I feel the answer is a certain "no". The strong men among managers are the exception, not the rule.' If only Moore had heeded his own advice.

Moore never was going to be one of those strong men he so admired like Matt Busby, Bill Nicholson or Bill Shankly, titans of the profession. Football had been his game, his area of expertise but, in several important ways, he was no more suited to the job of management than he was to running a country club.

The confrontations, the hard decisions, the need to stand up for himself did not come naturally, but Moore only learned that the hard way. He should have regarded his rejection by Watford as a lucky escape but twice he tried his luck in management and twice he failed.

Harry Redknapp shared part of the bruising journey and he shakes his head with bemusement as he recalls his life as

Moore's assistant manager down in the depths of non-league football. 'I'd sit there on a cold, rainy night playing against Aveley Town in front of a few hundred fans and think "how did I get into this?"' Redknapp says ruefully. 'Then I'd look at Bobby next to me and think "never mind me, how did *he* end up here?"'

How did England's World Cup-winning captain find himself flailing in a non-league dugout in charge of a ragbag squad of part-timers as manager of Oxford City? The simple answer is that Moore wanted work. Needed it, even. After eighteen months out of football following the Watford snub and the Herning debacle, Moore was ready to accept any job. Even this one.

He was ready to work out of a Portakabin at a club which was not even the biggest in Oxford. He was ready to coach part-time players in English football's sixth tier, in front of crowds you could almost count by hand.

Moore was the man for the big occasion, the guy whom Greenwood had said should play every game at Wembley. His first job in management was at the White House Ground, a 'stadium' nestled between family homes. It was a venue notable for the feature of St Matthew's Church in one corner, with windows protected by metal frames in case of wayward shots. These days it is a housing estate.

There had to be an attraction and it was a pay packet unheard of by non-league standards: a £5,000 signing-on fee, a salary of £14,000 a year plus a company Daimler. Most of Moore's counterparts were part-timers scratching around on £50 a week.

Given his financial predicament, Moore must have given thanks when Tony Rosser suddenly appeared from nowhere in December 1979. Rosser was the owner of a local newspaper group which had recently acquired Oxford City in the mis-guided belief that there was room for another professional club alongside Oxford United. In the city of dreaming spires, Rosser had a fantasy of City soaring up through the divisions.

Craving a big name to launch his doomed project, Rosser considered Malcolm Macdonald and Mike Summerbee as manager. But it was Moore he really wanted.

In terms of managerial qualifications, Moore had become one of the youngest holders of the full FA coaching badge, passing it by the age of twenty-one. He had attended coaching courses at Highbury and then extra sessions at the FA's centre in Lilleshall. But all that was a very long time ago.

'He hadn't actually any experience as a manager but, for the famously brilliant skipper of England's 1966 World Cup winning team, that surely wouldn't be a problem,' Rosser wrote in his memoirs. They were the familiar, naïve words of a football chairman about to part with his money.

Following countless meetings in which Rosser had to talk Moore into this peculiar job, England's World Cup-winning captain agreed to become Oxford City's one and only full-time member of staff. Speaking to local TV on the day of his appointment, Moore was typically grounded, saying that he had 'no divine right' to a bigger club just because of his playing achievements. 'It won't do me any harm to start my managerial career at the bottom,' he said.

But this was the bottom of the bottom. Moore was dropped straight into a relegation scrap in the Isthmian Premier league, leading a team which, according to one account of the club, had already suffered a 'catastrophic 5-1 reverse at Tooting & Mitcham'.

The crowd for Moore's debut in management was unprecedented for Oxford City – all 700 of them. The media massed to see England's World Cup winner take on Dulwich Hamlet. Alan Smith was in the opposing dugout, embarking on a managerial career that would take him into the top division with Crystal Palace.

Smith, a chartered surveyor who was coaching in his spare time, remembers using the presence of Moore to goad his team: 'I think I was a bit aggressive, telling my players we had to beat Bobby Moore's team. Bobby, of course, was very composed and polite.'

Moore's debut ended with a 2-1 defeat, and it didn't get any easier with one draw and four defeats in his first five games, including a 5-0 loss to Wycombe Wanderers on Boxing Day. The sight of Moore in the dugout meant that beating Oxford was a notable scalp, and many claimed it. He could hardly have started lower, yet still he managed to be relegated in his first season in management.

These must have been confusing times. Moore was working for a lowly non-league club, and struggling there, yet he told Rosser that he needed a six-week summer break to go and join Pelé, Sylvester Stallone and Michael Caine for the filming of *Escape to Victory*.

It was an enjoyable interlude as Moore flew to Hungary, especially because he had enticed his old mate Summerbee to take a part. 'Hey, Miguel, fancy being a film star?' Moore had asked. Summerbee was a willing drinking partner and, on the flight out to Budapest to start filming, they shared several bottles of Hungarian wine.

They had a riotous time off camera, and some fun on it, including Moore's role chipping the ball up to Pelé for the

Moore would enjoy many fun times in the company of George Best and Rodney Marsh at Fulham, and the football had some high points, too.

'It's still been a good day. We were there.' Moore consoles Alan Mullery after defeat to West Ham in the 1975 FA Cup final.

Moore signs an autograph for a young fan outside the sports shop opposite Upton Park, which was the starting point in an expanding commercial empire.

A partnership with Mike Summerbee took Moore into the shirt and tie business but, like many of his enterprises, it didn't last long.

An arson attack forced a delay to the opening of Mooro's in Stratford, but Rodney Marsh, Kenny Lynch, Frank Lampard Sr., Alan Ball, George Best and Malcolm Macdonald all joined the host once the fire damage had been repaired.

Bobby and Tina spent an estimated £100,000 on their dream house on Stradbroke Drive, Chigwell, including a drive-in porch. Moore had to contemplate selling up when he was hit by financial crisis.

In Denmark, they still marvel that England's World Cup-winning captain ended up playing alongside the part-timers of Herning Fremad in the third division.

Terry Brady, Captain John Colby and Hatch – more commonly known as Bobby Moore, Michael Caine and Sylvester Stallone – on the set of *Escape to Victory* in Hungary.

Elton John offered Moore the job of Watford manager but the musician was persuaded to change his mind, giving the position instead to Graham Taylor.

Moore's first managerial post was among the part-timers of Oxford City. He would quickly lead the team to relegation from English football's sixth tier.

As manager of Southend United, Moore was faced with numerous difficulties. Alongside director John Adams, he attempts to explain the club's dire financial predicament to fans.

(*Above*) In 1990, Moore left his position on the *Sunday Sport* to work for Capital Gold, travelling the country as a radio pundit.

(*Below*) Moore met Stephanie in the summer of 1979. They were married in December 1991 by which time he had been diagnosed with terminal cancer.

A shrine was built on the gates of Upton Park following Moore's death on 24 February 1993. One message read simply: 'I wanted to be like you.'

overhead kick which was the centre point of the highly improbable comeback by a team of POWs against the national team of the Wehrmacht. 'Bobby's character was called Terry Brady. Whenever we were in a crowd of people and I had to get his attention, I used to shout "Oi, Terry!"' Summerbee laughs. *Escape to Victory* may be the only time Moore was ever seen celebrating a goal, punching the air, leaping on the back of team-mates. It's fair to say that, when it came to acting, he was not a natural.

That long summer making friends with Caine, laughing at Stallone's Hollywood habits, was welcome levity before it was back to the struggles of Oxford. 'It was plain to see the poor chap was getting quite tense and was affected too by the feelings of the team,' Rosser noted.

The solution was a rescue call to Redknapp, Moore's old West Ham buddy, to come and help. Rosser agreed to reunite them, but only if Redknapp came as coach on a fraction of Moore's wages, and he would not have a company Daimler. Redknapp was given a bright green Ford Fiesta 950 he nicknamed Kermit.

Redknapp reflects ruefully on all the hours he would spend driving up to Oxford from his home in Bournemouth 'just to sit in that Portakabin waiting for Bobby to turn up really. The chairman wanted me in which was daft. We didn't have any full-time players.' Training was limited to Tuesday and Thursday nights after the players had finished work.

It is hard to tell if Redknapp is joking or not when he says that he took the job thinking it was Oxford United. The main attraction for him was working alongside Moore. 'He was Bobby Moore, wasn't he? He had that aura. But it was just an impossible situation he got into. We both did, really. We had no chance. We didn't know the league. We didn't know the players. We didn't have a clue.'

Redknapp is reluctant to admit it but he quickly became the more dominant member of the partnership. Rosser remarked that while Moore was 'a lovely, decent fellow', he was 'not a good motivator in the role of manager'. Presciently, given Redknapp's subsequent advance to the top of the profession, he noted that Redknapp was a much more effective coach and much more shrewd and knowledgeable in transfer dealings.

Barry Simmonds, the third and only other member of the staff, agrees that Redknapp had more impact. Now a top-level scout, Simmonds has a huge fondness for Moore. He talks of the way Moore never acted as though the non-league was beneath him; how Moore was unfailingly good-natured.

He laughs at the memory of eating sandwiches in the Portakabin with Moore, this icon of the English game. Simmonds was in awe of Moore the man but, like Rosser, he was more struck by the work of Redknapp. 'Bobby wasn't a great coach in the sense of putting a session on,' he says. 'He fed off Harry.'

Thanks to Redknapp's work rustling up a few players, Oxford stabilised and finished seventh in 1980–81 but the grand plan was dying, the club losing money as attendances fell to a few hundred. Rosser claims that he brought the union to an end in May 1981, ousting Redknapp and making Moore a consultant. 'Neither were happy with this. In fact Harry was plain angry,' he said. Redknapp insists he left of his own accord. Either way, the non-league's most expensive experiment had failed halfway through Moore's three-year contract.

Rosser had fond memories of Moore including a Christmas drinking session at the Blind Beggar with the former England captain 'crawling across the floor with enormous style' after a heavy session.

But perhaps the most poignant memory is one Simmonds has of Moore in in the spartan dressing room of the White Horse Ground after City's part-timers had been beaten once again. The crowd – a few hundred – had slipped away. The Oxford players were throwing their sports bags over their shoulders and heading off to the pub. Moore stood in the dressing room next to a pile of filthy kit heaped on the floor.

Out of habit, he started picking up the dirty socks and straightening them out. He put the muddy shorts neatly in a stack. He sorted through the shirts and scrunched up the used strapping and placed them in the bin. Old habits die hard, even when you have swapped a tumultuous night at Wembley for a game against Morris Motors in the Oxford Senior Cup.

Results picked up after Moore's departure but Rosser never did fulfil his dreams. His newspaper group folded a few years later and City were evicted.

A curious thing happened during Moore's spell at Oxford. The phone rang one day in the Portakabin in October 1980. On the line was John Bond, an old team-mate of Moore's from West Ham.

Bond brought news that he was about to resign as manager of Norwich City to leave for Manchester City. He was ringing to do his old friend Moore a favour, tipping him off about the imminent vacancy at Norwich.

Bond told Moore that he could smooth his way into the job,

running a solid club in the First Division. No more hanging around the dead men of the non-league. Simmons and Redknapp were there when Moore took the call.

Simmons recalls: 'Bob puts the phone down and we say, "well what was that about?" "Oh, do I want the Norwich City job as manager." Bob just said "no, we've taken this on at Oxford and we're going to see it through". I was taken aback.'

Simmonds took Moore's polite rejection of Bond's offer as a measure of the man's loyalty and dedication, a lesson in how to conduct yourself by not breaking a contract. If so, it was loyalty to a ludicrous degree.

Not even Rosser could have blamed Moore for jumping at the chance to swap a fixture against Walton & Hersham for the chance to take on Manchester United; the Oxfordshire Benevolent Cup for the First Division.

It is a bizarre episode. Was Moore really that committed to Oxford? Or, rather, was he reluctant to take on a big job? The question can be expanded to ask if Moore was ever cut out to be a manager.

His friends say that, just as he saved his best playing performances for the grandest stages, he needed to manage at the highest level. The case is made, vehemently, that the game betrayed him by not providing the opportunity.

They say that it was not Moore's fault his coaching career never took off but the failure of the big clubs, and the FA, to recognise his obvious gifts. Redknapp is insistent: 'I still believe that with the right support, he could have been the greatest manager in West Ham's history.'

Hadn't Moore read the game so beautifully as a player? Hadn't he worked under two of the greatest English managers in Greenwood and Ramsey? What better credentials than to be able to lay his World Cup winner's medal on the table? Yet the claims are based on little more than loyalty.

The argument might stand if Moore had demonstrated that he was totally committed to coaching as a career, but he never did. Malcolm Allison, back for a second spell as manager at Manchester City, had offered him a coaching job at Maine Road before Moore took the Oxford job. But Moore had declined it, reluctant to move north to be a number two.

Friends tried to push his coaching career when he was struggling to find work following his departure from Oxford. Kenny Lynch and Jimmy Tarbuck put in a word for Moore with their friend Lawrie McMenemy, the Southampton manager. McMenemy offered Moore a chance to coach the awe-struck members of the youth team, but he made only a fleeting visit and never went back. 'I got Bobby that job at Southampton but he didn't tell me he only went once,' Lynch recalls. 'I was really pissed off with him about that because he said he couldn't be bothered to go schlepping down there. I loved Bobby but he could be lazy.'

Management is not a job for the uncertain. To do it well requires obsessiveness; thousands of miles on the road every year scouting players, endless hours on the phone to contacts, many nights away from family. Redknapp reached the top because he never balked when faced with those demands.

Jimmy Armfield talked with Moore about coaching once and found his answers vague. Moore gave his England team-mate the impression that he was ambivalent about management. 'He was one of those people that when they ask "what was your profession?" even when you go for your old age pension, you say "professional footballer". Full stop. Even though it was thirty years ago. That's what Bob Moore was: professional footballer, full stop, nothing else. Coaching? He never really suggested that he'd like to do it.

'I always had a soft spot for Bob Moore but I don't think there was a great deal of depth to him and I think that was his problem after he finished playing. I'm forever telling people "you've got to think that one day you have to hang your boots up". We all have to finish one day, like we all have to die. You have to prepare for it.'

Temperamentally, Moore never seemed cut out for the job. An honest appraisal comes from Rodney Marsh, one of the most candid of Moore's friends, who saw him coach at close quarters. Marsh was running the Carolina Lightnin' in the North American Soccer League and, in the summer of 1983, Moore joined him for six months. He went principally as a coach but ended up pulling on his boots when the Lightnin' suffered a run of injuries. The matches feature in few records, with no reference on Wikipedia, but, aged forty-two, Moore played the final eight games of his career as a sweeper, winning four and losing four. Of Moore's work on the training ground, Marsh is unwavering: 'He would never have made a manager. Possibly never even made a top coach.'

The softness that made Moore such a great bloke to have around was his undoing. Moore had a preference for gentle persuasion, but it did not work on the training field. 'Bobby didn't like to say to somebody "what are you doing? Come on mark up!" He would go "have you thought about so and so?",' Marsh says.

It is the simplest summary of Moore's unsuitability for management, an air of detachment and his reluctance to confront. But those failings did not stop him trying again, with grim results.

Moore had lured Redknapp into the Oxford debacle, but the roles would be reversed. Anton Johnson, the Essex builder who was owner of Southend United, needed someone to run his club and he was implored by Redknapp, a friend, to 'give Bobby a chance'.

Oddly, Moore began as chief executive in August 1983 but became manager within six months. If Moore had doubts about the challenge they were flushed away by a reputed wage of £20,000 a year, one of the highest outside the top flight. His first job would be to oversee the club's relegation from the Third Division.

That was the unpromising start to a reign which lasted two years and two months, featuring Southend's lowest attendance in the bottom tier (2,103 fans), a finish of twentieth place in the Fourth Division and an investigation by the Fraud Squad into a fans' Christmas savings scheme because money had gone missing.

The club was in such a dire financial mess that the players were never certain they were going to be paid. There was no training ground so they wandered around, borrowing pitches from sports clubs and local companies. There is footage of Moore pulling aside a hole in the fence to take his players on to a park. It was a step up from Oxford, but not by much.

With few exceptions, the players loved Moore. He was full of warm encouragement. He was a legend yet behaved like one of the lads. He had no airs and graces. When Alan Ball became manager of Manchester City, the players used a stopwatch to time how long it would be before he mentioned that he was a

World Cup winner. It was a matter of seconds. With Moore they would have been waiting months, perhaps years, for him to bring up his own glories.

Alan Rogers was signed by Moore from Portsmouth on Ball's recommendation. Now running a hotel in Plymouth, Rogers recalls: 'Bobby seemed totally unaware of his level of fame. When I was signing, we arranged to meet at Waterloo station. He asked me how he would recognise me. I said, "Don't worry, Bob. You stand in the middle of Waterloo station and I think I'll recognise you".'

The players particularly loved it when Moore joined in training, though not the stomach-strengthening exercises that were still his speciality. For players at the bottom of the pile, it was a treat to watch Moore hit his unerring passes.

Glenn Pennyfather was one of the young Southend players Moore would sometimes take for extra training. 'I was just a young man looking up in awe at this man who had lifted the World Cup. He brought four, five of us back in for an afternoon session, dropping balls on to the chest of the centre-forward. We'd scuff it, or hit to the left or the right. He must have hit eighty to one hundred balls straight on the chest.'

Moore tried to pass on the lessons he had learned himself. He would tell the players about using their brains rather than rushing around. He told Pennyfather and the rest of the lads to slow the game down. He wanted them to be composed, in the style of their manager.

'For many of us, it was a privilege to play under Bobby but some of the senior players were old school, very cynical and in a rut with their own careers,' Pennyfather says. 'They thought they'd heard it all before. The club was sinking. It needed shaking up. Bobby wanted to change the style, to play nice football. When we couldn't make it happen, you could tell he was exasperated but he didn't want to show it.'

And that restraint was one of the biggest problems. When Moore did erupt after one defeat, it came as a shock to him as much as his players. Marching into the dressing room, furious at yet another poor performance, Moore hurled a plate of sandwiches across the dressing room, smashing it against the wall. There was a shower of egg and cress.

Instead of unleashing all his rage, Moore instantly checked himself, embarrassed by the loss of control. 'That's a shame,' he said. 'I was hungry.' The players smiled as Moore regained his familiar poise, but he was not going to succeed if he was inhibited.

Recruiting Malcolm Allison was not going to help either. Allison was down on his luck and, out of loyalty and compassion, Moore invited him down to Southend to help on the training ground. The brilliant, innovative coach was now a heavy-drinking eccentric.

Allison kept ordering the players to stop what they were doing and run on the spot 'to keep them on their toes'. Fine in the middle of the training session, but the players found it ludicrous when it happened in the middle of lunch or on the team bus.

'Freakin' disaster,' says Brian Dear of the decision to recruit Allison. Dear was running the Hope pub in Southend on behalf of Moore and Jimmy Quill and it was one of the venues, along with Southend's Spaghetti Club, that Moore and Allison would frequent for long lunches. It was after one of those sessions that Moore turned up late – and pissed – for a match.

Southend were preparing to face Newport County in an

evening fixture, but the manager had gone AWOL. Moore was missing and he hadn't left a team sheet. Pressed by the referee to submit a starting XI, Buster Footman, Southend's long-serving physio, had told the players to go with the same side as the previous week.

While the team wondered where on earth the manager had got to, Moore and Allison were boozing in the pub. Time slipped by. Kick-off got closer. Finally realising how late they were, the pissed duo screeched up to Roots Hall in a taxi with less than half an hour to kick-off.

The dressing-room door burst open and Moore walked in. It was obvious he was sozzled even before he slipped and almost fell into the team bath. As Allison lent against the wall in the shower room, eyes closed, head nodding, Moore tried to give a cohesive team talk through the alcoholic fog. The players say he was unusually exuberant that night.

Turning up drunk for a match was a one-off, they say, but the squad could hardly fail to notice how much Moore loved to drink. He would lead the boozing on the coach back after a match just as he had done in the old days at West Ham. The players knew that, in late 1983, Moore had been arrested for drink-driving for a second time because some of them had to give their manager lifts to work. Moore had driven up to Stamford to see his old mate Noel Cantwell who was opening a pub. They had plenty to chat about and, as one beer became half a dozen, Cantwell offered a bed for the night. Moore said he had to head south for a meeting the next morning and left.

He phoned Cantwell at 8 a.m. 'Oh, good, you're back'. 'Er, no,' Moore replied, 'I've just come out of the police station.' Reports from the time say that Biggleswade Magistrates fined

Moore £175 and banned him from driving for three years for a second offence and being twice the legal limit.

Being unable to drive inevitably restricted Moore's travelling whenever he needed to scout for players and check out opponents, further complicating a difficult job. He needed help and, just as he had recruited Redknapp to assist him at Oxford, the shrewdest move of his Southend tenure was to turn to another good friend, Frank Lampard.

His old West Ham team-mate arrived to play and coach for the 1985–6 season, with an instant uplift in fortunes. The signing of Richard Cadette from Leyton Orient was an immediate hit and Southend began the campaign with six wins and three draws in the first nine matches. They were chasing promotion. Perhaps Moore had found his managerial feet at last.

But results began to slip and the directors started to interfere. Vic Jobson, who had taken control of the club after Johnson had run into his legal difficulties, had great admiration for Moore the England hero, but could be heard complaining loudly about the decline in results and league standing. He was less than pleased when Moore said that he wanted to commute from London.

As Southend bumped along in a dire run which yielded just five wins out of twenty-one league games at the start of 1986, rifts at the top of the club began to show themselves openly. The directors started to voice their concerns so audibly that Moore was undermined in the eyes of his squad.

Alan Rogers remembers that the players became uncertain who was running the team: 'John Adams was vice-chairman. He'd done some coaching and he used to rip into Bobby about his team and tactics. We'd hear it when we went to fetch our wages from the club offices after training on a Friday. It was embarrassing.'

Moore, of course, declined to answer back and tell the directors to keep their nose out of team business. His acquiescence only made the situation worse.

'We were doing well then all of a sudden, whoosh, a bad run and it was Bobby's first time of not winning games. And though Vic Jobson meant well, he was starting to bully Bobby a bit,' Lampard says.

It all came to a head one Friday morning. Moore and Lampard were on the training pitch practising set pieces. Moore told Lampard that he had to see Jobson for a meeting, which turned out to be one of the most humiliating of his career.

'About an hour and a quarter later, Bobby still hadn't come out,' Lampard says. 'We'd finished the session when he finally appears. "You all right?" He said "I've got a problem. Vic doesn't want to play with these two players". I said "are you sure about this?" And Bobby was just non-committal.

'I could tell he was worried about it. I knew he'd give in. I went, "well, I'll leave it with you, Bob". I felt hurt by it a little bit, if I'm honest, because he could be a bit like that where he was too nice. He should have said "thanks for your advice, chairman, I'll bear it in mind but I've picked my team and that's how it is".

'Anyway, the next day these two boys didn't play. I went in on the Monday and said "Bob, I've had enough, mate. He's fucked us. I ain't having that". I thought "that's it I'm finished". I can't suffer people like that. I've always done my own thing, made my own mistakes. Bob said I should stay. But I went and he lasted about six more days.

'Bobby was a nice fellow and I think in some ways, not knocking him down, but sometimes he was too nice. That time he threw the sandwiches, I thought "about fucking time" because normally I'd be having a go at someone and Bobby would just listen to it. I'm not saying managers have got to be devious or horrible but Bobby was maybe too nice.'

Lampard departed and Moore resigned not long afterwards at the end of April 1986, saying that he would see out the season but not the remaining two years on his contract. 'I want to make it clear that there was no row,' Moore said to the media on his departure. 'We are parting on very friendly terms.'

Dave Webb was his replacement and the following season he took Southend out of the bottom division. According to Pennyfather: 'Dave Webb brought in a number of players who rolled their sleeves up. They would kick, bollock and bite to get things out of games. Bobby wasn't that person. He was an advocate of trying to play good football and, to be honest, with the standard of players he had, we weren't up to that.

'I don't think management came easily or naturally to him. He'd become exasperated. You could see his frustration but he didn't want to lose his temper so he kept it bottled up.' On the very rare occasions when he did let his anger out, Lampard says that 'it didn't really look like Bobby, it didn't have that same effect'.

No manager can survive when he is not free to pick his own team – or willing to stand up for the right to do so – though it was typical of Moore that he never held this interference against the directors. Other managers would have erupted; Moore agreed to stay on as a director and consultant to Southend for some years afterwards.

There is still a Bobby Moore lounge at Roots Hall which is

used by the directors on match day, but that, a broken plate and a couple of relegations on the lower rungs of English football, is all there is to show from his experiences in management. At forty-five, after those failed spells at Oxford and Southend, Bobby Moore walked away from football. He never came back.

22. Stephanie

If Bobby Moore's heart never seemed to be in football management, that may have been because it was being torn by domestic upheaval. Moore's home life was fracturing throughout his travails at Oxford and Southend, piling personal angst on top of his financial and professional worries.

The summer of 1979 was when he had first come across Stephanie. Moore's second wife talks now of the joy they would share; a blissful relationship from the day they met, and he acted with unusual impulsiveness. Romance bloomed at a party in Johannesburg where Moore was playing in a charity football game for a Bobby Charlton XI. An air stewardess, Stephanie had flown out with British Airways. As guests mingled and ageing footballers reminisced about the old days, an instant connection was made. Moore could conceal many of his emotions but not his attraction to the poised and confident woman who even shared a surname, Parlane-Moore. Both would come to talk of that first encounter in South Africa – eyes locking, hearts beating a little faster – as though reciting Mills and Boon.

She liked the kind, tall, handsome chap who seemed such a

gentleman – and he was persistent, too. When Stephanie told Moore that she was flying back to England in a couple of days via Nairobi, working at the front of the plane, he turned up with a ticket. He had booked himself into first class simply so that he could spend some more hours with her.

Moore flew straight on to Scandinavia where he joined in another invitation game involving Mike Summerbee. As soon as Moore arrived, his old friend noted a jauntiness in his step. 'What's happened to you?' Summerbee asked, as Moore beamed.

'I've met someone.'

'What d'you mean, you've met someone?'

'I'm in love.'

Summerbee did a double take. The Bobby Moore he knew was not given to sudden proclamations but his friend seemed utterly serious. Moore had a new woman in his life and he wanted to spend time with her. But first he had to extract himself from his marriage to Tina and it would take four tortuous years, a long, drawn-out agony.

From that first meeting with Stephanie, Moore agonised over his dilemma. He fretted over the effect on his children. He worried about the media fallout. He felt racked with guilt. Typically, he never discussed his agonies with Stephanie as their relationship developed from platonic evenings and walks in Richmond Park to a full-blown affair.

It was hard enough for Stephanie to prise from Moore what he did for a living or even that, yes, he was the footballer who had lifted the World Cup in 1966. For her it was just a vague memory. Whenever she tried to quiz him, he employed his old trick of asking all the questions and giving away little in return.

Stephanie relied on friends to fill in the details and background of Moore's career, and a few mentioned the disappearance of the bracelet in Bogotá. Troubled by the rumours, she decided one day to ask him the truth behind the accusations. It was, she says, a rare occasion when she felt a blast of cold anger. 'I can't believe you even had to ask me that,' he said. He did not elaborate, regarding the question as unworthy of a response. Stephanie still voices regret. 'He was disappointed in me that I would have so little faith.'

Never discussed was his collapsing marriage to Tina. Not once. Stephanie could only guess at Moore's domestic turmoil. She knew that he was not happy at home but he never talked about those strains or the financial pressures.

As their passion grew, Stephanie and Bobby would meet when she was not off flying around the world. Kenny Lynch's house near Henley-on-Thames was one convenient hideaway. But it was stolen time. Moore told Stephanie that he wanted to be together with her but he remained deeply conflicted by his marriage to Tina and responsibilities for Roberta and Dean, his teenage children.

'I found it very frustrating and confusing that so very early on he wanted to spend his life with me but very obviously had a family and nothing was discussed,' Stephanie says. 'I'd say to him, "you can't say you want to spend your life with me and want to marry me when you're actually living at home. How dare you say that sort of thing!" And he just wouldn't discuss it. I'd say "is there some sort of plan here or what?" It was very frustrating but I loved this man so much that I just accepted the status quo.'

As the frustrations grew too much to bear, they separated for six months. Then one day Stephanie was in the kitchen and heard Bobby talking football on the radio. Immediately she picked up the phone and left a message in his office. Moore rang back within minutes.

Eventually Tina's suspicions were bound to be aroused as Moore's movements became unpredictable, his moods even more so. She did not want to believe her own nagging doubts, but the signs became impossible to ignore. When Moore was on a work trip to Australia in between his jobs at Oxford and Southend, Tina rang to speak to him. A woman answered the phone. A flustered Moore explained that it was the wife of a work colleague. He told Tina to trust him. She was not so sure.

The marriage was heading towards a crisis point, and it came in late 1982 when Moore travelled to work in Hong Kong with Alan Ball, coaching Eastern Athletic. It was not a job to get excited about, but at least it kept him in football.

Ball sensed that there was something distracting his old friend as soon as Moore arrived. He seemed preoccupied. Ball became highly suspicious when Moore turned down invitations to go for beers after training. That was very much out of character. In an unfamiliar, foreign city, where on earth did Moore have to go that was better than a lager and a chat with his best pal?

The answer came in a series of excruciating rows between Bobby and Tina who had flown out to Hong Kong to find her husband even more aloof and distant than ever. When she could bear no more, and erupted in a screaming fury, Bobby admitted for the first time that there was someone else in his life.

'Tina, I've got a problem. I think I'm in love with somebody.'

'You've brought me two-thirds of the way around the world to tell me that?!'

It was as much as he would give away. The more Tina demanded to know, the less he would reveal.

He disappeared on nights away from their apartment to see Stephanie who had flown into Hong Kong. There were more slanging matches with Tina in public, which Moore hated. They tried to put on the pretence of a happy couple, but a meal out with the Balls deteriorated into a vicious row. Bobby said he had to go off to watch a game the next day. When Tina asked if he could not put her first, ahead of his work, he snapped back: 'What makes you think you're as high as second?' She knew her husband could be detached and indifferent at times, but now he was freezing her out, icy cold.

After another disastrous meal, with Tina storming out of the restaurant, Moore left and broke down in tears. They struggled through Christmas for the sake of the kids. Bobby and Tina got drunk and it was a wretched time. Tina flew home to Chigwell in January. Bobby gave up his job in Hong Kong and followed. He walked through the front door of Moorlands and went straight to bed.

The spring of 1983 in America with Rodney Marsh at the Carolina Lightnin' was a chance for Moore to work in football but also to escape his marital worries. Marsh was glad to have his mate with him but, as with Ball in Hong Kong, he could not understand why Moore kept disappearing after training. Marsh had expected long afternoons in the pub, but Moore was being elusive.

'I kept expecting Bobby to say "fancy a glass of wine tonight?" But nothing. After a couple of weeks I said "Bob, this ain't gonna fly, you've got to tell me the truth, something's going on". So we went to this little pub called the Barleycorn in

Charlotte and he poured out his life to me for five hours. How he'd met Stephanie, flown her to Charlotte, she was living with him in the townhouse and he just said "Rodney, I'm so much in love with Stephanie and I'm agonising with Tina and the kids". And that's when it all kicks off.'

When Stephanie left America, Moore invited Tina and the children to come over. Tina deluded herself into thinking there might be a chance to save the marriage. She knew she was fooling herself when she opened the fridge door and found Parmesan cheese. Since when had Moore shopped for that?

They started rowing again, sharing a bedroom, but they were no longer man and wife. Tina was relying on sleeping pills and booze. Then, in a drunken state, all the rage and resentment poured out at a party at Marsh's home. 'We've got this huge long outdoor balcony deck and everybody's there. Bobby is at one end, Tina at the other end and she suddenly starts "you fucking this, you effing that". It's like an East End pub scene. He didn't like it at all, everything out in public. Bobby was such a gentleman, he wouldn't want that.

'It's why he was horrified in the first place in terms of getting divorced. The stigma was something he really, really found difficult but he'd met Stephanie and he said to me that she was his soul mate. He said some phrase like it would be "inappropriate not to spend the rest of his life with her". It had to be done.'

Tina flew back home. In spite of everything, Moore returned to Moorlands again and Tina tried to salvage her marriage one last time. 'I actually said "have both of us. If you love her so much, have her and me". I was prepared to do anything,' Tina wrote. She was begging, pleading, cajoling.

After a week in which Moore barely unpacked his suitcase,

Tina gave him a final ultimatum with the words, 'this is killing all of us'. She went out and by the time she returned, Moore and his suitcase had gone.

'Bobby phoned me and said "would you like to go for a drive somewhere",' Stephanie says. 'He picked me up in the evening and said he had something to do, a pub he had to open or something. On the way home he dropped me off and I said "how long is it going to take you to get back to Essex from here?" He said "I'm not going back home. I left two days ago." And that was the first time he stayed at my house and that was all the notice I had.'

Living together lasted a fortnight. The newspapers had discovered that Moore had left Tina. 'Bobby said I wouldn't be able to handle the press,' Stephanie says. 'He said "when this becomes public, they will arrive in pairs on the doorstep, one will be a photographer and you won't be able to handle it". I said "of course I will", but he was right. I couldn't. I saw these two men standing on the doorstep and I thought "oh God, press" and I shut the door and then I was holed up for a week in my house unable to go out because we just had them camping everywhere. My neighbours were complaining. It was just a nightmare.'

Tina was also under siege and she, too, was struggling to cope. As she tried to find solace in drink, Roberta called her father to say that Tina had gone to pieces. The guilt kicked in, and Moore told Stephanie that he had to go home.

'I said "that's fair enough but you take everything". I just couldn't handle any of it. I thought "this is a nightmare, for her for me for him", and now it was public news it was horrendous. He went, though he phoned me quite regularly during this time.'

Two weeks later, Stephanie's phone went in a hotel room in Abu Dhabi where she was on another trip. She was semi-comatose.

'How do I fix the boiler?'

'With all due respect, Bobby, you can sort your own boiler out.'

'Er, actually it's your boiler that's the problem.'

Stephanie smiles. 'And that's when I knew he'd come back home.'

When Moore's separation from Tina became tabloid news, he did not fuel the media frenzy. 'The responsibilities for this situation are entirely mine,' he said. And he left it there. It was the same after the undefended divorce hearing on 6 January 1986: 'The only person to blame is myself.'

Moore had left home with only one suitcase of clothes. He had to retrieve his handmade shirts and a few bespoke suits from the Salvation Army. A distraught Tina had thrown them out in bags.

Otherwise, he left Tina with everything, including Moorlands. He left all his worldly possessions, including all his trophies and medals, which he would later regret. He had to ask Tina to hand over his World Cup medal some years later so that he could have it replicated for an item of jewellery. Apart from the England Youth caps, which he had given to Doss, and a miniature Jules Rimet Trophy, which his mother kept on the mantelpiece in Waverley Gardens, Tina kept it all stuffed in sacks.

For Moore, there was enough baggage just shouldering his guilt. 'He felt very guilty leaving his family,' Stephanie says. 'It caused him tremendous amounts of angst, I think, and indeed the next few years were also very difficult financially because Bobby left everything.'

Stephanie believes that separation was all the harder for Moore to confront because of the security of his East End upbringing. It pained him leaving the children because he had always been a doting father. Yet, among his friends, there was never any doubt that he had done the right thing.

They talk of his joy with Stephanie and how Moore blossomed in his new relationship. 'Stephanie took him to a different place,' Sir Michael Parkinson says. 'I don't want to say "classy" to upset Tina but . . . it gave him a different dimension.' Stephanie loved to travel and she opened up new worlds of travel and culture. They visited India, and many of the European cities Moore had been to as a player without having the time or inclination to see the sights. He began to visit galleries and museums. He had never been a great reader beyond the odd James Bond book or detective novel but he found new horizons far beyond Essex.

Stephanie talks of happy days walking a dog and how Moore, who had once seemed to put such value on having a fast car and a palatial house, was so content in a flat in London, able to stroll across the river to cafés and shops.

He began to resume closer relations with his family. Moore had drifted away from his cousins during the long years with Tina. Stephanie attempted to bridge the gap. She came to adore Doss who, even in old age, had lost none of her feistiness. 'She presented me with a set of tea towels one day,' Stephanie recalls, 'because she said mine were not clean enough.'

The family noticed that Moore had loosened up when they met. He had always been a little uptight at rare family gatherings, with Doss often putting up a protective shield around him. He had never wanted to sit around and talk about football but now he would crack open a beer with his cousins and chat.

'When I met them I said to Bobby "you come from a remarkable family, these are really good lovely people. Why don't you see much of them?"' Stephanie says. 'I don't know why that was.'

His insomnia seemed to have eased, too. 'Occasionally he used to have this recurring nightmare and because we were cuddled up together always and I slept very lightly,' Stephanie says, 'I was immediately aware and his skin would come up in goose bumps and I knew he was having a nightmare. Occasionally he would shout out. I just used to stroke him and they would disappear and you would hear him breathing again still asleep.'

Even though Moore had left everything for Tina, she quickly realised that she could not afford to run Moorlands. She auctioned off most of their possessions, put the house on the market and began to split her life between London and Florida. Tina admits that she took a long time to adjust to separation.

'I missed him,' she says. 'We had our rows. I was feisty. I would get angry. But he liked me because I was fun and I used to fight on his behalf. I don't mean physically but he always used to say to me "you handle people better, why don't you sort it out?". He would give me the bullets and I would fire them. I was protective of Bobby. He was vulnerable in a way and, especially after he finished playing, he accepted too much and got a bit trodden down.

'We really laughed together, we were buddies and I missed him enormously afterwards because it was like we were friends as well as everything else. We had a good marriage for a long, long time. And, listen, I thank every day I was with him. We had a great time and great kids and it was sad what happened but life goes on and then you find what you're made of. You have to. I remember once when we had separated and he said to me "you're really strong, you'll be all right". I didn't feel very strong but he thought I was. I just wish he'd been all right.'

23. Tits and Bums

'I used to hate the way the broadsheets would pontificate about Bobby "lowering himself" to work for the *Sunday Sport*, like he had prostituted himself. At least we gave him a job. We were proud to have him and he was very happy to join us. The snobs never offered him anything.'

David Gold, the West Ham United chairman and former publisher of the *Sunday Sport*, still fumes about how Moore's three years at the trashy tabloid are regarded as a symbol of how far a sporting icon had fallen. 'I loved him, as did everyone on the paper,' Gold says.

For his part, Moore certainly never gave any inkling that he saw the *Sunday Sport* as beneath him, not even on those days when he would come into the offices over an Ann Summers warehouse, walk past the poster screaming 'Topless – World's Fattest Woman!' and sit in on editorial conferences to decide whether to lead the front page with midget sex or Elvis Presley spotted on the moon.

'Honestly, Bob, you don't have to come in to these meetings,' one of the senior staff told him.

'I know,' he replied. 'But it's a right fucking laugh.'

It *was* a laugh. Moore enjoyed himself, demonstrating that he had tapped into the spirit of the paper when he interrupted one news conference, pointing to a commotion on the top of a building opposite. 'Are those two pigeons having a fuck?' he asked.

He was having fun and Stephanie Moore, like Gold, bridles at any suggestion that working on the country's sleaziest tabloid was an indignity. She hates the way that Moore's latter years are portrayed as a sad descent into obscurity. She tells of a happy man who never felt self-pity whatever his struggles in business or management. Personal contentment, she says, dwarfed any other frustrations.

Yet sitting in the offices of the *Sunday Sport* above a dildo factory was not the work Moore had aspired to, or anyone could have imagined for him. He was England's World Cup captain but, as far as mainstream football was concerned, he was now an outcast.

Management had not worked out but did Moore have nothing to offer the game? Friends insist that they tried on Moore's behalf to find him a job in football. They remain enraged that he was snubbed.

The FA was an obvious employer, if only to use Moore as an ambassador and glad-hander. Jimmy Tarbuck tells of pulling aside Peter Swales, chairman of the FA's international committee, when the two men bumped into each other in the directors' box at Manchester City. Tarbuck demanded to know why the FA did not get the unemployed Moore on board. He seethes as he tells of a brief exchange.

'I went "Peter, can I have a word? Why don't you take Bobby Moore on one of these England trips with you, an ambassador for football?". I said "Pelé's done it, Beckenbauer's done it. Bobby would be perfect".

'Do you know what he said? He said "are you serious? They'd all want to meet him". Honestly, those were his words. I said "well of course they would. Who would want to meet all you boring bastards?"'

Terry Venables says that he took up the same argument with Graham Kelly, the FA chief executive, asking why Moore was in the press box at Wembley when he should have been in the Royal Box among the VIPs. According to Venables, Kelly replied that it would be setting 'a difficult precedent' if he started inviting former England internationals into the inner sanctum. Venables fumed: 'I said "where is the precedent? I don't remember too many people captaining England to the World Cup".'

Venables says it was a hobby horse of his for many years that it took so long for the FA to understand the wider appeal of the game's heroes. He says the organisation did not have the foresight to see how they could harness the allure of their most famous captain because the game's hierarchy looked down snootily on the players.

'In South America, Italy, Spain they had understood the power of football and the power of great former players for years,' Venables says. 'Not in England, not till the last ten years. Was it snobbery? Probably. The class system always saw the game as the sweaty end of the market. You never saw a footballer come out of Weybridge. They realised it eventually. Football became huge, but too late for Bobby.'

Snobbery was undoubtedly the main reason behind the failure to honour Moore with a knighthood, which was in the gift of the FA and government. Yet this was not just a snub to him but reflected the Establishment's low regard for footballers in general.

Alf Ramsey was knighted in 1967, Matt Busby in 1969 but they were both honoured for achievements in management. After Stanley Matthews became a Sir in 1965, there was not a single playing knight for almost thirty years until Bobby Charlton in 1994.

Administrators could expect to be honoured, like Dr Andrew Stephen, chairman of the FA (knighted in 1972) or Denis Follows, secretary of the FA and chairman of the BOA (knighted in 1978). Walter Winterbottom became a Sir in 1978, rewarded for his work as England manager and for administration roles including the Sports Council.

But knighting players? Don't be ghastly. For several decades, the FA and politicians simply did not see the merit in honouring those who had sweated on the pitch. The Honours system defies sensible analysis but it does reflect trends in popularity, and one senior FA figure from the eighties says that Moore's name was simply not fashionable. There was no public clamour for him to be knighted, not while he was alive.

Without seeking to defend the indefensible, Graham Kelly puts the failure to honour Moore in some context: 'Bobby's name was just not at the forefront during my years at the FA. He had tried management, not altogether successfully. He was getting on with his life in media and business. Names were floated of people who had been more recently successful or done other outstanding things for the game.'

Kelly quotes the example of Tom Finney who, he says, was knighted in 1998 not just because of his distinguished football career but also because he had worked with the Football Trust charity and through years of public service in Preston. Moore, it seems, was looked down upon because of his failed businesses, his management struggles, working for the *Sunday Sport* and even the turbulence in his private life.

Another senior FA figure of the period believes that headlines about Moore's divorce from Tina and union with Stephanie did not help: 'I think perhaps it did not go down well with those "in power".' However ridiculous they may seem now, those were the attitudes of the time.

Harry Redknapp is certain that Moore's reputation for enjoying a night out played its part in the Establishment's refusal to embrace him. Perhaps the dark associations with Woolston Hall contributed. According to Rob Jenkins, the West Ham physio, Moore was even blackballed by Chigwell Golf Club, told that he was not welcome because he was not the right type.

Moore was ignored by the FA but this was not just about the organisation's failings. It was not his style to force his way into a role. The examples are often quoted of Michel Platini and Franz Beckenbauer, renowned players who became leading administrators, but Moore never had their political ambitions, or their guile.

The truth is that Moore never showed the inclinations, never mind abilities, to manoeuvre in football's corridors of power. Like management, the job would not have suited his personality.

Ken Jones was a great admirer of Moore but he acknowledges: 'Bob wouldn't have been cute enough to do that. You have to remember that the German Football Association didn't make a big fuss about Beckenbauer – Beckenbauer made a big fuss about himself. Franz had a way about him. He could be a bit of an arrogant bastard. I liked him but he was arrogant and Bob wasn't. And I think that held him back.'

Moore almost seemed resigned to his fate, not pushing himself forward or kicking up a fuss when others would have raged against football's unwillingness to find a position for him.

'If that was somebody like me, I'd have gone "you fucking arseholes",' Rodney Marsh says. 'Not that it would have done any good but it would have made me feel better. With Bobby, I think it was more disappointment. It was sadness rather than anger or frustration. I think it was naturally within him to get on and live life.'

Moore did not rage even when he was given the most outrageous snub of all, the cold shoulder from West Ham. Not many clubs excelled at cherishing their old heroes, though some did better than most. Bobby Charlton was invited back to Manchester United as a director in 1984. 'Come back to Old Trafford where you belong,' Louis Edwards, the chairman, told him.

West Ham's greatest captain never found that welcome at Upton Park. 'I think he was too big for some people at that club. I think they were a little bit frightened of him,' says Frank Lampard.

Harry Redknapp believes that John Lyall, who managed West Ham after Greenwood, did not want Moore back inside Upton Park because he would have been a threat. Redknapp still shakes his head with anger as he tells how Moore was finally alienated from the club that he had served as their most distinguished captain.

Back at Upton Park, visiting during a spell working in the United States, Redknapp went to watch his old team in the Second Division: 'It was half empty that evening, about twenty-six thousand people there I suppose and West Ham were struggling a bit. I forget who they were playing but it wasn't a great game.

'I'm sitting in E block, next to Frank Lampard's mum, and she suddenly says "Harry, look round it's Bobby". I wave "all right, Bob? See you at half-time for a cup of tea". I found this out later but while the game is going on, this steward comes up to Bobby and says "excuse me, Bob, it ain't me but I've been told you're not allowed to come in without a ticket". Bobby used to turn up, come late, walk in one of the gates and just go up and sit at the back. But he was asked to leave without a ticket, turfed out like a hooligan. And I don't think he ever went back.

'I found it hurtful and hard to understand. I'll be honest, I said to Terry Brown at West Ham one night in words much stronger than this, "you had the greatest ambassador you could have had for this football club, you could have made him a director, getting young kids into the club, somebody special at West Ham and you wasted the opportunity. You didn't want to know him".'

Redknapp says that after being asked to leave, Moore swore that he would never return to Upton Park unless he had to in a professional capacity. The club's greatest captain, the man who had lifted the only back-to-back trophies in their history, did not go back as a fan.

Football had no need for him, but the *Sunday Sport* did – and the newspaper was the only suitor offering Moore a salary of £50,000 for little more than a day's work each week. A few months after his departure from Southend, his phone not exactly ringing with job offers, Moore went to work for Gold and David Sullivan, the paper's co-owners, who launched their new title on 14 September 1986.

Moore joined as 'sports editor', a ludicrously overblown title for a job of columnist and match reporter, but they had to call him something grand given he was earning almost as much as the editor. Staff at the paper saw such generosity as an exercise in fan worship. Gold and Sullivan were both avid West Ham supporters, so much so that they would end up buying the club. The pair insist that Bobby's contract made commercial sense.

Sitting in his mansion in Essex, a diminutive figure almost hidden behind his vast desk, Sullivan says: 'It gave Bobby a good interest in life, put him back in the public domain. And it was good for us, too. We always wanted to make the sports section credible because we thought it was an excuse factor for buying the paper.'

Moore brought a dash of respectability to this new tabloid which was looked upon as downmarket even by its grubbiest rivals. This was the paper which handed out a free car sticker proclaiming 'I get it every Sunday!' and gave readers the chance to 'Meet the Gran who makes Joan Collins look like a Nun'. (It was also, incidentally, the paper that was obsessed by AIDS. Perhaps we all were back in 1986, though it was the *Sport* which revoltingly dubbed it 'the gay plague').

On the back page of the paper's first edition, Moore made his debut with a fierce critique of the game under the headline 'SOLD OUT'. Moore lamented that players were demanding £1,000 per week (how quaint!) and moaned about the quality of modern football which he derided as 'a shapeless mess, played by muscle-bound mediocrities who wouldn't know a dummy if someone stuffed it into their mouths'.

Were those really his words or those of an excitable ghostwriter? Moaning about modern failings, while waxing lyrical about everything being so much better in his day, was never Moore's style. He had his qualities of reserve and discretion, and they were bound to hamper his work as a tabloid columnist. Moore's refusal to badmouth people was a constant. 'Bobby didn't speak ill of anyone,' Kenny Lynch says. 'Not even the shithouses.'

When Stephanie once gave a withering assessment of a celebrity as she sat at home on the sofa watching television, Moore turned to her. 'I didn't realise you knew him,' he said.

'I don't,' Stephanie replied.

'So how come you are slagging him off?'

'That was Bobby,' Stephanie says. 'He had that attitude of "if you can't say anything nice . . ."'

That was Moore's gentle nature and it was reinforced by incidents like Blackpool and Bogotá when he felt his own reputation had been unfairly traduced. Rather than become bitter, he preferred to become even less judgemental.

For the *Sunday Sport* he might comment that Manchester United were having a stinker of a season when he reported from matches. Each Saturday, Moore and other former players, including Paddy Crerand, Ian St John and Gordon Banks, attended a top-flight game and phoned in some thoughts to be knocked into best tabloidese by sub-editors in the office.

But when Hugh Southon, who ghosted Moore's columns for two years, asked him to opine about an extra-marital affair involving an England player, Moore replied: 'I'm not going to hammer him for that. Everybody gets it wrong now and again.'

'Bobby was always reluctant go stick the boot in,' Southon says. 'It would have been easy for him to be high and mighty, passing down judgements, but that was never his style. He wasn't a hypocrite. He'd made a few mistakes of his own. He remarked a few times about "the old eleventh commandment – don't get caught".'

It is a line worth remembering when you read some of the outrage written in Moore's name; how the hero of '66 would be appalled at the various scandals involving England players and turning in his grave. Moore was far too worldly to indulge in sanctimonious humbug, though he did put his name to one piece that seems distinctly odd and out of character.

The striker Mark Hateley was considering a lucrative move to Monaco but had been warned that heading abroad might jeopardise his England career. Perhaps reflecting his own dismay at the way football was ignoring him – or maybe it told of his post-career financial crisis – Moore urged Hateley to set aside international ambitions and follow the money.

'Sporting patriotism is fine – but a few England international caps gathering dust on the sideboard can't compare with £1m in the bank, a life of luxury and a secure future,' Moore wrote. 'I know an England appearance is the greatest honour our game can offer. But DON'T BLAME those who settle for hard cash instead. Patriotism pays for nothing!' Words you never expected to hear from the hero of '66, until you recall his own financial struggles.

A piece Moore wished that he never had to contribute came from the Hillsborough disaster in April 1989. Moore was in the press box that day, watching the horror unfold as ninety-six Liverpool fans died in the crush.

Professional duty required him to ring in to provide a report, but he could barely speak through his tears. The copytaker had to console him repeatedly. 'This isn't football,' Moore sobbed down the phone. 'There are people here dying'.

In the following day's paper, the last few lines of his first-hand account read: 'I left Hillsborough a broken man. It doesn't matter who wins the Cup now. It's tainted. I'm shattered. God help football. God bless those who died.'

Moore stayed with the *Sport* for three years and, in the best Fleet Street traditions, enjoyed many long, liquid lunches. The paper also gave Dean a job as a page designer, though he was regularly threatened with the axe. 'Dean was a nice lad but not really up to the job,' one senior staff member recalls. 'He only survived because everyone had so much respect for Bobby.'

The *Sunday Sport* was a good home for Moore, looking after his son, taking him around the grounds and keeping him in the game when he had no other capacity in football. 'It worked out well for all of us,' Sullivan says. 'The paper did well and we gave Bobby decent money.'

When he left in 1989, it was for Capital Gold Radio who wanted a new pundit in the year running up to the World Cup in Italy. Moore travelled the country with Jonathan Pearce who became a very close friend as well as colleague, covering London clubs and taking to the road with England. Bobby loved that job, even if Pearce reckons that he was earning as little as £150 per match, plus expenses.

Moore's presence opened doors for Pearce. 'You'd have England players asking "what did Bobby say about me, what does he think of me as a player?"' he recalls. Moore was the straight, droll pundit to Pearce's famously excitable commentaries. The combination seemed to work. In 1991 Pearce and Moore picked up a Sony Radio Academy Award.

They covered thousands of miles together, Moore offering his sober reflections on air except for the match between Oxford United and West Ham United when he had drunk so much at lunchtime that he turned up late and fell asleep during the game.

Moore enjoyed the job even when he was travelling up to Grimsby Town on a freezing winter night to cover West Ham. Redknapp was manager, standing by the side of the pitch, watching his players warm up. He heard a familiar voice shout 'Harry'.

'I look up and it's this fella sitting with a great big peaked cap on eating his bit of fish and chips. Then I realise it's Bobby in Grimsby, doing his bit of commentary. Amazing, really, to see him like that.'

The scene jars with everything we might expect of the greatest legend of English football but this was not just about Moore. It would take the nineties boom for the game to appreciate its former players properly.

Suddenly the legends business took off. Roles started cropping up on television, and as ambassadors and corporate faces. No longer did retired players have to try to scrape together an audience in provincial cities, telling a few hackneyed yarns.

Moore would have finally been able to bask in recognition, including a knighthood. Like Sir Geoff Hurst with his enriching work for McDonald's as a corporate ambassador, Moore would finally have become the elegantly ageing face of big business. He would have been schmoozing alongside David Beckham on World Cup bids. Being a 'legend' would have become a full-time job.

After his sacking as Chelsea manager, Hurst had fallen into selling insurance for years but then his secretary began to take an increasing number of calls inviting him to speak at corporate functions or appear at golf days.

'It all changed in the early nineties with the Premier League, the Taylor Report and Sky TV all arriving to almost transform the game overnight to the unbelievable industry it is today,' Hurst says. 'The World Cup team from '66 has benefited hugely, both commercially and profile-wise because the industry has gone nuts for it. Mooro was seen as the golden boy and there would have been no end of opportunities.'

Moore would have cashed in. He would have enjoyed all the offers and attention fitting a man of his stature and achievements. Sir Trevor Brooking, another footballing knight, believes that Moore was starting to loosen up as he entered his fifties, losing some of his inhibitions in the public glare, and would have revelled in the attention.

Brooking says: 'When he got a bit older, people found him far more approachable. I certainly found that. He'd never been the easiest communicator but that humour we all knew was there seemed to be on the surface much quicker than it had been in the past. He didn't seem to feel he was on show, on edge. I think the next few years would have been a time when he could have that prominence which he should have as the England captain who lifted the World Cup.'

Moore could have been enriched by football's boom but, tragically, he never got that chance.

24. The Old Enemy

It is said that many sufferers of bowel cancer die of embarrassment. Critical time for early treatment is lost because they do not want to go to their GP with symptoms in such a delicate area. They do not want to talk of diarrhoea and rectal bleeding. You might well imagine that Bobby Moore would fit into that category, as a man of such privacy and discretion. You might think that he would be exactly the type to suffer in silence, as he did for months with his testicular cancer until the swelling and the pain became unbearably acute.

But the tragedy of Moore's bowel cancer is that he did everything by the NHS book. Moore gave himself the best possible chance of early detection and effective, life-saving treatment. It was the medical profession that failed him, and with grievous consequences.

Stephanie Moore reveals the story in all its heart-breaking detail in the hope that others can be better cared for, and lives saved. Steeling herself in a way that would make her husband proud, maintaining a steady voice despite her grief, she tells how Moore's cancer went undetected for four long years from the day he first told her he was feeling unwell.

Moore did not know what those early symptoms meant, when he suffered from bleeding and frequent night-time dashes to the toilet, but he had no hesitation in visiting the doctor. Stephanie and Bobby went together to see their GP in Battersea who did everything correctly in immediately referring Moore to a specialist in Harley Street. Within days they were sitting in the offices of an eminent rectal proctologist.

An examination was made, tests done and then the consultant imparted what seemed like happy news.

'It's irritable bowel syndrome,' he said. 'Go away and live your life.'

Moore left Harley Street reassured he was a healthy man, with problems that would disappear with a few alterations to his diet. He took the specialist at his word – until the symptoms kept recurring. He had moved to Putney with Stephanie and signed on with a new GP. Moore went to see him. 'A lovely, lovely man,' Stephanie says. 'But I know now that he was just looking at the specialist's notes and fobbing Bobby off with "there's nothing wrong with you".'

Moore went back, on several occasions. Still the advice came back to adapt his lifestyle and eat what didn't upset his stomach. If a Harley Street specialist was convinced the problem was IBS, the GP did not dream of overruling an expert.

Was this an understandable, forgivable mistake? Generously, Stephanie declines to blame the local GP. She acknowledges that there was an overlap in symptoms between IBS and bowel cancer. She notes that, in the eighties, there was not the recourse to scans which could have ended the confusion before it was too late.

But it is also true that Moore had all the obvious, high-risk symptoms of bowel cancer. 'Bobby would complain about it every couple of months and then we'd go back to the doctor. And each time we went he was told there was nothing wrong. We'd never heard of bowel cancer. Nobody had back then, it was a big taboo.

'Bobby would go back to work. He always put himself way down the list of priorities so he would attend to his commitments. Every now and then he'd say I've still got these symptoms and I think something's wrong but he wasn't losing weight at this point and I think our GP, if he'd even heard of bowel cancer, he couldn't understand it in someone so young. He didn't think Bobby would fit into that category. You'd think people over sixty got bowel cancer and didn't think he was in the right age to have it. A specialist had confirmed Bobby didn't have it.'

Her voice falters for the first time: 'Obviously I know now that the specialist made a tremendous error.'

Finally, Moore demanded a second specialist's opinion – effectively a fourth, including the two GPs. Still their friendly local doctor thought it unnecessary.

'I can assure you there's nothing wrong,' he told Moore. 'But if you insist.'

And so he ended up being referred to another specialist at Parkside hospital in Wimbledon. By now it was spring 1991 and the problems had been troubling him for several years. An appointment was arranged with Dr Barnardo, though first there was the important matter of Moore's fiftieth birthday on 12 April 1991. Stephanie arranged a surprise party, filling their home in west London with family and friends.

Jimmy Tarbuck and Kenny Lynch were there, old West Ham team-mates, Terry Venables and George Graham, East End mates mixing with heroes from 1966. Moore was determined to live up to his reputation as the last man standing, downing lager, champagne and wine into the early hours. 'How he got through that day I don't know,' Stephanie says, 'because he really was not well.'

It took a woman's eye to notice that Moore's usual bonhomie was masking a deeper problem. Terry Creasy recalls his wife's observant remark amid the celebrations. 'My Diane didn't see Bobby as much as I did and that night she says to me, "Bobby don't look right, you know". He had no bum, he'd lost a lot of weight. I said "Bobby, you all right?" "Yeah yeah. I'm going into hospital for a check up but I'm fine." Bobby just brushed it off, like he always did.'

Moore went into hospital a few days later to undergo a barium enema to find the cause of the bleeding that had been upsetting him for so long. It was the first time that he was beset with worry. He kept looking at the faces of the nurses and imagining that they were keeping a terrible secret. Stephanie tried to reassure him.

They both went back to work the following day. When Stephanie got home there was a call from the hospital. It was the sort of call you never forget. Dr Barnardo was 99 per cent sure that it was cancer. He needed to see them urgently. He would be available the very next morning. Really, they should not delay.

When Moore returned home, Stephanie said nothing. 'I thought, I'm not going to tell him tonight, we can't do anything and it just means we'll have a very disturbed night.' She told him the next morning, that the doctors were certain he had cancer. Moore sat there and barely flinched. 'He just looked at me and I saw tears well in his eyes, but that was the only sign,' Stephanie says. 'He just said "oh well, what do we do now?" That's all he said.'

They went into hospital that morning. After all the long years of misdiagnosis and delay, suddenly everything seemed a blur. Bobby was referred to a surgeon, Peter Hawley, and was under the knife within a week, but there was only so much the doctor could do. Hawley could remove the malignant growths from Moore's colon, but the cancer had spread. There was a secondary tumour in the right lobe of the liver. There were also spots on the other lobe and, though they could be removed, the news could hardly be worse. His cancer was almost certainly terminal.

Bobby and Stephanie decided to tell no one apart from Dean and Roberta, now in their twenties, and less than a handful of family members. And they clung to the last slender thread of hope. Three months after the operation, Bobby and Stephanie went back to Mr Hawley for a scan on Moore's liver. If only one lobe was still affected, they could cut it out and hope that the unaffected part would regrow. It was a long shot but all they had to cling to.

'So we went back, he had that scan and we went to see Mr Hawley. And he said to Bobby "unfortunately you're inoperable. They have grown back". And I knew then that was all hope gone,' Stephanie says.

They climbed into Moore's car. Typically, he was determined to go back to work where he shared an office with Roberta. Stephanie was also due to head off on a flight, looking after passengers and a crew.

'I remember we got in the car and drove back to his office. I knew there was no way I could go to work and pretend nothing was wrong in my life. I just burst into tears uncontrollably. It was the only time I ever broke down in front of Bobby, and Bobby just looked at me, somewhat alarmed, and got out of the car.

'I gathered myself together and that was that, I never broke down in front of Bobby again. I knew that wasn't helpful to him. I broke down a lot privately on my own by never in front of him again and that was not the way. He didn't want histrionics. He didn't even want to discuss it.'

It was characteristic of Moore to be so stoical, but to walk off and leave his wife sobbing in the car? Did Stephanie not feel it a little cold? Did she not want to be asked how she was coping? Did she not want a cuddle and to discuss what was *his* illness but *their* shared trauma?

'No, Bobby so dominated every aspect of my life and I adored him more than anyone could do, that whatever he did or said that's the way we were going to deal with things. Something as important as this I was totally led by him.'

Moore did not ask the doctors how long he had to live. He never discussed it with Stephanie. The doctors had told him that he had inoperable cancer so, as far as he was concerned, what was the point of wailing? He decided to enjoy life, not dwell on death. Only once did Moore ask Stephanie 'how do you feel about all this?'.

'He wanted to live every day to the full and we had such a fabulous life. It just pulled us closer together. Most of our life was fun, it really was. We were doing things and going places that most people would have given their eye teeth for and mixing with people that were really interesting and vibrant and achieving. We had a great life and this is what was so tragic, we had so much to live for still.

'We spent every moment we could together. I want people to know that Bobby's last two years were happy years, even during those last months when things couldn't get any worse, and I knew he was going to die, and he knew he was going to die.'

Post-operative treatment was under the care of Professor John Smythe, head of the Imperial Cancer Research Unit at the Western General Hospital in Edinburgh and recommended to Moore by a friend. Bobby and Stephanie would fly up to Scotland every fortnight, managing to do so incognito. Moore had stressed the need for privacy and, despite his regular visits to the outpatient clinic, the secret was not betrayed.

Smythe explained that the chemotherapy did not have much to offer Moore in terms of battling his own disease, but that he could take part in trials that could help future patients. Moore willingly agreed. 'The tragedy,' Smythe says, 'is that the developments since might have helped to overcome his illness.'

Smythe remembers Moore's coping strategy. 'I have always been a great believer in humour to deal with times of darkness and Bobby had a wonderful sense of humour. We had lots of laughs even as he was dealing with his illness. He had a good supply of East End one-liners.'

Moore began to put weight back on, and kept himself fit as part of his therapy. As well as playing golf, he took to regular jogging, swimming and squash. Malcolm Allison gave him a skipping rope which he used daily, hopping up and down, working up a sweat. For eighteen months of the next two years, he looked fit and well. He was on a programme of non-aggressive chemotherapy so his appearance was little changed. He mostly kept his hair, weight and good complexion. Fooled by his outward vitality, no one guessed that he was terminally ill.

In the midst of his treatment, Stephanie and Bobby tied the knot in December 1991. He was driving them along the King's Road when he stopped the car outside Chelsea Town Hall and suggested it was time to become man and wife. Their wedding was a small, private ceremony with a few family and friends followed by lunch at the Ritz.

They travelled extensively, with Moore drawing up a bucket list of golf courses he had always wanted to play and Stephanie supplying a long list of destinations they must visit; driving across India, snorkelling in the Maldives, touring Zimbabwe and Tahiti. Fifty things to do before you die. They flew to Union Island in the West Indies, blissful days in the sun and the sea even if Moore's health was starting to fade. There was a hill nearby and Moore vowed to climb it every day, to stand on the summit and gaze out over a turquoise ocean. Gasping at the top one morning, a fellow hiker remarked on Moore's breathlessness: 'You need to get fit, mate.' Moore felt like swearing. He smiled, politely.

Moore's horizons had expanded beyond holidays in Marbella and Stephanie introduced him to a new cultural world, too. Nights at the Royal Opera House in Covent Garden, evenings at the theatre. They decided it was essential to maintain privacy so that they could enjoy this full life without intrusion. At one point, Stephanie noted the work that Roy Castle was doing to raise awareness about lung cancer. They discussed whether Moore might do the same for his disease, but he was certain that he did not want to go public. 'He just thought he just didn't have that ability to go out and do what Roy was doing,' Stephanie says.

He kept his condition secret even from Doss who was in a nursing home with her own terminal cancer. 'She never knew and it was best that way,' Graham Hardwick, Moore's cousin, says. 'It would have slaughtered Doss if Bobby had gone before her.' Doss died in 1990 without knowing that her only son did not have long to live.

Moore was also dealing with the problems of Dean who had moved in with his father but was lazing on the sofa all day, drinking beer and leaving the house only to go to the pub. There had been problems with drink since his school days and now he had an addiction. One night Stephanie and Bobby forced him to answer an Alcoholics Anonymous questionnaire to judge the scale of his problem. Dean ticked almost every box. Having lost his job in newspapers, Dean was an unemployed alcoholic.

It was Dean's decline which dissuaded Moore from handing out the mementos of his life. He had not done much to prepare for the end but he did ask Tina to send all his caps and medals. He laid them out on the kitchen table, holding them, wondering how to divide them between his children but Dean was in no state to take them so Moore put them away, back in the sacks in which they had arrived.

Moore continued to work, still travelling around the country to give his thoughts on Capital Gold. He had also set up a sports marketing company, Mitchell–Moore Associates, with John Mitchell, an old Fulham team-mate. They were involved in various sporting ventures, working with Panini football stickers, assisting Mastercard's sponsorship of the World Cup. They had been setting up corporate hospitality events, including golf days, with some success. Moore's business fortunes seemed to have improved just as his health declined.

He stayed active but it became hard into the last few months. Old friends started to notice his deterioration. Jimmy Armfield bumped into him at Elland Road when they were both working in the press box. 'I always remember his eyes were yellow. He had a black beret on because he'd maybe lost some hair and he really looked ill. I thought to myself what the hell is he doing here? I hadn't maybe related to him so much before but it's funny, as we were leaving, we sort of grabbed hold of each other. I said "I'll come and see you when the season is over". We never got the chance.'

His old ghost writer from the *Sunday Sport*, Hugh Southon, came across Moore at a game at the Hawthorns. 'He was sat in the corner of the press room, flat cap on drinking a cup of tea out of some crap polystyrene cup. I thought then like I've thought so many times since "is this how we treat our heroes?".'

Nigel Clarke, his faithful ghost writer on the *Daily Mirror*, was in the gym they both used in south-west London when Moore walked in one day. 'I said "maestro, how are you?" He just said "look at my feet". He had an immaculate suit on with plimsolls because his feet were so swollen he couldn't get his shoes on. He asked me to help. This was not long before the end. When I walked away I cried. I just hated the idea of someone so noble being brought down by something like this.'

He was weakening and, privately, Moore began to say his farewells, without actually saying so. He asked Mike Summerbee to meet him for lunch in Manchester when he was up covering a game. They gathered at an Italian restaurant on Deansgate.

'I always remember, we were sat and talking and having a little bit of something to eat and I noticed a little bit of blood coming out of his nose,' Summerbee says. 'I leant over with my napkin and just wiped it away. We didn't say anything. We didn't need to. I knew then. So, when we were leaving, I didn't want to say goodbye as if it's the last time. I said goodbye as if I was going to see him in a week's time but I remember getting into the car and I waved and got onto the phone straight away.

'I phoned Jimmy Tarbuck and said "when did you last see

Bobby?" He said "I've not seen him for about a month or so". I said "well, you better get the lads together because he ain't gonna last long. I've just been with him, it's terrible". And I never saw Bobby after that.'

It had reached the point where the secret was going to be revealed on someone else's terms, if they were not careful. Moore was declining, and everybody could see it. Stephanie realised that something had to be done when they were on holiday in Florida in late January 1993.

Moore was sitting out in the sun, feeding ducks. He had been struggling to eat, feeling nauseous much of the time, and she was constantly on the phone to the doctors back home asking what more she could do to help him live comfortably. 'I still have a photo of him sitting there feeding these ducks. He turned round to talk to me and his eyes had gone yellow. I thought "jaundice. That means his liver is not functioning, we've got to get home".

'When we got home we took the dog out for a walk. Bobby was quite weak and our neighbour, lovely Patrick, said to Bobby, "My god you look ill, I think you ought to go and see a doctor". We went home and Bobby said "do I look that ill?" I said, "well you don't look well". And that's when he said "I think I'll have to make this public".'

Calls were made. Jeff Powell was invited round to draft the press statement, Jonathan Pearce to do his bit for the broadcasters. On 14 February, a public statement was released. Moore disclosed that he had undergone the operation on his colon in April 1991 and that he had cancer in his liver.

Moore gave the public no sense that he was losing that battle, or that he had limited time. Three days after his statement, on

17 February, he went to Wembley to watch England play San Marino. It was one last chance to look at the stadium where he had enjoyed his greatest moments. The place had been his stage as much as the National Theatre had been home to Laurence Olivier.

A photographer snapped him as he went in, the last image in a dark cap he had bought travelling around Lake Como and thick sheepskin coat. He looks drawn and haggard but he was determined to perform his duties, attending a dinner after the match where he made a presentation in front of hundreds of guests who had no idea that this was his last appearance in public. 'I don't know how he got through that,' Stephanie says. 'He was very unwell then, struggling to even put a sentence together. Bobby being Bobby had made this commitment and he was determined to see it through. I didn't expect him to be dead within a week.'

Moore went to work on the Thursday and Friday to the offices of Mitchell–Moore on Fulham Road, determined to keep up his routine right to the end but he was declining rapidly. He was supposed to go to West Ham United against Newcastle United that Saturday but Stephanie rang Jonathan Pearce to say that she did not want Bobby going. Between them, they talked Bobby out of a return to Upton Park.

The family spent the last few days and nights together in peace and affection. They refused the routine medical advice for him to be moved to hospital, but he was housebound. On the Sunday he got up but didn't get dressed. He was weakening but still there was a quiet stoicism about him. 'He was very strong, particularly at the end when he was so ill,' Stephanie says.

On the Monday he was unable to get up. One of the nurses

told Stephanie that she should tell the family to come to his bedside. Roberta was told to rush back from Italy, where she was travelling on holiday, as fast as possible.

'They said it could be tonight. It could be in two weeks' time, it's a matter of how strong his heart is now. So when Roberta phoned on the Tuesday morning I said you must come home your father is very ill,' Stephanie says. Moore's daughter came home and lay on the bed with her father as he drifted in and out of consciousness. The following morning, just after 6.30 a.m. on 24 February, Moore passed away.

Roberta spoke movingly about the scene for the *Hero* documentary: 'It sounds really odd but when he took his last breath and I knew he'd gone, I just had the most unbelievable surge of energy go through me. Just the most unbelievable warmth spread through me and I don't know and I know it might sound a bit cranky but I believe his soul passed through me. That's what I believe and that's what gives me comfort. And people just said to me "oh, it's an adrenalin rush". I just don't believe that. I'll never forget it and he just, he just went.'

Moore had died peacefully among his family less than a fortnight after he announced he was fighting cancer, and less than a week since he had visited Wembley. 'I don't know how helpful it is for people to know that,' Stephanie says. 'A lot of people with bowel cancer can be very ill at the end and they may think that they should be behaving and being like Bobby. But people can have the same prognosis and behave very differently. I wouldn't want people to think they hadn't managed like Bobby. It's really not like that at all. It's just the way the cookie crumbles.

'One thing I do regret in many ways, having spoken to lots of people since who have gone through something similar, is that they were able to properly say goodbye. We never did that because Bobby never fully accepted the fact that he was going to die. You know, he was a very silent man in many ways.'

Moore's body was moved to a funeral parlour. Booked under a false name, the family held a small, private funeral ceremony. Tina was invited but chose to pray alone in Miami, not wanting there to be any awkwardness with Stephanie on such a day.

While Moore was in his coffin at the funeral home, Dean took one last chance to say goodbye to his father. 'I walked in there and he looked, he looked immaculate but he had one hair out of place. So I put it back which he would have liked, put a flower on him, kissed him three times on each cheek and forehead. I'm sure, looking down, he would have appreciated that. He wouldn't have wanted to have been buried untidy.'

25. Aftermath

When Bobby Moore passed away in 1993, the England team was faring dismally under the management of Graham Taylor, the man who had once beaten him to the job at Watford. Taylor was on his way to the public stocks, to be ridiculed as a turnip, and England's star player was Paul 'Gazza' Gascoigne who had belched into an interviewer's microphone. When asked by a journalist if he had a message for Norway, he replied: 'Yes. Fuck off Norway.'

A nation mourned not just for Bobby Moore the player and the man, but for the standards and qualities he embodied. It longed for his elegance. It grieved for a time when England possessed the best team in the world and when heroes came unblemished, at least in the public perception. Sir Michael Parkinson called Moore 'last of the polite footballers' and, whether it was true or not, that was the impression left when he died.

'I think to many of us, Bobby was almost the demarcation line between one era and another,' Parkinson told me. 'People can make their own mind up which they prefer but I've lived through both. Football represents the nature of society around it and Bobby was very clearly the last well-mannered footballer, the last true hero.'

In death, Moore was no longer the pundit on local radio or the failed manager. Once again, he was the immaculate hero of 1966. A game, and a national audience, which had not had much use of him for twenty years began to glorify him more even than in his playing pomp. A nation suddenly woke up to what it had lost. His lustre was restored.

The speed with which Moore had deteriorated, passing away so soon after disclosing his cancer, made the grief all the more profound. There was sorrow, shock, and a heavy dose of guilt, too. It was as though there was a rush to make up for the failure to treat Moore better in those latter years. Death marked the start of the process of sanctification.

A shrine was built out of people's affections on the gates of Upton Park in Green Street, a vast array of flowers, wreaths, scarves and shirts with handwritten notes, proclaiming their admiration and love for Moore. On one of the cards among the multitude outside Upton Park, someone had written: 'I wanted to be like you'.

'Wherever people gathered on Wednesday, there was a pervasive sense of loss, an unforced emotion that suggested many had been taken unawares by the depth of their feelings,' Hugh McIlvanney wrote.

Suddenly, everything changed. The Establishment which had not felt Moore worthy of a knighthood now gave him a memorial service at Westminster Abbey, the first footballer to be granted that posthumous privilege. Almost two thousand mourners walked through the doors, entering between ranks of West Ham and Fulham youth players, for what felt like a state occasion.

The Dean of Westminster, Michael Mayne, who conducted the service, explained that Moore was a great national figure 'and I thought it right that such greatness should be recognised here. He made such a distinguished contribution to the life of the nation.'

Moore's caps and medals were borne in procession on pale blue cushions. Jonathan Pearce and Franz Beckenbauer read the lessons; Parkinson gave a reading from Kahlil Gibran's *The Prophet*. Bobby Charlton spoke along with Jimmy Tarbuck who drew damning parallels with the modern game as he addressed the congregation: 'He did not really know how to foul anyone. He did not know how to argue with referees. He did not know how to retaliate and, worst of all, he did not have a clue how to be negative.' There was a dig at a flailing England team. 'His team leadership was magnificent and I know how we need it now,' Tarbuck said.

A recording of BBC commentator Kenneth Wolstenholme describing the Wembley scene as Moore went up to accept the World Cup echoed through the Abbey towards the end of the service. They had resisted the temptation to play the famous line where Wolstenholme says 'they think it's all over', though Moore's friends say that he would have smiled if they had.

The only awkwardness of the day came after the ceremony. Tina and Stephanie had both arranged separate wakes nearby. Inevitably, many of Bobby's oldest friends had been invited to both and faced the delicate task of deciding which to attend. 'Terry Venables and I ended up having to go to both because we didn't want to be disrespectful,' Rodney Marsh says. 'One was at Langan's upstairs and one was in Scribes but they were competing at the same time. Tina showed up, she'd had a makeover for it, been to like a West End coiffeur.'

Tension between the pair had been exacerbated by Tina's revelations that Moore had suffered from testicular cancer. The story came out the day before the service. Stephanie remains deeply unimpressed. 'It sold the story at the time, it made headline news, but out of loyalty to Bobby I would not have made that public.'

Tina justified her actions by saying that the story demonstrated Bobby's courage. 'That's beside the point,' Stephanie says. 'Bobby made it very clear he didn't want it made public. Surely things are allowed to remain private? Even at the end of his life, very few people knew and I honoured that and would have done to this day had it not been made public, which I think is very sad.'

Moore's death marked a watershed. Within a year, Bobby Charlton became a Sir. Did political antennae twitch at the overwhelming public response to Moore's passing? It does not take a cynic to see that, in Westminster, someone detected a populist wave to catch.

Mention the theory to Charlton and he is suddenly struck by sorrow, as though he had not thought of Moore's missing knighthood before. 'Football just wasn't looked at in the same way in those years,' Charlton told me. 'That makes me sad now you mention it.'

It was not until 2000 that five of the heroes of 1966 – George Cohen, Roger Hunt, Ray Wilson, Nobby Stiles and Alan Ball – were finally recognised by the Establishment and made MBEs. That it took so long was a scandal, the World Cup winners forced to wait until the game enjoyed a mainstream boom.

Look around at the statues of great footballing figures and, with very few exceptions, they have all sprung up in the last twenty years. Busby at Old Trafford, Clough in Nottingham, Ramsey in Ipswich, Haynes at Fulham, Bremner at Elland Road, Shankly at Anfield; all sculpted and erected in the Premier League era.

There was something good in this belated acknowledgement of the game's greats but perhaps something a little cynical and self-serving, too, in the way that not just politicians but football clubs suddenly rediscovered their old heroes and heritage. It smacked of enhancing 'the brand'. Harry Redknapp could not disguise his disdain for some of those who now feted Moore. 'The hypocrisy that followed his tragically premature death sickens me,' he wrote.

At Upton Park, the way they celebrated Moore posthumously offended many of his old friends given how he had been ignored so long. West Ham retired Moore's number six shirt. They called one end behind the goal the Bobby Moore Stand and erected a statue of him holding the World Cup. All this at a club which had found no use for him during those long years when he was effectively exiled from the game.

More recently, West Ham have started using Moore's name for a BM6 hospitality suite and his image on posters. Moore's silhouette appears on tickets and posters, even though the family claim not to have granted approval. Some marketing whiz came up with the slogan 'MOORE than a football club' – turning it into a licensed trademark even though Stephanie says she was not properly consulted.

It would seem less like cynical exploitation if West Ham had done more to support the Bobby Moore Fund, which is perhaps his most uplifting legacy. Stephanie took all her grief and channelled it into this noble cause. 'They should have spotted the illness but after Bobby died I thought what do

I do about this?' she says. 'I didn't want to rant and rave at the doctors. I didn't want to claim money from the National Health on misdiagnosis. But I did want to change things and I'm sure Bobby would have felt the same way.'

She set up the Fund which raised £21 million in its first twenty-one years, advancing research into bowel cancer and spreading awareness. With almost 20,000 deaths a year in the UK, bowel cancer remains the second highest cancer killer but mortality rates have fallen by almost 30 per cent since Moore's death thanks to scientific advances. Nine out of ten cases can be successfully treated if caught early, but men remain the hardest group to educate about the illness and Moore is an ideal vehicle to promote national screening for colorectal cancer.

'It's hard to believe how far things have moved on in twenty years,' Stephanie says. 'But we still have to increase awareness and to make sure people don't fall foul of this disease unnecessarily. Lots of men still won't go to the doctor because they are told to "man up". In America it's not the case. They don't have the startling statistics from bowel cancer that we do in Great Britain.'

George Cohen, the dynamic right-back from 1966, was one of those who was treated in time. 'I got mine very, very quickly because I couldn't do the exercises that I normally do,' he said. 'I became ill overnight, I met the doctor and was in hospital within a week and operated on. Unfortunately for Bobby, his cancer moved up into his liver. Mine moved down. The poor guy became a statistic on the wrong side of the page.'

The Fund makes sure there are more who enjoy Cohen's good fortune and far less who must suffer from the misdiagnosis that resulted in Moore's tragically premature demise.

Stephanie was initially thrilled with West Ham's support for the Fund when the club was under Icelandic ownership, but that changed when David Gold and David Sullivan took over and Karren Brady became chief executive. In 2010, she expressed public disappointment at West Ham's replacing of the pre-season Bobby Moore Cup with the SBOBET Cup, ending one source of revenue (part of the ticket sales from that pre-season fixture had gone to the Fund). The club said that it simply could not afford to support charity when it had so many bills to pay.

In 2011, the Bobby Moore Fund was dropped from the front of children's replica shirts. West Ham explained that a formal three-year partnership had ended and that they were still supporting the charity in many ways. 'I'll be honest,' Sullivan explains. 'The problem on the kids' shirts was the club was £100 million in debt. I know the charity would like us to do a lot more but there's only so much you can do.'

Sullivan says that he has made his own donations, including a £10,000 cheque in 2012. West Ham promised to raise £50,000 in the 2012/13 season and delivered more than £60,000, but the majority came out of the pockets of the fans. Since then, West Ham have promised nothing despite their blanket use of Moore's name and image to promote the club and to sell hospitality packages. 'There's no ongoing financial contribution to the Fund,' Stephanie says. It is, frankly, not good enough.

If West Ham want to honour Moore properly, on top of supporting the Fund in his name, they might care to dig out his medals, caps and football jerseys from a bank vault and put them on public display. Stephanie says that her late husband would be appalled to find out how his cherished mementos have been traded, and then locked away.

Moore had always intended that they should be divided between his children. After his death, Stephanie passed them back to Tina, believing she should decide how best to split them. In 2000, Tina put them up for auction, though not Pelé's gold shirt from 1970 swapped in that famous embrace at the final whistle. That was lost, or stolen as the gear was shipped between two quarrelling wives and various places of storage.

What remained of the collection – including Moore's 1966 winner's medal, some of his 108 caps, the trophy as best player from the finals, the 1966 BBC Sports Personality of the Year award and more – was bought by Terry Brown, West Ham's chairman, for £1.7 million though odd items have subsequently come on sale. In November 2007, Christie's auctioned a cap from the 1962–3 season on Tina's behalf which sold for £5,000, along with other trinkets from Moore's career.

'He knew that whatever happened, I would protect and care for all his medals and treasures and that ultimately everything, including the memorabilia or the proceeds from their sale, would pass on to Roberta and Dean and our grandchildren,' Tina wrote. Dean, though, died in 2011. After his long years of alcoholism, he had become an insulin-dependent diabetic and collapsed through complications, found by a care worker alone in his flat in Notting Hill. He was forty-three and left a daughter, Poppy. Roberta has two children, Ava and Freddie, born after Moore died.

West Ham initially put the memorabilia on show in the club museum at Upton Park but the venue closed because it was not paying its way. The medals and shirts were put in storage, unseen for years, though the new regime did consider a sale to raise funds after their takeover. 'I was really alarmed when Karren Brady told me that they were going to sell it all,' Stephanie says. 'I think their research told them that they would get a lot of bad publicity if they were to do that. The fans would be up in arms.'

So they sit somewhere in a box, though one enduring mystery is whatever happened to the most valuable item of all, the shirt Moore wore in the 1966 World Cup final. Stephanie still has a pile of jerseys including a red England number six. Could that be the one? She smiles coyly.

Would she sell it? 'If I did, any money would go to the charity, wouldn't it? Though I feel quite strongly that if his memorabilia had to be sold, it should have gone somewhere where it would have been open to the public to see. I'm sure Bobby would be horrified if he knew what had happened.' Sullivan says that he hopes to put the caps and medals back on show at the Olympic Stadium when the club finally moves to Stratford, though there would be plenty of willing takers in the meantime, such as the National Football Museum in Manchester.

Eight of the team of 1966 have sold their medals: Cohen the first in 1998 to ease financial problems. Fulham, his old club, bought it for £80,000 and it is on display in the suite named after him at Craven Cottage. He meets and greets on match days.

Ray Wilson became an undertaker after retiring from football, selling his for a reported £80,000 in 2002. Gordon Banks said that auctioning his medal would spare his children from agonising over what to do when he was no longer around. Alan Ball wanted to leave money to his family. Nobby Stiles was the most recent seller, with Manchester United paying £160,000.

It seems desperately sad that they have had to cash in their treasured mementos, but they have not sold out their annual reunion. With no fanfare, media coverage or commercial deal (though they could easily attract one), England's surviving world champions meet up each year for a strictly private gathering. They wander out to tea or play golf, if wonky hips and knees allow, while their wives go shopping. They always end up with a formal dinner where they present prizes. Then they drink into the evening and, without fail, raise a glass to those no longer around.

There are a few empty seats these days. Ball died of a heart attack in 2007, aged sixty-one. Alf Ramsey passed away in a nursing home in Ipswich in 1999 after a long illness. But the first to go was the captain.

The FA has sought to make amends for its own failure to properly honour Moore during his lifetime. On the twentieth anniversary of his death in 2013, an evening marked by ceremonies at Wembley and Upton Park, David Bernstein, the FA chairman, released a letter of public apology: 'I am aware the Football Association has been criticised over its treatment of Bobby once he retired from football . . . it is clear to me the organisation could have done more,' Bernstein said. It felt rather like the Prime Minister appearing before the House to admit guilt for some ancient crime committed by our ancestors.

It sometimes feels as though the FA can never truly atone for the neglect of Moore, and it is too late to lobby for a knighthood because the honour is not awarded posthumously. But the organisation has tried to make up for lost time. For years, the FA has backed the Fund. One of the banqueting areas at the new Wembley was named the Bobby Moore Suite.

There is that magnificent statue which stands outside the stadium, unveiled in May 2007, though even that has become a money-making machine. Gaze up and you see the towering figure of Moore; look down and you see an advert for Global Reach Partners and H Murat Atac Med Supplies Ltd.

The FA gives fans and businesses the chance to carve their names on paving stones outside Wembley, ranging from £50 for the most basic to a top price of £999 for the 'first grade black granite' slabs on the floor around Bobby Moore. However much money is required to pay off the stadium debts, to sell the ground beneath Moore seems horribly tacky.

It is a particularly sad bit of commercialism because the statue itself is so striking, lauded ever since it was unveiled in the presence of, among others, Tony Blair, the Prime Minister. 'If you want a role model in public life, Bobby Moore is a pretty good one to take. He was a true gentleman,' Blair said.

'It's a remarkable sculpture, it really is,' Stephanie says. 'The first time I saw it when it was still clay in a cold environment in Philip's studio and I walked around the back and just looked at the muscles on Bobby's calf and it was as though you could reach out and touch him. It was him. I know it's more than life size but it was just an amazing piece of work. The fact that it should be there at Wembley, he would be very proud, I don't doubt.

'It's just a shame he was never alive to see it. That's very sad but one has to cling on to the fact that he has been acknowledged in this way now and his grandchildren, and son and daughter, saw it.'

Millions see it each year as they walk up to Wembley. They look up at the figure who stood on the top of the world in 1966. They see Moore in his prime, looking as though he never had a single worry or doubt. A man in control of all he surveys, radiating an air of supernatural calm. In that respect, it is a brilliant likeness. The trick of looking unflappable was one Bobby Moore mastered all his life, whatever turmoil was raging below the surface.

Epilogue: Under a Magnolia Tree

A few miles north of where it all began in Barking lies the
City of London Cemetery and Crematorium across 200
peaceful, green acres in Newham. Head through the ornate
arch at the main gate, into one of England's largest burial
grounds, and they give you a map of the Heritage Trail with
an index to the location of notable graves.

Number 14 is Elizabeth Ann Everest, who was nanny, and
beloved confidante of the young Winston Churchill. Britain's
most celebrated Prime Minister paid for the crucifix which
stands above her grave and arranged a constant supply of
fresh flowers. Number 15 is Percy Thompson, brutally stabbed
at thirty-two when walking home with his wife Edith from
a night at a theatre in 1922. At a notorious trial, Thompson's
wife was revealed to be having an affair with his killer. Both
were hanged.

Plot number 16 is where Bobby Moore's ashes are buried.
You walk along quiet lanes, past a mourner crouched over
a grave and staff tending the flower beds. Near the gothic
Burial Chapel, in a garden of remembrance, is a dark granite
headstone lying flat in the shade of a magnolia tree. It reads

simply: 'Bobby Moore O.B.E. 1941–1993. Also Robert Edward Moore 1913–1978, Doris Joyce Moore 1912–1992'. There is nothing elaborate or fussy, nothing to draw your attention, which is just how Moore would have wanted it. The grave is as modest as the man.

After two years of chasing the enigmatic icon of English sport, I came here to ponder what I had learned about Moore. It made me think of a friend who died terribly young. Like Moore, he declined to talk about his illness. He would not speak about his fears, or what he thought his death would mean for his family. He took his feelings to the grave. I found the reticence difficult, wanting to help and provide a shoulder to cry on.

I admired my friend's stoicism but his emotional reserve put up a barrier that I wanted to break down but never could. I felt that same combination of frustration, bursts of helplessness and, at times, irritation trying to get to know the buttoned-up Bobby Moore.

His friends found him private, often guarded, so I should not have been surprised to find myself kept at arm's length, too. It wasn't just the mythology which caused Moore to seem remote. It was Moore himself.

And the truth is it vexed me. The only person whose life story I had investigated to this degree was that of Diego Maradona. He is a slightly unhinged former drug addict (and drug cheat) who kept me waiting eight hours for an interview and still did not turn up. But when I finally caught up with him following two fruitless trips to Buenos Aires, all was forgiven (well, not quite everything. That handball still hurts). Maradona was compelling and unforgettably charismatic. He stirred a passion in me. His poster adorns my office wall. I was drawn to him. After getting to know Bobby Moore, it felt more like respect; a polite handshake.

Perhaps if I'd had the chance to meet Moore, I would have felt that warmth that his friends love to reminisce about. I would have seen the generous man relaxing over a lager, or seven, and the mischief-maker. I am sure I would have sensed the charisma which arose from a quiet aura, the combination of stellar reputation and unfailingly down-to-earth manner. Just because you are good at something, he once said, doesn't mean you have to tell the world about it. As Hugh McIlvanney once wrote of Moore, he 'left the swaggering to lesser men'.

Moore's personal qualities were unmistakeable, if not unique. As a player, he was a devoted self-improver. He put in his 10,000 hours of practice long before that terminology became fashionable. He bore his indignities in later life with Job-like stoicism, never overcome with self-pity as the game found no use for him, and not even as the medics failed to diagnose his cancer. As the disease ravaged his body, he was strong and silent.

I could appreciate why his contemporaries adored him but, from a distance, Moore felt a very awkward man to bring back to life. He rarely said much that grabbed the attention. What little film survives of him shows a reserved man, so deliberately bland they might have hesitated even to invite him on to the *Match of the Day* sofa.

His post-playing days had revealed Moore to be just a man – decent, likeable and increasingly at ease – but not a leader away from the pitch or a thinker, not a coach of distinction or someone with compelling views about the game. I had come to this project hoping to discover hidden depths and finished wondering if, in truth, I had spent all that time looking for something that was not there.

The wife of one of the 1966 players told me that she liked Moore immensely – he was well-mannered and charming in a laddish world – but added, insightfully, that she always wondered if there was much behind that polite façade. One of the 1966 squad said something very similar (though not for quotation in case it got him into trouble). I came to question, too, what depths there were to Moore.

Maybe I was expecting too much. Perhaps this was just the gripe of a frustrated biographer. It was certainly an uncomfortable feeling given the adoration for him, and his achievements. Moore had excelled at one thing in his life to an extraordinary degree, which is more than the rest of us can hope to accomplish. He was no saint, but he *was* one of the supreme footballers of his generation. One of the best English footballers of all time.

That should be enough to put any man on a pedestal. When will England enjoy such glory again? When will they stand on top of the sporting world? Excuse the pessimism but probably not in my lifetime. In sporting terms, Moore stood on Everest, he walked on the moon, and did so with immense style.

It is reason enough to celebrate Moore's life but we seem to have a need to go further, to hold him up as a perfect role model and, of course, his terribly premature death ensures that we always picture him as the young, handsome god of Wembley; not a struggling manager or a radio pundit or a corporate ambassador for Visa or Pepsi, as he might have become in recent years.

He will remain an unblemished hero and perhaps people have a need for that. These days we know too much about our sports stars. It is hard to be saintly when you are super-injuncting your love life. As Frank Deford, the great American sports writer, noted: 'It is a lot easier now to be notorious than famous.'

Moore came from an age when we knew little, and he ensured that we knew even less. That is how he wanted it and, standing at his grave, it occurred to me that perhaps we do, too, choosing to revel in the idyll of England's greatest captain rather than the more complicated truth.

Postscript

West Ham United were quick to the telephone. Sensitive to the depiction of how Bobby Moore, and his legacy, had been handled by the club, a spokesman wanted to make a few clarifications. He explained that West Ham were establishing a new foundation with Tina and Roberta Moore – the West Ham United Moore Family Foundation – which would be launched in October 2014 and be the club's principal charity through the 2014/15 season. A statement said that David Sullivan would be making a five-figure donation to establish a project that would provide 'life-changing opportunities for targeted young people' in the East End. It would include free tickets and 'football and educational experiences' at the Olympic Stadium in Stratford, which will be the club's new home from August 2016. The formation of the new foundation followed 'extensive consultation with Bobby Moore's family' – though that depends, of course, on which part of the family you are talking about.

In announcing that they had gone into partnership with Bobby's daughter and first wife, West Ham could hardly avoid distancing themselves from his second, Stephanie. The Bobby

Moore Fund for Cancer Research UK, established by Stephanie, was to become a 'second-tier partner', which would give them some publicity and matchday collections but not the direct financial backing Stephanie believes should be forthcoming.

Stephanie has her reasons to feel dismayed and yet Roberta has described the West Ham slogan 'Moore than a Football Club' as 'a very inspired and clever piece of branding'. Behind these fresh tensions and differences of opinion about the handling of Moore's name lie some old wounds.

Remembering Moore remains a delicate issue, even among his family, and the topic never goes away. There will be further discussions about what is right and fitting in 2015, which marks 50 years since his finest hour as captain of West Ham; and certainly into 2016 with the 50th anniversary of the World Cup triumph. Those historic dates and Moore's glories will, rightly, be celebrated but his legacy will remain a source of fresh angst and sensitivity, too.

Acknowledgements

Bobby Moore was not an easy fellow to get to know so I am hugely grateful to all his friends, family, former team-mates and opponents who delved into their memories and spoke candidly on and, sometimes off, the record, as well as many Fleet Street colleagues.

I am especially indebted to Stephanie Moore, Bobby's widow. A donation has been made to the Bobby Moore Fund which seems only right given how the story ends.

Some people gave me five minutes, some hours, and they follow in no particular order of importance, but I do want to place on record that Rodney Marsh, Harry Redknapp and Frank Lampard senior were particularly helpful and candid. The film-maker Tony Palmer allowed me access to transcripts from his *Hero* documentary, which was hugely beneficial, and I am very thankful for his generous assistance. Tina Moore has written her own account of life with Bobby but kindly spared the time to answer my many questions.

Among the World Cup winners I spoke to were Sir Bobby Charlton, Jack Charlton, George Cohen and Martin Peters. Sir

Geoff Hurst offered some fascinating insights, as did Jimmy Armfield, Francis Lee and Peter Thompson.

My thanks to former West Ham United team-mates including Brian Dear and Eddie Bovington. Among Moore's close friends who opened up were Morris Keston, Jimmy Tarbuck, Kenny Lynch, Mike Summerbee, Terry Venables and the unforgettable Terry Creasy. Rob Jenkins, Clive Lewis and Tony McDonald filled in many details about the West Ham years while Graham Hardwick and Peter Buckle, two of Moore's cousins, helped me to understand the family.

In Denmark, Leif Clausen, Ole Nielsen, Jesper Nielsen and Helge Sander recreated that odd period at Herning Fremad. Graham Taylor and Muir Stratford enlightened me about Watford. Glenn Pennyfather, Alan Rogers and Robert Jobson were among those who talked me through the Southend episode.

I had help from too many people to mention, and some who prefer to remain anonymous, but they include Graham Kelly, Pat Smith, Lawrie McMenemy, Paddy Crerand, Jimmy Gabriel, Barry Simmonds, Alan Smith, Mike England, David Sullivan, Professor John Smythe, Peter Hawley and, not least, Pelé. Thanks to my sister Louise for introducing me to Tim Oliver, and to him for his oncology expertise.

I owe a debt to many journalists including Hugh Southon, Ken Jones, Nigel Clarke, Jonathan Pearce, Tony Livesey, Lawrie Hacker, Jeff Powell, Brian Scovell, Michael Hart, Brian Glanville and Hugh McIlvanney, whose stature as the greatest of British sportswriters became even more apparent reading his brilliant, humbling reportage of Moore's career.

Thanks to Terry Byrne and Suzanne Collins, and to Richard Scudamore for sharing his rare collection of *Shoot!* magazines; and to the staff at the National Archives, Kew, and the various outlets of the British Library, especially the much-missed Newspaper Library at Colindale.

I would like to thank Luis Restrepo, Sir Keith Morris, and particularly Carl Worswick for his attempts, far beyond the call of duty, to try to solve the mystery of the missing bracelet in Bogotá. If any man deserves to find that jewellery it is Carl.

To Richard Whitehead, sincere thanks for devoting so much time to help with the manuscript and for all the wise words of advice. I am indebted to Paul McCarthy for his unwavering support and guidance, not just on this book but over many years. To my colleagues and dear friends on the road including Oliver Holt, Marc Aspland and Matt Lawton and all the gang – you know who you are – thanks for making it such fun.

I want to take this opportunity to thank Keith Blackmore and David Chappell not just for giving me my chance at *The Times* but for being mentors and friends. To Tim Hallissey and all in the sports department for their support over many years.

My half-baked idea for this book might have remained just that without the energy and enthusiasm of David Luxton who has provided not just professional advice but friendship. I cannot imagine there are many better literary editors out there than Matt Phillips whose patience, understanding and wisdom felt like a godsend. Thanks to Matt and all his colleagues at Yellow Jersey Press for believing in the idea, and carrying it over the line.

Most of all, thanks to my family. To Joseph and Finlay for all the joy you bring to my life every day. And especially to Helen, who came to know England's greatest captain as 'effing Bobby Moore' as I disappeared on book duty. I truly couldn't have done it without you.

Bibliography

Books:

Malcolm Allison, *Colours of My Life* (Everest, 1975)

Alan Ball, *Playing Extra Time* (Pan Books, 2004)

Brian Belton, *The First and Last Englishmen* (Breedon Books, 1998)

George Best, *Best of Both Worlds* (Corgi, 1968)

—— *Blessed: The Autobiography* (Ebury Press, 2001)

Gordon Burn, *Best and Edwards* (Faber & Faber, 2006)

Noel Cantwell, *United We Stand* (Stanley Paul, 1965)

Sir Bobby Charlton, *The Autobiography: My Manchester United Years* (Headline, 2007)

—— *The Autobiography: My England Years* (Headline, 2008)

Jack Charlton, *The Autobiography* (Corgi, 1996)

Phil Daniels, *Moore than a Legend* (Goal Publications, 1997)

Jeff Dawson, *Back Home: England and the 1970 World Cup* (Orion, 2001)

David Downing, *The Best of Enemies, England v Germany* (Bloomsbury, 2000)

Edson Arantes do Nascimento, *Pelé: The Autobiography* (Simon & Schuster, 2006)

Clive Everton, *Black Farce and Cue Ball Wizards: The Inside Story of the Snooker World* (Mainstream, 2007)

Norman Giller, *Bobby Moore – The Master* (NGB Publishing, 2013)

Brian Glanville, *Soccer Nemesis* (Secker & Warburg, 1955)

—— *England Managers – The Toughest Job in Football* (Headline, 2007)

David Gold, *Pure Gold* (Highdown, 2006)

David Goldblatt, *The Ball Is Round: A Global History of Football* (Penguin Books, 2007)

Jimmy Greaves, *'This One's On Me'* (Arthur Baker, 1979)

—— *Don't Shoot the Manager* (Boxtree, 1993)

—— *Greavsie: The Autobiography* (TimeWarner, 2003)

Geoffrey Green, *Great Moments in Sport: Soccer* (Pelham Books, 1972)

—— *Pardon Me for Living: An Autobiography* (George Allen & Unwin, 1985)

Ron Greenwood, *Yours Sincerely* (Willow Books, 1984)

Geoff Hurst, *My Autobiography: 1966 and All That* (Headline, 2001)

—— *1966 World Champions* (Headline, 2006)

Morris Keston and Nick Hawkins, *Superfan: The Amazing Life of Morris Keston* (Vision Sports Publishing, 2010)

Tony Livesey, *Babes, Booze, Orgies and Aliens* (Virgin, 1998)

Tony McDonald, *West Ham United – The Managers* (Football World, 2007)

Hugh McIlvanney, *McIlvanney on Football* (Mainstream Publishing, 1994)

—— and Arthur Hopcraft (eds), *World Cup '70* (Eyre & Spottiswoode, 1970)

Leo McKinstry, *Sir Alf* (HarperSport, 2006)

David Miller, *The Boys of '66 – England's Last Glory* (Pavilion, 1986)

Bobby Moore, *My Soccer Story* (Stanley Paul, 1966)

—— *Soccer the Modern Way* (Stanley Paul, 1967)

—— *England! England!* (Stanley Paul, 1970)

—— *Moore on Mexico: World Cup 1970* (Stanley Paul, 1970)

Tina Moore, *Bobby Moore – By the Person Who Knew Him Best* (HarperSport, 2005)

John Moynihan, *The Soccer Syndrome* (McGibbon & Kee, 1966)

Alan Mullery, *The Autobiography* (Headline, 2006)

John Pearson, *Notorious. The Immortal Legend of the Kray Twins* (Arrow, 2011)

Martin Peters, *Mexico 1970* (Littlehampton, 1970)

—— *The Ghost of '66, Martin Peters – The Autobiography* (Orion, 2006)

Ivan Ponting, *The Book of Football Obituaries* (Pitch Publishing, 2012)

Jeff Powell, *Bobby Moore: The Authorised Biography* (Everest, 1976)

—— *Bobby Moore: The Life and Times of a Sporting Hero* (Robson Books, 2002)

Harry Redknapp, *'ARRY: The Autobiography of Harry Redknapp* (CollinsWillow, 1998)

—— *Always Managing. Harry, My Autobiography* (Ebury Press, 2013)

Bobby Robson, *Farewell But Not Goodbye* (Hodder & Stoughton, 2005)

Terry Roper, *West Ham in the Sixties: The Jack Burkett Story* (Football World, 2009)

Tony Rosser, *The £20 Million Stitch of a Family Business* (Phoenix Publications, 2004)

Dominic Sandbrook, *White Heat* (Abacus, 2006)

Phil Shaw, *The Book of Football Quotations* (Ebury Press, 2008)

Rob Steen, *The Mavericks* (Mainstream, 1994)

Mike Summerbee, *The Autobiography* (Optimum Publishing Solutions, 2010)

David Tossell, *Big Mal: The High Life and Hard Times of Malcolm Allison, Football Legend* (Mainstream, 2009)

Martin Tyler, *Cup Final Extra!* (Hamlyn, 1981)

Jonathan Wilson, *Inverting the Pyramid: A History of Football Tactics* (Orion, 2008)

—— *The Anatomy of England: A History In Ten Matches* (Orion, 2010)

Ray Wilson, *My Life in Soccer* (Pelham Books, 1969)

David Winner, *Those Feet – A Sensual History of English Football* (Bloomsbury, 2005)

Billy Wright, *One Hundred Caps and All That* (Robert Hale, 1962)

Magazines:

EX Magazine

BACKPASS

SHOOT!

TV, Film:

This Is Your Life, Thames Television, broadcast January 1971

Melvyn Bragg on Class and Culture, BBC2, March 2012

Hero, directed by Tony Palmer, BBC, released 2010

Melvyn Bragg on Class and Culture, BBC2 (March 2012)

List of Illustrations

teammates as he lifts the Jules Rimet Trophy (Getty); Moore, Ramsey and Stiles (Getty)

12. Moore poses with his wife Tina (Terry O'Neill/Getty Images); Moore with Sean Connery and Yul Brynner (Getty); the Moore family pose as Pearly Kings and Queens (Mirrorpix)

13. Bobby Moore jogging (Rex); West Ham United footballers at a social function (Getty); Moore lifts model (PA)

14. Moore talks to the press in Essex after hearing news from Bogotá, Colombia that he may face a trial for allegedly stealing a gold bracelet (PA); England players enjoy a game of cards, 1970 (Popperfoto/Getty)

15. Moore tackles Brazil's Jairzinho at the 1970 World Cup (Offside); Moore and Pelé exchange shirts (Offside); Bobby Charlton and Alf Ramsey look dejected after England's 3-2 loss to West Germany (PA)

16. Moore poses with ninety-nine children from a primary school near Upton Park on the eve of his 100th England appearance (Action Images); Moore leads West Ham United out for his final game for the club (PA)

17. Moore with George Best and Rodney Marsh (Getty); Fulham captain Alan Mullery and Moore console each other after they were defeated 2-0 by West Ham United in the 1975 FA Cup final (PA)

18. Moore signs an autograph outside Bobby Moore Sports Wear (PA); Moore shows off one of his line of stylish fashion products (PA)

19. The opening of Mooro's in Stratford, 1976 (PA); Moore outside his home at Chigwell, Essex, 1978 (Getty)

20. Moore playing for Herning (Scanpix); Moore, Michael Caine and Sylvester Stallone (All Star Picture Library)

21. Moore with Elton John (Getty); Moore as Oxford City Manager (Rex)

22. Moore at Southend United (Action Images); Moore with Southend United director John Adams (PA)

23. Moore working for Capital Gold (Offside); Moore with Stephanie Moore (Rex)

24. Bobby Moore shrine (Rex)

Index